Keys to Success

BUILDING SUCCESSFUL INTELLIGENCE

for College, Career, and Life

BRIEF FOURTH EDITION

Carol Carter

Joyce Bishop

Sarah Lyman Kravits

PEARSON

Prentice
Hall

Upper Saddle River, New Jersey

Columbus, Ohio

Library of Congress Cataloging-in-Publication Data
Carter, Carol.
    Keys to success : building successful intelligence for college,
    career, and life / Carol Carter, Joyce Bishop, Sarah Lyman Kravits.—Brief 4th ed.
        p. cm.
    Includes bibliographical references and index.
    ISBN 0-13-171524-0
    1. College student orientation—United States—Handbooks, manuals,
    etc. 2. Study skills—Handbooks, manuals, etc. 3. College students—
    United States—Life skills guides. 4. Career development—United
    States—Handbooks, manuals, etc. I. Bishop, Joyce
    (Joyce L.). II. Kravits, Sarah Lyman. III. Title.

    LB2343.32.C3694 2006
    378.1'98—dc22   2005001756

Vice President and Publisher: Jeffery W. Johnston
Senior Acquisitions Editor: Sande Johnson
Assistant Editor: Susan Kauffman
Development Editors: Jennifer Gessner, Charlotte Morrissey
Production Editor: Holcomb Hathaway
Design Coordinator: Diane C. Lorenzo
Cover Designer: Jeff Vanik
Cover Photos: SuperStock, PhotoDisk
Interior Design: Aerocraft Charter Art Service
Production Manager: Pamela D. Bennett
Director of Marketing: Ann Castel Davis
Marketing Manager: Amy Judd

Credits and acknowledgments appear on page xii, which constitutes an extension of the copyright page.

All chapters have been adapted for use in this book from *Keys to Success: Building Successful Intelligence for College, Career, and Life*, Fifth Edition, by Carter, Bishop, Kravits, copyright © 2006 by Pearson Education, Inc.

This book was set in Sabon by Carlisle Communications, Ltd. It was printed by Courier Kendallville, Inc. The cover was printed by Phoenix Color Corp.

Pearson Education Ltd.
Pearson Education Australia Pty. Limited
Pearson Education Singapore Pte. Ltd.
Pearson Education North Asia Ltd.

Pearson Education Canada, Ltd.
Pearson Educación de Mexico, S. A. de C.V.
Pearson Education–Japan
Pearson Education Malaysia Pte. Ltd.

10 9 8 7 6 5 4 3 2 1
0-13-171524-0

Our Mission Statement

Our mission is to help students know and believe in themselves, successfully retain and use what they learn, and take advantage of resources and opportunities. With these abilities, we are confident that all students can achieve their goals, become lifelong learners, build fruitful and satisfying relationships with others, and experience the challenges and rewards that make life meaningful.

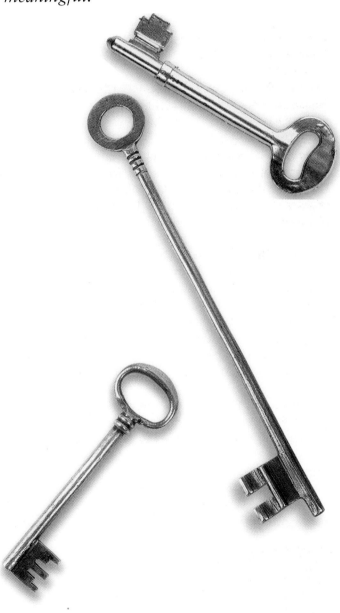

Foreword

Everyone's experience in college is different. My experience was not that of a traditional student because I volunteered for four years of military service prior to going to college full-time. The Marine Corps gave me discipline and instilled in me the motivation I needed to continue my education. By the time I had finished my enlistment, I had also finished my freshman year at the University of South Carolina.

The time I took to serve our country also gave me the opportunity to decide what type of college atmosphere best suited my needs. In the end, I chose to attend a small university with close ties to the businesses in Denver. The information in *Keys to Success* was important to my college education. While acting as student editor on this book, I learned how to be a better student, employee, and person. I graduated feeling ready for the rest of my life.

I took advantage of the worksheets and personal stories by applying them to my everyday life. After working with this book, I was more inclined to take active steps toward improving my education and my ability to learn. The most important thing I learned in college is, in fact, how to learn. I have a goal to learn throughout my lifetime. I want my life to be a series of new lessons about my profession and myself.

Someone once told me that a college education can be valued by the amount of effort the student puts into it. Anyone can go to class, take notes, and pass the tests. In my experience, the students who succeed in the long term make every assignment a learning challenge. I encourage you to take advantage of every opportunity to learn. Your efforts and dedication to learning are in direct relation to your degree of happiness and success in college, career, and life.

Best Wishes,

Dylan Lewis

UNIVERSITY OF COLORADO, DENVER

Contents

Chapter 1

WELCOME TO COLLEGE   2
Opening Doors to Success

Chapter 2

VALUES, GOALS, TIME, AND STRESS   26
Managing Yourself

Chapter 3

LEARNING STYLES, MAJORS, AND CAREERS   58
Knowing Your Talents and Finding Your Direction

Chapter 4

Chapter 5

Chapter 6

LISTENING, NOTE TAKING, AND MEMORY   152
Taking In, Recording, and Remembering Information

Chapter 7

TEST TAKING   186
Showing What You Know

Chapter 8

RELATING TO OTHERS 216
Communicating in a Diverse World

Chapter 9

CREATING YOUR LIFE 248
Building a Successful Future

NOTE: *Every effort has been made to provide accurate and current Internet information in this book. However, the Internet and information posted on it are constantly changing, so it is inevitable that some of the Internet addresses listed in this textbook will change.*

Preface

Since the last edition of *Keys to Success, Brief Edition*, we have focused our energies and research on the following question: How can students get the most out of college and use what they learn to achieve their goals in an ever-changing world? We found an important answer in the concept of successful intelligence, developed by psychologist Robert Sternberg.[1]

This book builds successful intelligence

Successful people, says Sternberg, are more than their IQ score. Focus on the two most important parts of Sternberg's message and you can change your approach to education in a way that will maximize your learning and *life success*.

One: *Successful intelligence gives you tools to achieve important goals.* Successful intelligence goes beyond doing well on tests (analytical thinking). Only by combining that analytical skill with the ability to come up with innovative ideas (creative thinking) and the ability to put ideas and plans to work (practical thinking) will you get where you want to go.

Two: *Intelligence can grow.* The intelligence you have when you are born does not stay the same for the rest of your life. You can build and develop your intelligence in the same way that you can build and develop physical strength or flexibility.

Every chapter of *Keys to Success* helps you to build successful intelligence. How?

- *Chapter coverage:* The theme is introduced in Chapter 1 and covered in more detail in the thinking chapter (Chapter 4). Successful intelligence concepts are referenced throughout all chapters of the text.
- *In-text exercises:* Three exercises within the chapter text—"Get Analytical!," "Get Creative!," and "Get Practical!"—develop each skill in the context of the chapter material and your personal needs.
- *Synthesis exercise:* At the end of each chapter, the "Putting It All Together" exercise gives you an opportunity to combine all three skills and apply them toward a meaningful task.

This book connects you with the ideas and experiences of others

To help you excel in a world that is increasingly diverse, this edition of *Keys to Success* introduces the concept of *cultural competence*, using the following features:

- *Chapter-opening Q & A* highlights questions posed by actual students as they begin college. Each question is answered by another person who offers ideas and advice.
- *Descriptions of real students' experiences*, often accompanied by quotes from the students, have been woven into the text in areas where they enhance the topic being discussed.
- *A focus on cultural competence*, in Chapter 8, shows the value of going beyond tolerance to actively adapt to and learn from people different from you. References to cultural competence and diversity are also woven throughout every chapter, showing how diversity is part of many aspects of school, the workplace, and personal life.
- *Personal Triumph* stories, real-life accounts of how people have overcome difficult circumstances in the pursuit of education and fulfillment, appear near the end of selected

chapters. These inspiring stories motivate you to step up your personal efforts to succeed.

- *Chapter summaries* introduce a word or phrase from a language other than English and suggest how you might apply the concept to your own life.

- *A continuing focus on multiple intelligences* highlights individual diversity and confirms that each individual has a unique way of learning, with no one way being better than another. Chapter 3 introduces and explains this concept, and subsequent chapters include grids with strategies for applying various learning styles to the chapter content.

This book provides strategies and resources that help you do your work

With successful intelligence as the foundation of this edition and cultural competence as an underlying theme, *Keys to Success* presents these learning tools and materials that will help you succeed in college and beyond:

Skills that prepare you for college, career, and life.

The ideas and strategies that help you succeed in college also take you where you want to go in your career and personal life. The three parts of this text help you develop a firm foundation for lifelong learning.

- *Defining yourself and your goals:* Chapter 1 provides an overview of today's college experience and an opportunity to evaluate your personal starting point. Chapter 2 gets you on track with ways to manage yourself effectively, focusing on values, goal-setting strategies, time-management skills, and handling stress. Chapter 3 helps you identify complementary aspects of your learning style (your Multiple Intelligences and your Personality Spectrum), choose strategies that make them work for you, and begin to think about your major.

- *Developing your learning skills:* Chapter 4 puts your learning into action by exploring the concept of successful intelligence in depth, helping you to build analytical, creative, and practical thinking skills and to put them together in order to solve problems, make decisions, and achieve goals. The next

few chapters build crucial skills for the classroom and beyond—Reading and Studying (Chapter 5), Listening, Note Taking, and Memory (Chapter 6), and Test Taking (Chapter 7).

- *Creating success:* Recognizing that success includes more than academic achievement, Chapter 8 focuses on developing the interpersonal and communication skills you need in a diverse society. Finally, Chapter 9 helps you explore wellness, career, and money issues and encourages you to think expansively: What path have you traveled during the semester? What plans do you have for your future?

Skill-building exercises.

Today's graduates need to be effective thinkers, team players, writers, and strategic planners. The set of exercises at the end of each chapter—"Building Skills for College, Career, and Life Success"—encourages you to develop these valuable skills and to apply thinking processes to any topic or situation:

- *Developing Successful Intelligence: Putting It All Together.* These exercises encourage you to combine your successful intelligence thinking skills and apply them to chapter material.

- *Team Building: Collaborative Solutions.* This exercise gives you a chance to interact, problem solve, and learn in a group setting, building your teamwork and leadership skills in the process.

- *Writing: Discovery Through Journaling.* This journal exercise provides an opportunity to express your thoughts and develop your writing skills.

- *Career Portfolio: Plan for Success.* This exercise helps you gather evidence of your talents, skills, interests, qualifications, and experience. The Career Portfolio exercises build on one another to form, at the end of the semester, a portfolio of information and insights that will help you in your quest for the right career and job.

This book changes with your needs

As we revise, we are in constant touch with students and instructors who tell us how we can improve. From our work with students, student editors, instructors, and experts all over the country, we have made important changes to better focus this new edition on what you need to succeed now. Here's what's new:

- The text-wide theme of successful intelligence—the way to achieve goals and success through analytical, creative, and practical thinking
- A new focus in Chapter 1 on how to use and benefit from the text and its theme
- Three in-chapter exercises in each chapter—one building analytical thinking skill, one building creative thinking skill, and one building practical thinking skill
- A new first exercise at the end of each chapter— "Developing Successful Intelligence: Putting It All Together"—to encourage the synthesis of successful intelligence thinking skills
- Earlier placement (in Chapter 2) of values, goal setting, time management, and basic stress-management strategies
- Revision of learning styles material in Chapter 3 to more clearly delineate the two learning styles assessments and enhance their usefulness
- Extensive revision of Chapter 4—the thinking chapter—to focus on successful intelligence and how it makes problem solving and decision making happen
- Revision of Chapter 8—the diversity chapter—to focus on cultural competence, along with added cultural references throughout the text
- New student stories included within the text to heighten relevance of the material and the reader's ability to connect to it
- Newly revised end-of-chapter exercises to increase relevance and usefulness and to help students build on what they learn throughout the semester

This book is just a start—only you can create the life of your dreams

As you work through this course and move forward toward your goals, keep this in mind: Studies have shown that when students feel that they have a fixed level of intelligence, they improve less, put less effort into their work, and have a harder time in the face of academic challenges. However, students who feel that they can become more intelligent over time are more likely to improve, tend to work harder, and handle academic challenges with more success.[2] *Believe that your intelligence can grow*—and use this book to develop it this semester, throughout your college experience, and afterward as you build the future of your dreams.

Students and instructors: Many of our best suggestions have come from you. Send your questions, comments, and ideas about *Keys to Success* to Carol Carter at caroljcarter@lifebound.com or call our toll-free number at 1-877-737-8510. We look forward to hearing from you, and we are grateful for the opportunity to work with you.

Notes

1. Successful intelligence concepts from Robert Sternberg, *Successful Intelligence*. New York: Plume, 1997.
2. David Glenn, "Students' Performance on Tests Is Tied to Their Views of Their Innate Intelligence, Researchers Say," *The Chronicle of Higher Education*, June 1, 2004 [on-line]. Available: http://chronicle.com/daily/ 2004/06/ 2004060103n.htm (June 2004).

Credits and Acknowledgments

Successful intelligence excerpts and themes reprinted with permission of Simon & Schuster Adult Publishing Group from SUCCESSFUL INTELLIGENCE by Robert J. Sternberg. Copyright © 1996 by Robert J. Sternberg.

Photo Credits

Acknowledgments

This significant revision has been produced through the efforts of an extraordinary team. Many thanks to:

- Robert J. Sternberg, IBM Professor of Psychology and Education at Yale University, for his ground-breaking work on successful intelligence and for his gracious permission to use and adapt that work as a theme for this new edition.

- Our reviewers, whose input is invaluable.

Fourth edition reviewers: Peg Adams, Northern Kentucky University; Veronica Allen, Texas Southern University; Angela A. Anderson, Texas Southern University; Robert Anderson, The College of New Jersey; Joyce Annette Deaton, Jackson State Community College; Ray Emett, Salt Lake Community College; Jacqueline Fleming, Texas Southern University; Ralph Gallo, Texas Southern University; Jennifer Guyer-Wood, Minnesota State University; Laura Kauffmann, Indian River Community College; Quentin Kidd, Christopher Newport University; Patsy Krech, University of Memphis; Curtis Peters, Indiana University Southeast; Margaret Quinn, University of Memphis; Corliss A. Rabb, Texas Southern University; Rebecca Samberg, Housatonic Community College; Karyn L. Schulz, Community College of Baltimore County–Dundalk; Jill R. Strand, University of Minnesota–Duluth; Toni M. Stroud, Texas Southern University; Cheri Tillman, Valdosta State University

Reviewers from previous editions: Fred Amador, Phoenix College; Manual Aroz, Arizona State University; Glenda Belote, Florida International University; Todd Benatovich, University of Texas at Arlington; John Bennett, Jr., University of Connecticut; Ann Bingham-Newman, California State University–LA; Mary Bixby, University of Missouri–Columbia; Barbara Blandford, Education Enhancement Center at Lawrenceville, NJ; Jerry Bouchie, St. Cloud State University; Mona Casady, SW Missouri State University; Kara Craig, University of Southern Mississippi; Leslie Chilton, Arizona State University; Jim Coleman, Baltimore City Community College; Sara Connolly, Florida State University; Janet Cutshall, Sussex County Community College; Valerie DeAngelis, Miami-Dade Community College; Rita Delude, NH Community Technical College; Marianne Edwards, Georgia College and State University; Judy Elsley, Weber State University in Utah; Skye Gentile, California State University, Hayward; Bob Gibson, University of Nebraska–Omaha; Sue Halter, Delgado Community College; Suzy Hampton, University of Montana; Karen Hardin, Mesa Community College; Patricia Hart, California State University, Fresno; Maureen Hurley, University of Missouri–Kansas City; Karen Iversen, Heald Colleges; Laura Kauffman, Indian River Community College; Kathryn K. Kelly, St. Cloud State University; Nancy Kosmicke, Mesa State College; Frank T. Lyman, Jr., University of Maryland; Marvin Marshak, University of Minnesota; Kathy Masters, Arkansas State University; Barnette Miller Moore, Indian River Community College; Rebecca Munro, Gonzaga University; Sue Palmer, Brevard Community College; Bobbie Parker, Alabama State University; Virginia Phares, DeVry of Atlanta; Brenda Prinzavalli, Beloit College; Jacqueline Simon, Education Enhancement Center at Lawrenceville, NJ; Carolyn Smith, University of Southern Indiana; Joan Stottlemyer, Carroll College; Thomas Tyson, SUNY Stony Brook; Eve Walden, Valencia Community College; Marsha Walden, Valdosta State University; Rose Wassman, DeAnza College; Angela Williams, The Citadel; Don Williams, Grand Valley State University; William Wilson, St. Cloud State University; Michelle G. Wolf, Florida Southern College

- Our student editor, Dylan Lewis, for his wisdom, guidance, and hard work.

- The PRE 100 instructors at Baltimore City Community College, Liberty Campus, for their ideas and support, especially college President Dr. Jim Tschechtelin, and coordinator Stan D. Brown.

- Those who generously contributed personal stories, exhibiting courage in being open and honest about their life experiences:

Stephen Beck, Learn-to-Learn Company; Joyce Bishop, Golden West College; Carol Carter, LifeBound Inc.; Peter Changsak, Sheldon-Jackson College; Rosalia Chavez, University of Arizona; Carol Comlish, University of Alabama; Darrin Estepp, Ohio State University; Rachel Faison, Bard College; Jacqueline Fleming, Texas Southern University; Parisa Malekzadeh, University of Arizona; Joe A. Martin, Jr., University of West Florida; Gustavo Minaya, Community College of Baltimore County, Essex Campus; Afsaneh Nahavandi, Arizona State University West; Nisar Nikzad, Community College of Denver; Julia Nolan, University of California, Davis; Michael Nolan, Oregon State University; Morgan Paar, Academy of Art College; Shyama Parikh, DePaul University; Joe Pullen, University of Detroit; Lisa Rabinowitz, Bloomfield College; Dr. Benjamin Victorica, University of Florida; Tonjua Williams, St. Petersburg College

- Jessica Ovitz, Cynthia Nordberg, Dr. Frank T. Lyman, and Dan Laukitis for their invaluable advice and assistance.

- Our terrific editor Sande Johnson, who through her leadership was able to put together a team of people whose combined efforts took this edition to a new level. Special thanks to developmental editors Jennifer Gessner and Charlotte Morrissey for their comprehensive vision, hard work, and insightful ideas, and to editorial assistant Erin Anderson for all her efforts and attention to detail.

- The education professionals who contributed to the development and enhancement of the supplementary materials for this book, including Karyn Schultz and Charlotte Morrissey (Instructor's Manual) and Susan Bierman (Companion Website).

- Alison Pendergast of Pearson Education and Phyllis Colazzo and Peter Simmons of *The New York Times* for their roles in making stellar *New York Times* photographs available for our photo program.

- The following reviewers of and contributors to the instructor's manual, for their insight:

Todd Benatovich, University of Texas at Arlington; Amy Bierman, student, Old Dominion University; Jennifer Cohen; Jodi Levine, Temple University; Geri MacKenzie, Southern Methodist University; Gene Mueller, Henderson State University; Tina Pitt, Heald College; Dan Rice, Iowa State University; Michael and Frances Trevisan, Washington State University; Karen Valencia, South Texas Community College; Eve Walden, Valencia Community College; Don Williams, Grand Valley State University; William Wilson, St. Cloud State University; Nona Wood, North Dakota State University

- Our production team for their patience, flexibility, and attention to detail, especially Gay Pauley, John Wincek, Tammy Levins, JoEllen Gohr, and Pam Bennett.

- Our marketing gurus, especially Amy Judd, our Marketing Manager; Ann Davis, Director of Marketing; and our student success sales directors Joe Hale, Deb Gravely, Brian McGarry, and Connie James.

- Publisher Jeff Johnston, President of Education, Career, and Technology Robin Baliszewski, and Prentice Hall President Tim Bozik, for their leadership and their interest in and commitment to the Student Success list.

- The Prentice Hall representatives and management team, who help us to bring our mission to instructors all over the country.

• Our families and friends, who have encouraged us and put up with our commitments.

• We extend a very special thanks to Judy Block, whose research, writing, and editing work was essential and invaluable.

Finally, for their ideas, opinions, and stories, we would like to thank all of the students and professors with whom we work. Joyce in particular would like to thank the thousands of students who have allowed her, as their professor, the privilege of sharing part of their journey through college. We appreciate that, through reading this book, you give us the opportunity to learn and discover with you—in your classroom, in your home, on the bus, and wherever else learning takes place.

Best-Selling Titles in the
KEYS TO SUCCESS Series

About the Authors

Carol Carter is founder of LifeBound, a career coaching company that offers individual coaching sessions and seminars for high school students, college students, and career seekers. She has written *Majoring in the Rest of Your Life: Career Secrets for College Students* and *Majoring in High School*. She has also co-authored *Keys to Preparing for College, Keys to College Studying, The Career Tool Kit, Keys to Career Success, Keys to Study Skills, Keys to Thinking and Learning,* and *Keys to Success*. She has taught welfare-to-work classes, team taught in the La Familia Scholars Program at the Community College of Denver, and conducted numerous workshops for students and faculty around the country. Carol is a national college and career expert and is interviewed regularly in print, on the radio, and for television news programs. In addition to working with students of all ages, Carol thrives on foreign travel and culture; she is fortunate enough to have been a guest in more than 40 foreign countries. Please visit her Web site and write her at www.lifebound.com.

Joyce Bishop holds a Ph.D. in psychology and has taught for more than 20 years, receiving a number of honors, including Teacher of the Year for 1995 and 2000. For five years she has been voted "favorite teacher" by the student body and Honor Society at Golden West College, Huntington Beach, California, where she has taught since 1987 and is a tenured professor. She worked with a federal grant to establish Learning Communities and Workplace Learning in her district, and she has developed workshops and trained faculty in cooperative learning, active learning, multiple intelligences, workplace relevancy, learning styles, authentic assessment, team building, and the development of learning communities. Joyce is currently teaching on-line and multimedia classes, and she trains other faculty to teach on-line in her district and region of 21 colleges. She co-authored *Keys to College Studying, Keys to Success, Keys to Thinking and Learning,* and *Keys to Study Skills.* Joyce is the lead academic of the Keys to Lifelong Learning Telecourse, distributed by Dallas Telelearning.

Sarah Lyman Kravits comes from a family of educators and has long cultivated an interest in educational development. She co-authored *Keys to College Studying, The Career Tool Kit, Keys to Success, Keys to Thinking and Learning,* and *Keys to Study Skills* and has served as Program Director for LifeSkills, Inc., a nonprofit organization that aims to further the career and personal development of high school students. In that capacity she helped to formulate both curricular and organizational elements of the program, working closely with instructors as well as members of the business community. She has also given faculty workshops in critical thinking. Sarah holds a B.A. in English and drama from the University of Virginia, where she was a Jefferson Scholar, and an M.F.A. from Catholic University.

Keys to Success

BUILDING SUCCESSFUL INTELLIGENCE

for College, Career, and Life

BRIEF FOURTH EDITION

1

IN THIS CHAPTER. . .

you will explore answers to the
following questions:

Welcome to College

OPENING DOORS TO SUCCESS

Welcome—or welcome back—to your education. You are embarking on a new phase of life—one that presents challenges, promises hard work, and offers extraordinary rewards. As you contemplate the course of the next two to five years, you may wonder: How am I going to get from freshman orientation to graduation? How am I going to make it?

Here's one important part of the answer to that question: *With the help of this book.* Why? Because it will make your life easier. This book, and the course for which you are reading it, have a primary goal: To help you learn successfully, graduate, and reap the personal and professional rewards of a solid education. This chapter gives you an overview of how that will happen—how being a successfully intelligent, motivated, and forward-thinking student will help you face the challenges of college and achieve more than you could have imagined.

On the following page, read about student Joe Pullen, who is wondering how much grades matter and how hard he will have to focus to earn good grades in college.

- Where are you now—and where can college take you?
- How can successful intelligence help you achieve your goals?
- How will *Keys to Success* help you build successful intelligence?
- What will motivate you to make the most of college?
- How can what you learn now help you succeed in school, work, and life?

How important is it to have a high GPA in your first year?

In high school I was considered a pretty smart student but I didn't try that hard. I always waited to the last minute to do things, but I got them done. My GPA was okay but I feel it could have been twice as good. I'm nervous about what will happen in my first year of college. Everyone tells me that freshman year is fun but distracting. Knowing myself, I don't think I can take too much distraction.

I am a very energetic person so I try to get involved in everything I can. In high school I was active in the basketball team, football team, school newspaper, student council, forensics, chess team, student chapel organization, and baseball. I was able to balance athletics and academics in my high school but in college it seems like it will be different. Can I get involved in as many activities as I can without hurting my grades? How important is having a high GPA going to be for me to be able to continue my education?

Joe Pullen
Freshman, University of Detroit

Grades reflect the depth and focus of your learning.

You expect college to be more challenging than high school, and you are right! College As may be harder to earn. They may also represent greater commitment to subject and depth of understanding. Although a poor grade may reflect a lack of commitment, sometimes it means that you were exploring a subject in which you were not gifted but were brave enough to try!

When I began college, I found the courses more demanding than in high school. There was harder reading and more of it, more preparation required before class, more participation in class, and the teachers had higher expectations. Attractive events and activities distracted me. I had to study much harder and there never seemed to be enough time before an exam.

To get good grades, I learned, you have to make time—to write and revise papers, work out answers to problems, or plan and then finish a challenging project. Getting good grades shows that you have eliminated distractions, made school work a priority, demonstrated some natural or hard-earned ability in the subject, and met the professor's requirements.

It's important for you, and for all freshmen, to understand how grades work at your college. How free are you to study in an area that you are weak in but that interests you? Can you take a course for pass–fail? Do you need a certain GPA to major and/or to graduate? When you are not doing well in a course, can you drop it without facing a penalty? Remember, it is always a good idea to meet with your professor about problems and to avoid dropping a course unless you have consulted with your professor and your advisor.

So, back to your question: You don't want fear of a bad grade to prevent you from exploring whatever interests you, but you need to adjust your time to put your best effort into your academics. Good grades and a high GPA show that you are meeting college standards. You are right to be concerned, not because the grade itself is everything but because making smart choices about grades reflects maturity and growth as a learner.

Lisa Rabinowitz, Ed. D., Chair, Creative Arts and Technology, Bloomfield College, Bloomfield, New Jersey

Where are you now— and where can college take you?

You are standing at the gateway to a new phase of life. Before you think about moving forward, though, take a look at the road that brought you here. You completed high school or its equivalent. You may have built life skills from experience as a partner or parent. You may have been employed in one or more jobs or completed a tour of duty in the armed forces. You have enrolled in college, found a way to pay for it, signed up for courses, and shown up for class. And, in deciding to pursue a college degree, you made the choice to believe in your ability to accomplish important goals. You have earned this opportunity to be a college student!

If your work in college only helped you succeed in the classroom, the benefit of your learning wouldn't last beyond graduation day. However, learning is a tool for life, and a college education is designed to serve you far beyond the classroom. Here are a few important "life success goals" that college can help you achieve:

Life Success Goal: Increased employability and earning potential. Getting a degree greatly increases your chances of finding and keeping a high-level, well-paying job. College graduates earn, on average, around $20,000 more per year than those with a high school diploma (see Key 1.1). Furthermore, the unemployment rate for college graduates is less than half that of high school graduates (see Key 1.2).

More education is likely to mean more income.

key 1.1

Median annual income of persons with income 25 years old and over, by gender and highest level of education, 2000.

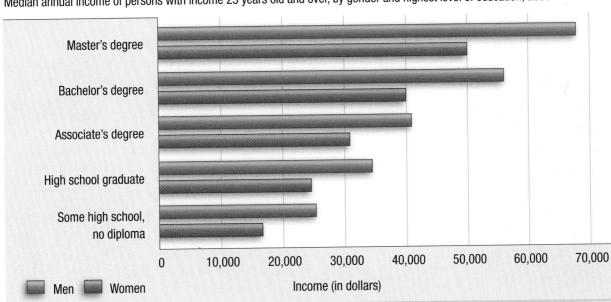

Source: U.S. Department of Commerce, Bureau of the Census, *Current Population Reports*, Series P-60, "Money Income of Households, Families, and Persons in the United States," 2002.

More education is likely to mean more consistent employment.

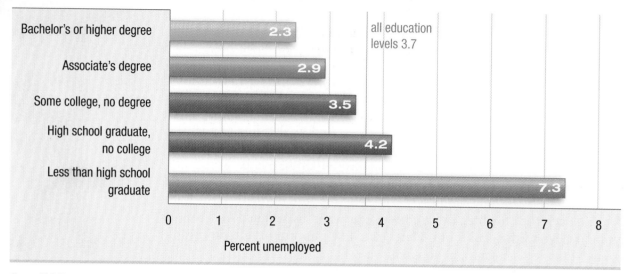

Unemployment rates of persons 25 years old and over, by highest level of education, 2001.

all education levels 3.7

Education Level	Percent unemployed
Bachelor's or higher degree	2.3
Associate's degree	2.9
Some college, no degree	3.5
High school graduate, no college	4.2
Less than high school graduate	7.3

Source: U.S. Department of Labor, Bureau of Labor Statistics, Office of Employment and Unemployment Statistics, unpublished tabulations of annual averages from the Current Population Survey, 2002.

Life Success Goal: Preparation for career success. Your course work will give you the knowledge and hands-on skills you need to achieve your career goals. It will also expose you to a variety of careers related to your major, many of which you may not have even heard of. Completing college will open career doors that are closed to those without a degree.

Life Success Goal: Active community involvement and an appreciation of different cultures. Going to college prepares you to understand complex political, economic, and social forces that affect you and others. This understanding is the basis for good citizenship and encourages community involvement. Your education also exposes you to the ways in which people and cultures are different and how these differences affect world affairs.

Thinking about these big-picture goals should help you begin to brainstorm, in more detail, what you want out of college. What courses do you want to take? What kind of schedule do you want? What degree or certificate are you shooting for? Think about academic excellence and whether honors and awards are important goals. If you have a particular career in mind, then consider the degrees and experience it may require. Finally, consider personal growth, and think about the importance of developing friendships with people who will motivate and inspire you.

A journey of a thousand miles begins with a single step.

LAO TZU

Now you are beginning to develop a picture of what you want to have gained by the end of your college experience. The biggest question remains: What gets you from here to there? Not everyone arrives successfully. However, with dedication, hard work, and the power that comes from something called *successful intelligence,* you can make it.

How can *successful intelligence* help you achieve your goals?

Think about how you would define *intelligence*. Chances are, like many people, you believe that people are born with a certain, unchangeable amount of intelligence, and that this has a significant effect on the ability to succeed. Another fairly common belief is that standardized tests, such as IQ (intelligence quotient) tests, accurately measure a person's intelligence and are predictors of success.

Psychologist and Yale professor Robert J. Sternberg views intelligence differently. His life experiences convinced him that traditional intelligence measurements lock people into poor performances and often do not accurately reflect their potential for life success.

According to Sternberg, the IQ, Scholastic Assessment Test (SAT), American College Test (ACT), and other standardized tests measure *inert intelligence*—that is, they require passive repetition rather than goal-directed thinking. He further explains that those who score well on tests may have strong recall and analytical skills but do not necessarily have the power to make things happen in the real world.[1] That power to put information to work is critical to your success. No matter how high you score on a library science test, for example, your knowledge won't serve you unless you can use it to research a topic successfully.

Defining successful intelligence

In Sternberg's view, intelligence is not a fixed quantity; people have the capacity to increase intelligence as they learn and grow. In his book *Successful Intelligence: How Practical and Creative Intelligence Determine Success in Life*, Sternberg focuses on what he calls *successful intelligence*—"the kind of intelligence used to achieve important goals."[2] Successful intelligence better predicts life success than any IQ test because it focuses on actions—what you *do* to achieve your goals—instead of just on recall and analysis.

Everyone knows people who fit the conventional definition of "smart." They score well on tests and get good grades. Teachers expect them to achieve academically, and they do. However, these students may have limited success outside the classroom if they can't translate their "smarts" into real-world actions.

In contrast, other students have a hard time making the grade but are seen as "offbeat," "creative," or "street smart." Some of these students use their practical or creative intelligence to lift themselves above the crowd. Successful people such as Bill Gates, Ellen DeGeneres, and Woody Allen, despite difficulties in school, built extraordinary success by creatively using their strengths and developing practical ways to reach their goals.

Sternberg breaks successful intelligence into three parts or abilities: *Analytical* thinking, *creative* thinking, and *practical* thinking.

- *Analytical thinking*—commonly known as critical thinking—involves analyzing and evaluating information, often in order to work through a problem or decision. Analytical thinking is largely responsible for school success and is recognized and measured through traditional testing methods.
- *Creative thinking* involves generating new and different ideas and approaches to problems, and, often, viewing the world in ways that disregard convention.
- *Practical thinking* means putting what you've learned into action in order to solve a problem or make a decision. Practical thinking enables you to accomplish goals despite real-world obstacles.

These ways of thinking work together to move you toward a goal, as Sternberg describes:

> Analytical thinking is required to solve problems and to judge the quality of ideas. Creative intelligence is required to formulate good problems and ideas in the first place. Practical intelligence is needed to use the ideas and their analysis in an effective way in one's everyday life.[3]

Here are two examples that illustrate how this works.

Successful intelligence in a study group— reaching for the goal of helping each other learn.

- **Analyze** the concepts you must learn, including how they relate to what you already know.
- **Create** humorous memory games to help you remember key concepts.
- **Think practically** about who in the group does what best, and assign tasks according to what you discover.

Successful intelligence in considering an academic path— reaching for the goal of declaring a major.

- **Analyze** what you do well, what you like to do. Then analyze the course offerings in your college catalog until you come up with one or more that seem to match up with your strengths.
- **Create** a dream career, then work backward to come up with majors that might support it. For example, if you want to be a science writer, consider majoring in biology and minoring in journalism.
- **Think practically** about your major by talking with students and instructors in the department, looking at course requirements, and interviewing professionals in the fields that interest you.

Why successful intelligence is your key to success

When you understand how learning helps you achieve goals that are important to you, you want to learn. When you want to learn, you work hard to make it happen. When you make the effort to learn, you are most likely to succeed.

Successful intelligence powers this entire process, from understanding to success. By helping you to focus on how your learning propels you toward specific goals, it boosts your desire to learn. By giving you an action plan with which you can think through problems or pursue goals, successful intelligence inspires you to work hard and aim high. By helping you to make the most of your strengths and compensate for or correct your weaknesses, it helps you capitalize on who you are and what you can do.

More good news for all kinds of learners lies in the fact that successful intelligence has three equally important elements. Students who have had trouble with tests and other traditional analytical skills can take heart, knowing that creative and practical thinking can help them forge new paths to success. Students who test well can turn their analytical skills into real tools for success through creative thinking and practical action plans.

How will *Keys to Success* help you build *successful intelligence?*

The goal of *Keys to Success* is to help you build the analytical, creative, and practical thinking skills that will get you where you want to go in school and in life. Each element of the book contributes to this goal.

The chapter material

Through your exploration of the various topics in *Keys to Success*, you will develop all three aspects of successful intelligence. The material will often connect a topic to analytical, creative, or practical thinking. Accounts and examples from students, professors, and professionals show how people use various analytical, creative, and practical skills to accomplish personal goals. In addition, Chapter 4—the chapter on thinking—goes into detail about how you can evaluate and build analytical, creative, and practical skills.

Key 1.3 provides some examples of the practical, analytical, and creative thinking skills that lie within chapter topics.

The in-chapter activities

As you work through each chapter, you will find three activities designed to help you turn ideas you read into news you can use.

- *Get Analytical* gives you an opportunity to analyze a chapter topic.
- *Get Creative* prompts you to think creatively about chapter material.
- *Get Practical* provides a chance to consider a practical application of a chapter idea.

Working through these activities gives you a double benefit. While building successful intelligence skills, you are also deepening your understanding of chapter material, making it more useful to you in pursuing your goals.

Keys to Success *chapters develop successful intelligence.*

CHAPTER	ANALYTICAL SKILLS	CREATIVE SKILLS	PRACTICAL SKILLS
2	• Thinking about whether your values reflect who you are or want to be • Analyzing how successful a time manager you are	• Coming up with creative ways to manage stress • Thinking about different paths toward a goal	• Planning steps toward a goal • Keeping an effective calendar
3	• Examining how you learn • Matching your learning style to courses, skills, and environments	• When thinking about a major, considering departments or types of majors that are off the beaten path • Opening your mind to new perceptions of you as a learner	• Creating a step-by-step plan toward declaring a major • Linking your learning style to study skills that will help you most
4	• Distinguishing fact from opinion • Evaluating assumptions	• Brainstorming • Using strategies that enhance creative abilities	• Practical problem solving • Making a well-considered decision
5	• Evaluating arguments • Analyzing the hidden perspectives found in all media messages	• Thinking of different ways to review reading material • Finding innovative ways to work with study group members	• Using a practical plan—SQ3R—for maximizing reading comprehension • Expanding your vocabulary
6	• Deciding which information is important enough to record in notes • Examining your particular listening challenges	• Coming up with interesting mnemonic devices • Brainstorming ways to listen more effectively when you don't agree with the speaker	• Memorizing by grouping information • Knowing when and how to use different note-taking systems
7	• Analyzing why you made a particular mistake on a test • Selecting the most important material to study for a test	• Brainstorming a study schedule • Coming up with a variety of review techniques	• Knowing how to handle different types of test questions • Combating test anxiety
8	• Examining how prejudice leads to discrimination • Evaluating the accuracy of your judgments of others	• Finding ways to think expansively about diversity • Brainstorming methods for managing anger	• Making connections with diverse people • Adjusting to different communication styles
9	• Thinking through the consequences of drugs and alcohol • Linking your learning style to related career areas	• Brainstorming careers that interest you and suit your talents • Coming up with people with whom you can network	• Keeping credit card use under control • Living your personal mission

The end-of-chapter exercises

The end-of-chapter exercises give you several opportunities to combine what you have learned and apply it to important tasks.

- *Developing Successful Intelligence: Putting It All Together* unites analytical thinking ("Think it through"), creative thinking ("Think out of the box"), and practical thinking ("Make it happen"). This exercise builds your understanding of successful intelligence as an active process and strengthens your ability to direct its elements toward a goal.
- *Team Building: Collaborative Solutions* encourages you to apply various successful intelligence elements to a group setting, building both thinking skills and your ability to work successfully with others.
- *Writing: Discovery Through Journaling* provides an opportunity to put your analysis, creative thoughts, and practical ideas down in words, building writing skills as well as thinking skills.
- *Career Portfolio: Plan for Success* is a chance to see how your analytical, creative, and practical skills will help you prepare for workplace success. Through the chapters you will build a tangible and useful portfolio—analyzing workplace opportunities, coming up with creative ideas about careers, and creating practical items that you will use in your job search.

With the power of your mind and the tools waiting for you in this book, you possess the keys to success. What remains is to turn the key and get moving toward your goals—and this requires motivation. Here are some ways to find that motivation and put it to work.

get creative!

SEE YOURSELF AT YOUR BEST

Use your creative powers to improve your opinion of yourself and inspire action.

You probably have some idea of where you fit into the student body—your age, stage of life, and educational background. However, your "student status" is only a small part of who you are.

Imagine that students gained entry into college by writing personal ads and posting them on the admissions Web site. Write a personal ad that you feel would give you the best possible chance to get in. In it, talk about

- what makes you unique and anything but "average."
- what is special about you that will make the college a better place.
- how your college education will bring you personal and professional success.

_____

_____

_____

_____

_____

_____

What will *motivate you* to make the most of college?

Success is a process, not a fixed mark—and **motivation** keeps the process in motion. Successfully intelligent people find ways to motivate themselves to learn, grow, and work toward what they want.

Everyone has the potential to be motivated. The following strategies will help boost your motivation now, as you begin college, and in the future.

Focus on your self-esteem

When people believe in themselves, their **self-esteem** fuels their motivation to succeed. Belief, though, is only half the game. The other half is the action and effort that help you feel that you have earned your self-esteem, as basketball coach Rick Pitino explains: "Self-esteem is directly linked to deserving success. If you have established a great work ethic and have begun the discipline that is inherent with that, you will automatically begin to feel better about yourself."[4]

Think positively

Your attitudes influence what you will learn from your courses, instructors, and fellow students. A positive attitude—reinforced by **positive self-talk**—can open your mind to learning and inspire you to action. How can you talk positively to yourself even when times get tough?

- **Stop negative talk in its tracks.** If you catch yourself thinking, "I can never write a decent paper," replace this negativity with, "I can write better than that and next time I will." Then think about specific steps you can take to improve your writing.

- **Pay yourself a compliment.** Note your successes. Be specific: "I can now create an outline that helps me organize my thoughts for a paper."

- **Replace words of obligation with words of personal intent.**

  I should   *becomes*   I choose to
  I'll try   *becomes*   I will

Words of intent give you power and control because they imply a personal decision to act. A nursing student at Palo Alto College in San Antonio, Texas, understands the relationship between positive self-talk and success. "To stay motivated I will always remember that I

After working hard to win the school's first women's national title, Purdue basketball players have earned their self-esteem.

am doing this to better myself and to learn what I need to in order to be the best nurse that I can be. Making a (commitment) and staying true to it is not easy, but I know that an uncommitted person will never finish anything."[5]

Take action

Although thinking positively sets the tone for success, taking action gets you there. Without action, positive thoughts become empty statements.

Consider, for example, a student in a freshman composition class. This student thinks positive thoughts: "I write well. I can get at least a B+ in this class." She even posts her positive thoughts where she can see them. Then, during the semester, she misses about one-third of the class meetings, turns in papers late, and completely forgets to hand in two assignments. *She did not back up her intentions with action.* At the end of the course, when she barely passes the class, she wonders how someone with such a positive attitude could have done so poorly.

Following are some ways to get moving in a positive direction:

- Take responsibility. See yourself as being in charge of your success. Create personal guidelines that support that success—for example, "I pay attention to deadlines."
- Translate general statements into specific actions. Success will come when you make your guidelines real through action. If one of your personal guidelines is "I pay attention to deadlines," one action might be turning in assignments when they are due.

Be responsible

College requires that you take personal responsibility for your academic success in ways that you never did in high school. Even if you have lived on your own and held a job, helped raise a family, or both, college adds to that responsibility. You, as your own manager, are responsible for making decisions that keep you on track toward achieving what you want.

The theme of responsibility stands out in how several New Mexico State University students describe their personal transitions:[6]

- Angie Miller (majoring in Biology): "The hardest part of my freshman courses was doing all my work myself with nobody telling me every day that my homework was due. Also, there was more material covered in a shorter time, so it was more study time than in high school."
- Jason Roach (majoring in Business Computer Systems): "Your classes don't meet as many times a week as they did in high school. As a result, you get more homework. Since you only meet for a minimum of three hours a week, you have a great deal more time to read the book and complete the homework. It is sort of like a 'learn on your own' concept."
- Daniel Estrada (majoring in Latin American History and Spanish): "Are the classes harder than high school? Yes and no. I find that they can be easier because they are more to my interest since I picked them. The catch is that it is not up to the instructor to keep you on task. It is left unsaid that it is our responsibility to keep up with the reading and homework and to actually show up for class."

Taking responsibility is about living up to obligations. Through action, you prove that you are responsible—"response-able"—able to respond as efficiently as possible and to the best of your ability. Responsible college students can be trusted to fulfill obligations like these:

- attending class and participating in activities and discussions
- completing reading and assignments on time
- communicating with instructors and fellow students

Why are these basic actions the building blocks of school success? First, completing everyday responsibilities promotes good (habits). The more you do something, the more it becomes second nature. Second, small accomplishments make a big impression. When you show up to class, pay attention, contribute, and put in the hours necessary to master the material, you show your instructor and fellow students that you are committed to learning.

HABIT

A preference for a particular action that you do a certain way, and often on a regular basis or at certain times.

Develop positive habits

"Bad" habits stall motivation and prevent you from reaching important goals. Some bad habits, such as chronic lateness, cause obvious problems. Other habits, such as surfing the Internet, may not seem bad until you realize that you needed to spend those hours studying.

"Good" habits bring you closer to your goals. You often have to wait longer and work harder to be rewarded for good habits, which makes them harder to maintain. If you reduce your nights out to gain study time, for example, your grades won't improve in a week.

Define and evaluate your habits to see whether you need to make a change. If a habit is getting in the way of your goals, make a decision to change it. Pick a day to make the change, and then keep it up. To become accustomed to a new habit, be consistent for at least three weeks. Use positive self-talk to encourage your progress, and reward yourself for steps in the right direction.

It's never too late to make an important change in your habits. Returning student Sunny Hobbs is determined and serious, although she had neither trait 30 years ago, when she first enrolled in college and failed nearly every course. Sunny's personal problems, including her troubled marriage, were insurmountable barriers. Now divorced, she arrives early at Joliet Junior College in Joliet, Illinois. Sitting in the second row of her intermediate-algebra course, she works hard to take comprehensive notes. Her positive habits reflect a determination to earn an ascciate's degree from Joliet and to transfer to the University of Saint Francis where she plans to study elementary education.[7]

Try not to get discouraged if the process seems difficult. Rarely does someone make a change without setbacks. Take it one step at a time; when you lose steam, reflect on what you stand to gain. With persistence and positive thinking, you can reach your goal.

FACE YOUR FEARS[8]

Use practical skills to conquer a fear of yours that stems from the experience of starting college.

First, describe your fear—and be specific.

_____

_____

Now, list three small activities that get you closer to working through that fear. If you don't want to start a project because you fear failure, for example, you can begin by reading a book on the subject, brainstorming what you already know about it, or making up a project schedule.

1. _____

2. _____

3. _____

Commit yourself to one step that you will take within the next two days. State it here. Include the time and date you will begin and how much time you will spend.

_____

_____

What reward will you give yourself for taking this step?

_____

Did taking this step help ease your fear? If so, describe how.

_____

_____

Affirm that you have taken that first step and are on the way to success by signing your name here and writing the date.

Name _____   Date _____

Face your fears

Everyone experiences fear. Anything unknown—new people, experiences, situations—can be frightening because it involves risk. As you begin college, for example, you may wonder if you can handle the work, if you have chosen the right school, or if your education will prepare you for a well-paying job.

Nobody succeeds beyond his or her wildest expectations unless he or she begins with some wild expectations.

RALPH CHARELL

The challenges you will face in college may require that you face your fears and push your limits. The first step is to acknowledge what you fear. Look for fears that may lurk under symptoms like putting

things off and not trying very hard. Then, be specific about what you're afraid of. Focusing on a fear of working in the science lab, for example, helps you to brainstorm useful ways of coping.

Once you know what you fear, evaluate what will help you overcome it. For example, if you are concerned about working in the science lab, arrange to work with another student who is comfortable there and willing to be a mentor to you.

As you work through your fears, talk about them with people you trust. Everyone has fears, and when people share strategies, everyone benefits.

What do you do if you lose motivation during the semester? Refocus your attention on the practical steps that lead you toward your goals—attend class, complete your assignments when due, challenge yourself to do your best. Also, remind yourself of the connection between your work in school and your ability to achieve goals in your life beyond graduation.

How can *what you learn now* help you succeed in school, work, and life?

In his book *Techno Trends—24 Technologies That Will Revolutionize Our Lives*, futurist Daniel Burns describes a tomorrow that is linked to continuing education: "The future belongs to those who are capable of being retrained again and again," he says. "Think of it as periodically upgrading your human assets throughout your career. . . . Humans are infinitely upgradeable, but it does require an investment" in lifelong learning.[9]

In other words, you will need to continue to learn and grow in order to succeed. Here are some ways in which your college experience will develop your ability to stay open to new information and experiences.

College helps you value diversity

For most students, college provides an opportunity to question the "givens" of life and to open your mind and heart to people who are different from you. Learning to appreciate the similarities and differences among people and within people, and to value diversity in all its forms, is critical for life success.

Diversity means differences among people. On an interpersonal level, diversity refers to the differences between ourselves and others, between the groups we belong to and the groups we are not part of. Differences in gender, skin color, ethnicity and national origin, age, physical characteristics and abilities, and sexual orientation define this most obvious level of diversity.

Students often meet and work with instructors and other students representing a variety of ethnicities, cultural backgrounds, and stages of life.

Other differences—many of which define people and affect relationships in fundamental ways—lie beneath the surface. Among these are:

- cultural and religious backgrounds and beliefs, reflected in different values and behaviors
- differences in educational background and socioeconomic status
- differences in family background (for example, two-parent versus single-parent households)
- differences in marital and parental status

Diversity refers to the differences within people. Another layer of diversity lies within each person. Among the factors that define this layer are:

- personality traits—Are you shy or assertive, a social butterfly or a loner, thoughtful and cautious or impulsive and a risk taker?
- learning style—Are you a verbal, visual, or logical learner? Do you learn by talking with others, thinking on your own, or performing hands-on tasks?
- strengths and weaknesses in analytical, creative, and practical abilities
- natural talents and interests

As you will see in Chapter 8, accepting people for who they are means accepting all aspects of their diversity. In Chapter 3, you will gain a greater understanding of your own and others' learning styles, and in Chapter 4 you will explore differences in analytical, creative, and practical abilities.

College prepares you to learn from failure and celebrate success

Even the most successful people make mistakes and experience failures. In fact, failure is one of the greatest teachers. Failure provides an opportunity to realize what you didn't know so that you can improve. What you learn from a failure will most likely stay with you more intensely and guide you more effectively than many other things you learn.

Learning from failure

Learning from your failures and mistakes involves successfully intelligent thinking.

Analyze what happened. For example, imagine that after a long night of studying for a chemistry test, you forgot to complete an American History paper due the next day. Your focus on the test caused you to overlook other tasks. Now you may face a lower grade on your paper if you turn it in late, plus you may be inclined to rush it and turn in a project that isn't as good as it could be.

Come up with creative ways to change. You can make a commitment to note deadlines in a bright color in your planner and to check due dates more often. You can also try arranging your study schedule so that it is more organized and less last-minute.

Put your plan into action. Do what you have decided to do—and keep an eye on how it is working. If you rearrange your study schedule, for example, look carefully at whether it is improving your ability to stay on top of your responsibilities.

Your value as a human being does not diminish when you make a mistake. People who can manage failure demonstrate to themselves and others that they have the courage to take risks and learn. Employers often value risk takers more than people who always play it safe.

In order to succeed you must fail,

so that you know what not to do the next time.

ANTHONY J. D'ANGELO

Celebrating success

Acknowledging your successes, no matter how small, is as important as learning from your mistakes. Earning a B on a paper after you had received a C on the previous one, for example, is worth celebrating. Take a moment to acknowledge what you have accomplished, whether it is a

---

get analytical!   **LEARN FROM A MISTAKE**

SUCCESSFUL INTELLIGENCE
CREATIVE
PRACTICAL
ANALYTICAL
SUCCESSFUL INTELLIGENCE

Analyze what happened when you made a mistake in order to avoid the same mistake next time.

Describe an academic situation—you didn't study enough for a test, you didn't complete an assignment on time, you didn't listen carefully enough to a lecture and missed important information—where you made a mistake. What happened?

_____

_____

_____

What were the consequences of the mistake?

_____

_____

_____

What, if anything, did you learn from your mistake that you will use in similar situations?

_____

_____

_____

_____

good grade, a job offer, or any other personal victory. Let your success help you to build your confidence that you can succeed again.

As you would when working to change a habit, reward yourself when you succeed. "Take it seriously and work hard, yes. But don't forget to enjoy yourself every now and then," advises a Palo Alto College freshman taking a First Year Experience class. "Take a break and see a movie. Read a book that's deliciously trashy, not scholarly. Take a bubble bath as you pat yourself on the back for a job well done. This is a special time. It's costing you time, money, sacrifices to be in college. Enjoy it and embrace it. You're making memories now, so make it count."[10]

College helps you apply successful intelligence in a changing world

As a college student, you are making sacrifices—including a significant investment of time and money as well as a dramatic lifestyle change—to achieve success throughout your life. You are building the analytic, creative, and practical intelligence you need to cope with a changing world:

- Knowledge in nearly every field is doubling every two to three years. That means that if you stop learning, for even a few years, your knowledge base will be inadequate to keep up with the changes in your career.
- Technology is changing how you live and work. The Internet and technology will shape communications and improve knowledge and productivity during the next 20 years—and will require continual learning.
- The global economy is moving from a product and service base to a knowledge and talent base. Jobs of the past are being replaced by knowledge-based jobs, in the United States and abroad, that ask workers to think critically to come up with solutions.
- Workers are changing jobs and careers more frequently. The National Research Bureau reports that currently the average employee changes jobs every three to four years, and it is estimated that a 22-year-old college graduate in the year 2000 will have an average of 8 employers in his or her first 10 years in the workplace.[11] Every time you decide to start a new career, you need new knowledge and skills.

All of these signs point to the need to become lifelong learners—individuals who continue to build knowledge and intelligence as a mechanism for improving their lives and careers. Through successful intelligence, you will maintain the kind of flexibility that will enable you to adapt to thedemands of the twenty-first century.

Facing change means taking risks. When you enter college, you accept certain challenges and risks as necessary hurdles on the path toward success. As a successfully intelligent lifelong learner, you will find ways to continue to learn and strive toward what you want. Welcome to the beginning of the road to your dreams.

In Chinese writing, this character has two meanings: One is "chaos"; the other, "opportunity." The character communicates the belief that every chaotic, challenging situation in life also presents an opportunity. By responding to challenges actively, you can discover the opportunity within the chaos.

Let this concept reassure you as you begin college. You may feel that you are going through a time of change and chaos. Take heart. No matter how difficult the obstacles, you can choose to persevere. You can build the kind of successful intelligence that helps you learn, grow, and realize your dreams.

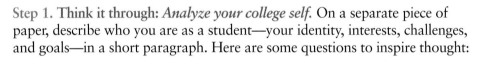

BUILDING SKILLS

FOR COLLEGE, CAREER, AND LIFE SUCCESS

Developing Successful Intelligence

Make your first semester count. Academics is only part of college. Campus resources, clubs, student activity groups, and other organizations can enrich your experience. Remember that students who make social connections tend to do better in college. Put a toe in the water sooner rather than later and you will begin to benefit from what your school has to offer.

Step 1. Think it through: *Analyze your college self.* On a separate piece of paper, describe who you are as a student—your identity, interests, challenges, and goals—in a short paragraph. Here are some questions to inspire thought:

- How would you describe your culture, ethnicity, gender, age, lifestyle?
- How long are you planning to be in college?
- What family and work obligations do you have?
- What is your current living situation?
- What do you feel are your biggest challenges in college?
- What do you like to study, and why does it interest you?

Step 2. Think out of the box: *Brainstorm your ideal extracurriculars.* On a second piece of paper, write ideas about how you want to spend your time outside of class. To inspire creative ideas, try using one or more of the following questions as a starting point:

- If you had no fear, what horizon-broadening experience would you sign up for?
- When you were in elementary school, what were your favorite activities? Which activities might translate into current interests and pursuits?
- What kinds of organizations, activities, groups, experiences, or people make you think, "Wow, I want to do that"?

create your future

- Think about the people that you feel bring out the best in you. What do you like to do with them? What kinds of things are they involved with?
- Who are the people with whom you have little in common? How could you benefit from getting to know them?

Step 3. Make it happen: *Take practical steps toward the activities you like.* Thinking about how you have described yourself in terms of both academics and extracurricular pursuits, look in your student handbook at the resources and organizations your school offers. These may include some or all of the following:

Academic centers (reading, writing, etc.)	Organizations for students with a disability
Academic organizations	Religious organizations
Adult education center	School publications
Arts clubs (music, drama, dance, etc.)	School TV/radio stations
Fraternities/Sororities	Sports clubs
International student groups	Student associations
Minority student groups	Student government
On-campus work opportunities	Volunteer groups

In the left-hand column on the grid that follows, list the five offices or organizations you most want to check out this semester. Then—through your school publications and/or a little legwork—fill in the information on the grid, answering the questions shown across the top for each item you listed. Notice that the last column requires action—fill it in when you have made initial contact with each office or organization.

Office or Organization	Location	Hours, or times of meetings	What it offers	Phone number or e-mail	Initial contact—date and what happened

Let this exercise be a jumping-off point for real involvement this semester. If after your initial contact you wish to become more involved, go for it. Remember that the activities that inspire you are often a clue to your career path—and that knowing how to work with others is one of the most important skills you will build in college.

Team Building

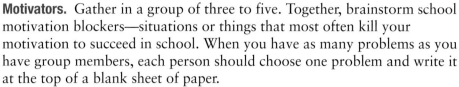

Motivators. Gather in a group of three to five. Together, brainstorm school motivation blockers—situations or things that most often kill your motivation to succeed in school. When you have as many problems as you have group members, each person should choose one problem and write it at the top of a blank sheet of paper.

Look at the motivation blocker on your page. Under it, write one practical idea you have about how to overcome it. When everyone is finished, pass the pages one person to the left. Then write an idea about the new blocker at the top of the page you've received. If you can't think of anything, pass the page as is. Continue this way until your page comes back to you. Then discuss the ideas as a group, analyzing which ideas might work better than others. Add other ideas to the lists if you think of them.

The last step: On your own, keeping in mind your group discussion, list three specific actions that you commit to taking in order to keep motivation high when the going gets rough.

1. _____

2. _____

3. _____

Writing

Record your thoughts on a separate piece of paper or in a journal.

Reasons for college. People attend college for technical training, the sake of learning, increased earning power, and more. Think about your own reasons. Why are you here, and what do you want out of the experience? On a scale of 1 (lowest) to 10 (highest), rank your commitment to succeeding in college. What sacrifices—in terms of time, hard work, finances—are you willing to make to get what you want and to persevere in your quest for success?

Career Portfolio

This is the first of 9 career portfolio assignments you will complete, one for each chapter. By the end of the semester, you will have compiled a portfolio of documents that will help you achieve your career goals.

Type your career portfolio work on a computer and store the documents electronically, on a disk or in a specific file on your hard drive. If you do not have access to a computer, type or write your work on sheets of paper and keep them together in one file folder. Use paper for assignments that ask you to draw or make collages.

Setting career goals. Whether you have a current career, have held a few different jobs, or have not yet entered the workplace, college is an ideal time to take stock of your career goals. The earlier in your college education that you consider career goals, the more you can take advantage of how college can help prepare you for work, in both job-specific and general ways. Having a strong vision of where you wish to go will also be a powerful motivator as you face some of the inevitable challenges of the next few years.

Take some time to think about your working life. Spend 15 minutes brainstorming everything that you wish you could be, do, have, or experience in your career 10 years from now—the skills you want to have, money you want to earn, benefits, experiences, travel, anything you can think of. List your wishes, draw them, depict them using cutouts from magazines, or combine these ideas—whatever you like best.

Now, look at your list. To discover how your wishes relate to one another, group them in order of priority. Label three computer "pages" or three pieces of paper Priority 1, Priority 2, and Priority 3. Write each wish where it fits, with Priority 1 being the most important, Priority 2 the second most important, and Priority 3 the third.

Look at your priority lists. What do they tell you about what is most important to you? What wishes are you ready to work toward right now? Circle or highlight the three highest-priority wishes. Write down the trade-offs you will have to make today to make these wishes come true. Don't let yourself off the hook—be realistic and direct.

SUGGESTED READINGS

Evers, Frederick T., James Cameron Rush, and Iris Berdow. *The Bases of Competence: Skills for Lifelong Learning and Employability.* San Francisco, CA: Jossey-Bass, 1998.

Jeffers, Susan. *Feel the Fear . . . And Beyond: Mastering the Techniques for Doing It Anyway.* New York: Ballentine, 1998.

Lombardo, Alison. *Navigating Your Freshman Year.* New York: Natavi Guides, 2003.

Simon, Linda. *New Beginnings: A Guide for Adult Learners and Returning Students,* 2nd ed. Upper Saddle River, NJ: Prentice Hall.

Sternberg, Robert. *Successful Intelligence: How Practical and Creative Intelligence Determine Success in Life.* New York: Plume, 1997.

Tyler, Suzette. *Been There, Should've Done That II: More Tips for Making the Most of College.* Lansing, MI: Front Porch Press, 2001.

Weinberg, Carol. *The Complete Handbook for College Women: Making the Most of Your College Experience.* New York: New York University Press, 1994.

INTERNET RESOURCES

Student Center: www.studentcenter.org

Student.Com: College Life Online: www.student.com

Prentice Hall Student Success Supersite: Student Union: www.prenhall.com/success/StudentUn/index.html

Success Stories: www.prenhall.com/success/Stories/index.html

1. Robert J. Sternberg, *Successful Intelligence*. New York: Plume, 1997, p. 11.

2. Ibid, p. 12.

3. Ibid, pp. 127–128.

4. Rick Pitino, *Success Is a Choice*. New York: Broadway Books, 1997, p. 40.

5. From student essay submitted by the First Year Experience students of Patty Parma, Palo Alto College, San Antonio, Texas, January 2004.

6. "Are the Classes Really That Much Harder Than High School?" New Mexico State University, June 1999 [on-line]. Available: www.nmsu.edu/aggieland/students/faq_classes.html (March 2004).

7. Jamilah Evelyn, "A Clean Slate: Many Colleges Start Programs to Forgive Poor Grades," *The Chronicle of Higher Education*, October 11, 2002 [on-line]. Available: http://chronicle.com/weekly/v49/i07a03901.htm (March 2004).

8. Rita Lenken Hawkins, Baltimore City Community College, 1997.

9. Cited in Colin Rise and Malcolm J. Nicholl, *Accelerated Learning for the 21st Century*. New York: Dell, 1997, pp. 5–6.

10. From student essay submitted by the First Year Experience students of Patty Parma, Palo Alto College, San Antonio, Texas, January 2004.

11. Jay Palmer, "Marry Me a Little," *Barron's*, July 24, 2000, p. 25.

2

IN THIS CHAPTER . . .

*you will explore answers
to the following questions:*

Values, Goals, Time, and Stress

MANAGING YOURSELF

Achieving your most important goals depends on your ability to manage yourself. As an effective self-manager, you take charge of your life much like a CEO heads up a top-performing business. This chapter divides the indispensable skill of self-management into four parts: using values to guide your goal setting, working through a process to achieve goals, managing time in a way that propels you toward your goals, and, throughout the journey, managing the stress that will often arise.

The reality of school, workplace, and personal life will often bring problems that create obstacles and produce stress. Everyone has problems; what counts is how you handle them. Your ability to manage yourself—accompanied by a generous dose of motivation—will help you cope with what you encounter, achieve your goals, and learn lasting lessons in the process.

On the following page, read how student Rosalia Chavez is working to overcome her real-life obstacles.

- Why is it important to know what you value?
- How do you set and achieve goals?
- How can you effectively manage your time?
- How do you cope with the stress of college life?

How can I stay focused on my school goals?

I married at 18 and didn't finish high school. After our two sons were born, I decided to get my G.E.D., but my husband didn't want me to. At this point, I knew I had to start making opportunities for myself. Shortly after I had begun to further my education, my husband died. I am now taking classes full-time and I work part-time in the Chicano/Hispano Student Affairs Office. I would like to empower future generations of Hispanic women to follow their dreams by telling them my story.

I have to make daily decisions about priorities, and my life situations often get in the way of my schoolwork. Recently, I had to drop a class because my children were sick and I couldn't keep up. My son, who is 11, has ADHD (attention deficit hyperactivity disorder). I can no longer afford his medicine because I was denied state medical assistance. Can you offer suggestions about how I can manage my life and stay focused on my school goals?

Rosalia Chavez
University of Arizona,
Tucson, Arizona

The key to everything is to decide what is most important to you and let all else fall in line.

I want to applaud you for trying to do so much under difficult circumstances. First, to minimize the sense of conflict and frustration, I suggest that you sit with your children and make a *written* list of your priorities. If you have too many things on the list, eliminate some. Simplicity is an important key to life management. If your first priority is your children, then don't sweat the fact that you had to stop school when one child was sick. You can always finish school.

Second, make a *written weekly schedule* so that you can see how you spend your time. Look at the schedule as your primary problem-solving tool. Monitor it to see how well it works and what it tells you about how you are managing. If how you spend your time does not reflect your priorities, or if you do not have enough time to accomplish tasks, revise your schedule.

Third, enlist your children to help with your management activities. For instance, your 11-year-old is old enough to help with most household tasks. I know of a woman who was divorced with four children. She discovered that they could do most everything as well as she could, including cleaning and paying bills. Her children are now a rocket scientist, a doctor, and two are lawyers. She credits their having learned responsibility at an early age. See what your children can do.

Finally, your son's ADHD problem can be approached from more than one angle. Changing diet or particular exercises may be effective. You may not need the medicine eventually. In the meantime, there are companies such as Medco that provide drugs at reduced rates. You and your son should research this issue thoroughly.

Dr. Jacqueline Fleming
Director, General University Academic Center
Texas Southern University, Houston, Texas

Why is it important to know *what you value?*

Y ou make life choices—what to do, what to believe, what to buy, how to act—based on your personal values. Your choice to pursue a degree, for example, reflects that you value the personal and professional growth that come from a college education. Being on time for your classes shows that you value punctuality. Paying bills regularly and on time shows that you value financial stability.

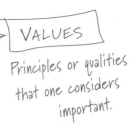

VALUES

Principles or qualities that one considers important.

Values play a key role in your drive to achieve important goals, because they help you to:

- Understand what you want out of life. Your most meaningful goals should reflect what you value most.
- Build "rules for life." Your values form the foundation for your decisions. You will return repeatedly to them for guidance, especially when you find yourself in unfamiliar territory.
- Find people who inspire you. Spending time with people who share similar values will help you clarify how you want to live and find support as you work toward what's important to you.

Now that you have an idea of how you can use values, focus on how to identify yours.

Identifying and evaluating values

Ask yourself questions: What do you focus on in a given day? What do you consider important to be, to do, or to have? What do you wish to accomplish in your life? Answers to questions like these will point you toward your values. The exercise on page 31 will help you think through values in more detail.

After you determine your values, evaluate them to see if they make sense for you. Many forces affect your values—family, friends, culture, media, school, work, neighborhood, religious beliefs, world events. No matter how powerful these external influences may be, whether a value feels right should be your primary consideration in deciding to adopt it.

Answering the following questions about a value will help you decide if it "feels right."

- Where did the value come from?
- What other different values could I consider?
- What might happen as a result of adopting this value?
- Have I made a personal commitment to this choice? Have I told others about it?
- Do my life goals and day-to-day actions reflect this value?

If you let your values shift to fit you as you grow, you will always have a base on which to build achievable goals and make wise decisions.

How values affect your educational experience

Well-considered values can lead to smart choices while you are in school. Your values will help you:

● **Keep going when the going gets tough.** Translate your value of education into specific actions, as a student at Palo Alto College did. "Success takes much hard work and dedication," he says. "Since I have a hard time with writing, and I can't understand algebra, I've made a commitment to write in a journal every day and attend math tutoring at least three times a week."[1]

Great minds have purposes; others have wishes.

WASHINGTON IRVING

● **Choose your major and a career direction.** If you've always been an environmentalist, then you may choose to major in environmental science. If you feel fulfilled when you help people, then you might consider a career in social work.

● **Choose friends and activities that enrich your life.** Having friends who share your desire to succeed in school will increase your motivation and reduce your stress. Joining organizations whose activities support your values will broaden your educational experience.

● **Choose what you want out of school and how hard you want to work.** What kinds of skills and knowledge do you wish to build? How hard are you willing to work to achieve your goals? Going above and beyond will build your drive to succeed and hone your work habits—two items that will be useful in a competitive job market.

Finally, your values affect your success at school and beyond, because the more ethical a student you are, the more likely you are to stay in school and to build lasting knowledge and skills.

Academic integrity: How ethical values promote success at school

ACADEMIC INTEGRITY
Following a code of moral values, prizing honesty and fairness in all aspects of academic life—classes, assignments, tests, papers, projects, and relationships with students and faculty.

Having academic integrity promotes learning and ensures a quality education based on ethics and hard work. Read your school's code of honor, or academic integrity policy, in your student handbook. When you enrolled, you agreed to abide by it.

The Center for Academic Integrity, part of the Kenan Institute for Ethics at Duke University, defines academic integrity as a commitment to five fundamental values: honesty, trust, fairness, respect, and responsibility.[2] These values are the positive actions that define academic integrity.

● **Honesty.** Honesty defines the pursuit of knowledge and implies a search for truth in your class work, papers and lab reports, and teamwork with other students.

● **Trust.** Mutual trust—between instructor and student, as well as among students—makes possible the free exchange of ideas that is fundamental to learning. Trust means being true to your word.

EXPLORE YOUR VALUES

get analytical!

Evaluate what you think is most important to you, and connect educational goals to your top values.

Rate each of the values in the list on a scale from 1 to 5, 1 being least important to you and 5 being most important.

___ Knowing yourself	___ Being liked by others	___ Reading
___ Self-improvement	___ Taking risks	___ Time to yourself
___ Improving physical/mental health	___ Time for fun/relaxation	___ Lifelong learning
___ Staying fit through exercise	___ Competing and winning	___ Getting a good job
___ Pursuing an education	___ Spiritual/religious life	___ Making a lot of money
___ Good relationships with family	___ Community involvement	___ Creative/artistic pursuits
___ Helping others	___ Keeping up with the news	___ Other (write below)
___ Being organized	___ Financial stability	___

Write your top three values here:

1. _____

2. _____

3. _____

Values often affect your educational choices. Choose one top value that is a factor in an educational choice that you have made. Explain the choice and how the value is involved. Example: A student who values mental health makes a choice to pursue a degree in psychology with a future plan to work as a school counselor.

_____

_____

_____

_____

Name an area of study that you think would help you live according to this value.

_____

- **Fairness.** Instructors must create a fair academic environment where students are judged against clear standards and in which procedures are well defined.
- **Respect.** In a respectful academic environment, both students and instructors accept and honor a wide range of opinions, even if the opinions are contrary to core beliefs.
- **Responsibility.** You are responsible for making choices that will provide you with the best education—choices that reflect fairness and honesty.

Choosing to act with integrity has the following positive consequences:

- **Increased self-esteem.** Self-esteem is tied to action. The more you act in respectful and honorable ways, the better you feel about yourself, and the more likely you are to succeed.
- **Acquired knowledge.** If you cheat you might pass a test—and a course—but chances are you won't retain the knowledge and skills you need for success. Honest work is more likely to result in knowledge that lasts—and that you can use to accomplish career and life goals.
- **Effective behavioral patterns.** When you condition yourself to play fair now, you set a pattern for your behavior at work and with friends and family.
- **Mutual respect.** Respecting the work of others will lead others to respect your work.

The last two bullet points reflect the positive effect that integrity has on your relationships. This is only one way in which values help you to successfully relate to, work with, and understand the people around you. Here's another way: Being open to different values, often linked with different cultures, can enhance your understanding of cultural diversity.

Values and cultural diversity

At college, you may meet people who seem different in ways that you may not expect. Many of these differences stem from attitudes and behaviors that are unfamiliar to you. These attitudes <u>and behaviors are rooted in the values that people acquire from their</u> culture, either from the continuing influence of family and community in the United States or from their homeland.

Cultural misunderstandings can interfere with the relationships and friendships you form in college, career, and life. As someone who accepts and appreciates diversity, your goal is to develop the cultural competence to understand and appreciate these differences so that they enhance—rather than hinder—communication.[3]

A simple model to help you avoid communication problems with people from other cultures was developed by Edward Hall, an anthropologist and an authority on cross-cultural communication. Hall linked communication styles to what he called high-context and low-context cultures:[4]

- People from *high-context* cultures rely heavily in their communication on context and situation as well as on body language and eye contact. Time (past, present, and future), fate, personal relationships and status, gender roles, trust, gestures, and sense of self and space are just some of the factors that influence communication in these cultures. High-context countries span the world and include China, Japan, Brazil, Saudi Arabia, Italy, and France.
- In contrast, people from *low-context* cultures focus on what is explicitly said or written and pay little attention to context and nonverbal cues. Countries with low-context cultures include the United States, Canada, England, Australia, Germany, and the Scandinavian countries.

CULTURE

A set of values, behaviors, tastes, knowledge, attitudes, and habits shared by a group of people.

CULTURAL COMPETENCE

The ability to understand and appreciate differences and to respond to people of all cultures in a way that values their worth, respects their beliefs and practices, and builds communication and relationships.

As you continue to read *Keys to Success*, look for examples of how cultural diversity impacts everything from teamwork and relationships, to listening, questioning, and more. Then think of the wisdom of cultural diversity consultant Helen Turnbull on turning differences into strengths:

> We must suspend our judgment. We should not judge others negatively because they are indirect, or their accents aren't clear, or their tone of voice is tentative, or they avoid eye contact. We must learn patience and suspend judgment long enough to realize these differences don't make one of us right and the other wrong. They simply mean that we approach communication from a different frame of reference and, many times, a different value system.[5]

Although clarifying your values will help you choose your educational path, goal-setting and goal-achievement skills will help you travel that path to the end. Goals turn values into tools and put them to practical use.

How do you *set and achieve* goals?

When you identify something that you want, you set a goal. Actually *getting* what you want—from college, career, or life—demands working to *achieve* your goals. Achieving goals, whether they are short term or long term, involves following a goal-achievement plan. Think of the plan you are about to read as a map; with it helping you to establish each segment of the trip, you will be able to define your route and follow it successfully.

Set long-term goals

Start by establishing the goals that have the largest scope, the *long-term* goals that you aim to attain over a period of six months, a year, or more. As a student, your long-term goals include attending school and earning a degree or certificate. Getting an education is a significant goal that often takes years to reach.

Some long-term goals have an open-ended time frame. For example, if your goal is to become a better musician, you may work at it over a lifetime. These goals also invite more creative thinking; you have more time and freedom to consider all sorts of paths to your (goal.) Other goals, such as completing all the courses in your major, have a shorter scope, a more definite end, and often fewer options for how to get from A to Z.

GOAL

An end toward which effort is directed; an aim or intention.

The following long-term goal statement, written by Carol Carter, a *Keys to Success* author, may take years to complete:

My goal is to build my own business in which I create opportunities for students to maximize their talents. In this business, I will reach thousands of students and teachers through books, the Internet, teacher seminars, and student-oriented programs.

Carol also has long-term goals that she hopes to accomplish in no more than a year:

Develop and publish one book. Design three seminars for teachers with accompanying PowerPoints and other materials. Create Internet-based materials that encourage student success and use them in student seminars.

Just as Carol's goals are tailored to her personality, abilities, and interests, your goals should reflect your uniqueness. To determine your long-term goals, think about what you want to accomplish while you are in school and after you graduate. Think of ways you can link your personal values and professional aims, as in the following examples:

- Values: Health and fitness, helping others

  Goal: To become a physical therapist
- Values: Independence, financial success

  Goal: To obtain a degree in business and start a company

Basing your long-term goals on values increases your motivation. The more your goals focus on what is most important to you, the greater your drive to reach them.

Set short-term goals

Short-term goals are smaller steps that move you toward a long-term goal. Lasting as short as a few hours or as long as a few months, these goals help you manage your broader aspirations as they narrow your focus and encourage progress. If you had a long-term goal of graduating with a degree in nursing, for example, you may want to accomplish the following short-term goals in the next six months.

- I will learn the names, locations, and functions of every human bone and muscle.
- I will work with a study group to understand the muscular-skeletal system.

These same goals can be broken down into even smaller parts, such as the following one-month goals:

- I will work with on-screen tutorials of the muscular-skeletal system until I understand and memorize the material.
- I will spend three hours a week with my study partners.

In addition to monthly goals, you may have short-term goals that extend for a week, a day, or even a couple of hours in a given day. To support your month-long goal of regularly meeting with your study partners, you may wish to set the following short-term goals:

- **By the end of today:** Call study partners to ask them about when they might be able to meet
- **One week from now:** Have scheduled each of our weekly meetings this month
- **Two weeks from now:** Have had our first meeting
- **Three weeks from now:** Type up and send around notes from the first meeting; have the second meeting

As you consider your long- and short-term goals, notice how all of your goals are linked to one another. As Key 2.1 shows, your long-term goals establish a context for the short-term goals. In turn, your short-term goals make the long-term goals seem clearer and more reachable.

At any given time, you will be working toward goals of varying importance. Setting priorities helps you decide where and when to focus your energy and time.

Reviewing animal physiology while caring for her son is just part of how this single parent and premed student juggles responsibilities on a daily basis.

Prioritize goals

When you prioritize, you evaluate everything you are working toward, decide which goals are most important, and focus your time and energy on them. What should you consider as you evaluate?

PRIORITIZE

To arrange or deal with in order of importance.

- **Your values.** Thinking about what you value will help you establish the goals that take top priority—for example, graduating in the top 25 percent of your class or developing a strong network of personal contacts.
- **Your personal situation.** Are you going to school and working part-time? Are you taking three classes or five classes? Are you a parent with young children who need your attention? Are you an athlete on a sports team? Every individual situation requires unique priorities and scheduling.
- **Your time commitments.** Hours of your day may already be committed to class, team practices, a part-time job, or sleep. Your challenge is to make sure these commitments reflect what you value and to establish priorities for the remaining hours.

As you will see later in the chapter, setting clear priorities will help you manage your time and accomplish more.

Goals are dreams with deadlines.

DIANA SCHARF HUNT

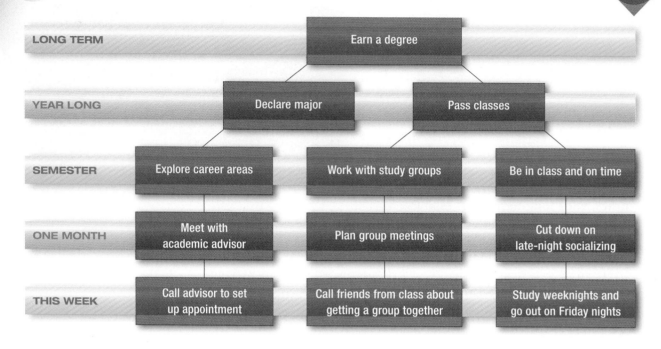

LONG TERM			Earn a degree		

YEAR LONG — Declare major — Pass classes

SEMESTER — Explore career areas — Work with study groups — Be in class and on time

ONE MONTH — Meet with academic advisor — Plan group meetings — Cut down on late-night socializing

THIS WEEK — Call advisor to set up appointment — Call friends from class about getting a group together — Study weeknights and go out on Friday nights

Work to achieve goals

When you've done all the work to think through a goal you want to achieve, these practical steps will help you achieve it. Remember, the more specific your plans, the more likely you are to fulfill them.

- **Define your goal-setting strategy:** *How do you plan to reach your goal?* Brainstorm different paths that might get you there. Choose one; then map out its steps and strategies. Focus on specific behaviors and events that are under your control and that are measurable.

- **Set a timetable:** *When do you want to accomplish your goal?* Set a realistic time line that includes specific deadlines for each step and strategy you have defined. Charting your progress will help you stay on track.

- **Be accountable for your progress:** *What safeguards will keep you on track?* Define a personal reporting or buddy system that makes accountability a priority.

- **Get unstuck:** *What will you do if you hit a roadblock?* Define two ways to get help with your efforts if you run into trouble. Be ready to pursue more creative ideas if those don't work.

Through this process, you will continually be thinking about how well you are using your time. In fact, goal achievement is directly linked to effective time management.

MAP OUT A PERSONAL GOAL

Work backwards to find an interesting path toward an important goal.

Name one important personal goal you have for this year.

_____

Now imagine that you have made it to the end—you already achieved your goal—and an impressed friend asks you to describe how you did it. Write your answer here, in a paragraph, as though you were telling this person about the specific steps you took to achieve your goal.

_____

_____

_____

_____

_____

_____

_____

Finally, examine what you've written. You just created a potential plan! Consider putting it—or a plan similar to it—to work. As you begin, let the image of the success you created in this exercise motivate and inspire you.

How can you effectively *manage your time?*

Time is a universal resource; everyone has the same 24 hours in a day, every day. Depending on what's happening in your life, however, your sense of time may change. On some days you feel like you have hours to spare, while on others the clock becomes your worst enemy.

Your challenge is to turn time into a goal-achievement tool by making smart choices about how to use it. Think of each day as a jigsaw puzzle: You have all of the pieces in a pile, and your task is to form a picture of how you want your day to look. Successful time management starts with identifying your time-related needs and preferences. This self-knowledge sets the stage for building and managing your schedule, avoiding procrastination, and being flexible in the face of change.

Identify your time-related needs and preferences

Body rhythms and habits affect how each person deals with time. Some people are night owls; others are at their best in the morning. Some people are chronically late; others get everything done with time to spare. An awareness of your needs and preferences will help you create a schedule that maximizes your strengths and cuts down on stress. If you are a morning person, for example, look for sections of required courses that meet early in the day. If you work best at night, schedule most of your study time at a library that stays open late.

Daniel Estrada, a student at New Mexico State University, arranged his schedule to maximize his personal strengths and minimize his weaknesses. Estrada explains: "An ordinary day is getting up around 9:00 A.M. to get ready for my 10:30 A.M. class. I have two classes on Monday-Wednesday-Friday and three on Tuesday-Thursday. Knowing that the classes on Tuesdays and Thursdays are longer, I schedule my more difficult classes on those days and leave Monday-Wednesday-Friday for those that I find easier to work with."[6]

Take the following steps to identify your time-related needs and preferences:

Create a personal time "profile." Ask yourself these questions: At what time of day do I have the most energy? The least energy? Do I tend to be early, on time, or late? Do I focus well for long stretches or need regular breaks? Your answers will help you find the schedule setup that works best for you.

Evaluate the effects of your profile. Which of your time-related habits and preferences will have a positive impact on your success at school? Which are likely to cause problems?

Establish what schedule preferences suit your profile best. Make a list of these preferences—or even map out an ideal schedule as a way of illustrating them. For example, one student's preference list might read: "Classes bunched together on Mondays, Wednesdays, and Fridays. Tuesdays and Thursdays free for studying and research. Study time primarily during the day."

Next, it's time to build the schedule that takes all of this information into account, helping you maximize your strengths and compensate for your weaker time-management areas.

Build a schedule

You've set up your "goal map," with all of the steps that you need to accomplish to reach your destination. With a schedule you place each step in time and, by doing so, commit to making it happen. Schedules help you gain control of your life in two ways: They provide segments of time for tasks related to the fulfillment of your goals, and they remind you of tasks, events, due dates, responsibilities, and deadlines.

Use a planner

A planner is the ideal practical tool for managing your time. With it, you can keep track of events and commitments, schedule goal-related tasks, and rank tasks according to priority. Time-management expert Paul Timm says that

"rule number one in a thoughtful planning process is: Use some form of a planner where you can write things down."[7]

There are two major types of planners. One is a book or notebook in which to note commitments. If you write detailed daily plans, look for the kind that devotes a page to each day. If you prefer to see more days at a glance, try the kind that shows a week's schedule on a two-page spread.

The other option is an electronic planner or personal digital assistant (PDA). Basic PDA functions allow you to schedule days and weeks, note due dates, make to-do lists, perform mathematical calculations, and create and store an address book.

Keep track of events and commitments

Your planner is designed to help you schedule and remember events and commitments. A quick look at your notations will remind you when items are approaching. Among the events and commitments worth noting in your planner are:

- test and quiz dates; due dates for papers, projects, and presentations.
- details of your academic schedule, including semester and holiday breaks.
- club and organizational meetings.
- personal items—medical appointments, due dates for bills, birthdays, social events.
- milestones toward a goal, such as due dates for sections of a project.

Include class prep time—reading and studying, writing and working on assignments and projects—in the planner. According to one reasonable formula, you should schedule at least two hours of preparation for every hour of class—that is, if you take 15 credits, you should study about 30 hours a week, making your total classroom and preparation time 45 hours. Surveys have shown, however, that most students study 15 or fewer hours per week, and some study even less—often not enough to master the material.

William Imbriale was such a student. As a freshman at Boston College, he had priorities other than studying and writing papers. "I got a D on my first philosophy paper," said William. "That woke me up, big time." With the aid of a professor who helped him plan his time more effectively, William found ways to increase his study time and received an A− on the final paper. He says "I felt like I earned that. The professor gave me a sense of achievement," but William was the one who did the work and put in the time.[8]

Students who hold jobs have to fit study time in where they can. Lisa Marie Webb, a University of Utah student, prepares for class while commuting from her job as a clerk at ShopKo to school and to home. Athletes, too, have to work hard to fit everything in. "I get up at 6:30, go to study hall from 7:30 to 9, have class from 9:30 to 1:15, then have practice at 2," says Ohio State defensive back A. J. Hawk. "Then we lift after practice every day through Thursday."[9] These kinds of situations demand creative time management and close attention to following your schedule.

Monday	Tuesday	Wednesday	Thursday	Friday	Saturday	Sunday
9 AM: Economics class Talk with study group members to schedule meeting.	3–5 PM: Study econ chapter 3.	9 AM: Economics class Drop by instructor's office hours to ask question about test	6 PM: Go over chapter 3 7–9 PM: Study group meeting.	9 AM: Economics class—Test 3:30 PM: Meet w/advisor to discuss GMAT and other business school requirements	Sleep in— schedule some down time	5 PM: Go over quiz questions with study partner

Schedule tasks and activities that support your goals

Linking the events in your planner to your goals will give meaning to your efforts and bring order to your schedule. Planning study time for an economics test, for example, will mean more to you if you link the hours you spend to your goal of being accepted into business school.

Here is how a student might translate his goal of entering business school into action steps over a year's time:

This year: Complete enough courses to meet curriculum requirements for business school and maintain class standing

This semester: Complete my economics class with a B average or higher

This month: Set up economics study group schedule to coincide with quizzes and tests

This week: Meet with study group; go over material for Friday's test

Today: Go over Chapter 3 in econ text

The student can then arrange his time to move him in the direction of his goal. He schedules activities that support his short-term goal of doing well on the test and writes them in his planner as shown in the example above. Achieving his overarching long-term goal of doing well in a course he needs for business school is the source of his motivation.

Before each week begins, remind yourself of your long-term goals and what you can accomplish over the next seven days to move you closer to them. Key 2.2 shows parts of a daily schedule and a weekly schedule.

Indicate priority levels

On any given day, the items on your schedule have varying degrees of importance. Prioritizing these items boosts scheduling success in two ways. First, it helps you to identify your most important tasks and to focus the bulk of your energy and time on them. Second, it helps you plan when in your day to get things done. Since many top-priority items (classes, work) occur at designated times, prioritizing helps you lock in these activities and schedule less urgent items around them.

Indicate level of importance using three different categories. Identify these categories by using any code that makes sense to you. Some people

Note daily and weekly tasks.

Monday, March 14

TIME	TASKS	PRIORITY
6:00 A.M.		
7:00		
8:00	Up at 8am — finish homew	
9:00		
10:00	Business Administration	
11:00	Renew driver's license @ D	
12:00 P.M.		
1:00	Lunch	
2:00	Writing Seminar (peer editi	
3:00	↓	
4:00	check on Ms. Schwartz's of	
5:00	5:30 work out	
6:00	↳6:30	
7:00	Dinner	
8:00	Read two chapters for	
9:00	Business Admin.	
10:00	↓	
11:00		
12:00		

Monday, March 28

8		Call: Mike Blair	1
9	BIO 212	Finanical Aid Office	2
10		EMS 262 *Paramedic	3
11	CHEM 203	role-play*	4
12			5

Evening   6pm yoga class

Tuesday, March 29

8	Finish reading assignment!	Work @ library	1
9			2
10	ENG 112	(study for quiz)	3
11	↓		4
12			5

Evening   ↓ until 7pm

Wednesday, March 30

8		Meet w/advisor	1
9	BIO 212		2
10		EMS 262	3
11	CHEM 203 *Quiz		4
12		Pick up photos	5

Evening   6pm Dinner w/study group

use numbers, some use letters (A, B, C), and some use different-colored pens. The three categories are as follows:

- *Priority 1* items are the most crucial. They may include attending class, completing school assignments, working at a job, picking up a child from day care, and paying bills. Enter Priority 1 items on your planner first, before scheduling anything else.

- *Priority 2* items are important but more flexible parts of your routine. Examples include library study time, completing an assignment for a school club, and working out. Schedule these around Priority 1 items.

- *Priority 3* items are least important—the "it would be nice if I could get to that" items. Examples include making a social phone call, stocking up on birthday cards, and cleaning out a closet. Many people don't enter Priority 3 tasks in their planners until they know they have time for them. Others keep a separate list of these tasks so that when they have free time they can consult it and choose what they want to accomplish.

Use scheduling techniques

The following strategies will help you turn your scheduling activities into tools that move you closer to your goals:

Plan regularly. Spending time planning your schedule will reduce stress and save you from the hours of work that might result if you forget something important. At the beginning of each week, write down specific time commitments as well as your goals and priorities. Decide where to fit activities like studying and Priority 3 items. For example, if you have a test on Thursday, you can plan study sessions on the preceding days. If you have more free time on Tuesday and Friday, you can plan workouts or other low-priority tasks. Your planner only helps you when you use it—keep it with you and check it throughout the day.

Make and use to-do lists. Use a to-do list to record the things you want to accomplish on a given day or week. Write your to-do items on a separate

Keep track of your time with a monthly calendar.

			MARCH			
SUNDAY	MONDAY	TUESDAY	WEDNESDAY	THURSDAY	FRIDAY	SATURDAY
	1 WORK	**2** Turn in English paper topic	**3** Dentist 2pm	**4** WORK	**5**	**6**
7 Frank's birthday	**8** Psych Test 9am WORK	**9**	**10** 6:30 pm Meeting @ Student Ctr.	**11** WORK	**12**	**13** Dinner @ Ryan's
14	**15** English paper due WORK	**16** Western Civ paper—Library research	**17**	**18** Library 6 p.m. WORK	**19** Western Civ makeup class	**20**
21	**22** WORK	**23** 2 p.m. meeting, psych group project	**20** Start running program: 2 miles	**25** WORK	**26** Run 2 miles	**27**
28 Run 3 miles	**29** WORK	**30** Western Civ paper due	**31** Run 2 miles			

piece of paper so you can set priorities. Then transfer the items you plan to accomplish each day to open time periods in your planner.

To-do lists are critical time-management tools during exam week and when major projects are due. They will help you rank your responsibilities so that you get things done in order of importance.

Post monthly and yearly calendars at home. Keeping track of your major commitments on a monthly wall calendar will give you the overview you need to focus on responsibilities and upcoming events. Key 2.3 shows a monthly calendar. If you live with family or friends, create a group calendar to stay aware of each other's plans and avoid scheduling conflicts.

Avoid time traps. Try to stay away from situations that eat up time unnecessarily. Say "no" graciously if you don't have time for a project; curb excess social time that interferes with academics; delegate chores if you find yourself overloaded. Pay special attention to how much time you spend surfing the Internet and chatting on-line, because these activities can waste hours.

Schedule down time. Leisure time is more than just a nice break—it's essential to your health and success. A little (down time) will refresh you and actually improve your productivity when you get back on task. Even half an hour a day helps. Fill the time with whatever relaxes you—reading, watching television, chatting on-line, playing a game or sport, walking, writing, or just doing nothing.

> DOWN TIME
> Quiet time set aside for relaxation and low-key activity.

MAKE A TO-DO LIST

get practical!

Accomplish practical goals with a to-do list and reduce stress as a result.

Make a to-do list for what you have to do on your busiest day this week. Include all the tasks and events you know about, including attending class and study time, and the activities you would like to do (working out at the gym, watching your favorite TV show) if you have extra time. Then prioritize your list using the coding system of your choice.

Date: _____

1. _____   7. _____
2. _____   8. _____
3. _____   9. _____
4. _____   10. _____
5. _____   11. _____
6. _____   12. _____

After examining this list, record your daily schedule in your planner. Include a separate list for Priority 3 items that you can fit into empty time blocks if you finish all your higher priority commitments. At the end of the day, evaluate this system. Did the list make a difference? If you liked it, use this exercise as a guide for using to-do lists regularly.

Fight procrastination

It's human, and common for busy students, to put off difficult or undesirable tasks until later. If taken to the extreme, however, procrastination can develop into a habit that causes serious problems. This excerpt from the Study Skills Library at California Polytechnic State University at San Luis Obispo illustrates how procrastination can quickly turn into a destructive pattern.

PROCRASTINATION

The act of putting off a task until another time.

> The procrastinator is often remarkably optimistic about his ability to complete a task on a tight deadline. . . . For example, he may estimate that a paper will take only five days to write; he has fifteen days; there is plenty of time, no need to start. Lulled by a false sense of security, time passes. At some point, he crosses over an imaginary starting time and suddenly realizes, "Oh no! I am not in control! There isn't enough time!"
>
> At this point, considerable effort is directed toward completing the task, and work progresses. This sudden spurt of energy is the source of the erroneous feeling that "I work well only under pressure." Actually, at this point you are making progress only because you haven't any choice. . . . Progress is being made, but you have lost your freedom.
>
> Barely completed in time, the paper may actually earn a fairly good grade; whereupon the student experiences mixed feelings: pride of accomplishment (sort of), scorn for the professor who cannot recognize substandard work, and guilt for getting an undeserved grade. But the net result is reinforcement: The procrastinator is rewarded positively for his poor behavior ("Look what a decent grade I got after all!"). As a result, the counterproductive behavior is repeated time and time again.[10]

Among the reasons people procrastinate are:

Perfectionism. According to Jane B. Burka and Lenora M. Yuen, authors of *Procrastination: Why You Do It and What to Do About It*, habitual procrastinators often gauge their self-worth solely by their ability to achieve. In other words, "an outstanding performance means an outstanding person; a mediocre performance means a mediocre person."[11] To the perfectionist procrastinator, not trying at all is better than an attempt that falls short of perfection.

Fear of limitations. Some people procrastinate in order to avoid the truth about what they can achieve. "As long as you procrastinate, you never have to confront the real limits of your ability, whatever those limits are,"[12] say Burka and Yuen. If you procrastinate and fail, you can blame the failure on waiting too long, not on any personal shortcoming.

Even if you're on the right track, you'll get run over if you just sit there.

WILL ROGERS

Facing an overwhelming task. Some projects are so big that they create immobilizing fear. If a person facing such a task fears failure, she may procrastinate in order to avoid confronting the fear.

Avoiding procrastination

Although it can bring relief in the short term, avoiding tasks almost always causes problems, such as a buildup of responsibilities and less time to complete them, work that is not up to par, the disappointment of others who are depending on your work, and stress brought on by the weight of the unfinished tasks. Particular strategies can help you avoid procrastination and the problems associated with it.

Analyze the effects of procrastinating. What may happen if you continue to put off a responsibility? Chances are you will benefit more in the long term from facing the task head-on.

Set reasonable goals. Unreasonable goals can intimidate and immobilize you. Set manageable goals and allow enough time to complete them.

Break tasks into smaller parts. If you concentrate on achieving one small step at a time, the task may become less burdensome. Setting concrete time limits for each task may help you feel more in control.

Get started whether or not you "feel like it." The motivation techniques from Chapter 1 might help you take the first step. Once you start, you may find it easier to continue.

Ask for help. You don't have to go it alone. Once you identify what's holding you up, see who can help you face the task. Another person may come up with an innovative way that you can get moving.

Don't expect perfection. No one is perfect. Most people learn by starting at the beginning, making mistakes, and learning from those mistakes. It's better to try your best than to do nothing at all.

Reward yourself. Find ways to boost your confidence when you accomplish a particular task. Remind yourself—with a break, a movie, some kind of treat—that you are making progress.

Be flexible

No matter how well you plan your time, sudden changes can upend your plans. Any change, whether minor (a room change for a class) or major (a medical emergency), can cause stress. As your stress level rises, your sense of control dwindles.

Although you can't always choose your circumstances, you have some control over how you handle them. Your ability to evaluate situations, come up with creative options, and put practical plans to work will help you manage the changes that you will inevitably encounter. For changes that occur frequently, think through a backup plan ahead of time. For surprises, the best you can do is to keep an open mind about possibilities and rely on your internal and external resources.

When change involves serious problems—your car breaks down and you have no way to get to school; you fail a class and have to consider summer school; a family member develops a medical problem and needs you more at home—use problem-solving skills to help you through. As you will see in Chapter 4, problem solving involves identifying and analyzing the problem, brainstorming and exploring possible solutions, and choosing the solution you decide is best. There are resources available at your college to help you throughout this process. Your academic advisor, counselor, dean, financial aid advisor, and instructors may have ideas and assistance.

Change is one of many factors associated with stress. In fact, stress is part of the normal college experience. If you take charge of how you manage stress, then you can keep it from taking charge of you.

How do you *cope with the stress* of college life?

If you are feeling more stress in your everyday life as a student, you are not alone.[13] Stress levels among college students have increased dramatically, according to an annual survey conducted at the University of California at Los Angeles. More than 30 percent of the freshmen polled at 683 two- and four-year colleges and universities nationwide reported that they frequently felt overwhelmed, almost double the rate in 1985. Stress factors for college students include being in a new environment; facing increased work and difficult decisions; and juggling school, work, and personal responsibilities.

Stress refers to the way in which your mind and body react to pressure. Pressure comes from situations like heavy workloads (final exam week), excitement (being a finalist for the lead in a play), change (new school, new courses), being short on time (working 20 hours a week at a job and finding time to study), or illness (having a head cold that wipes you out for a week).

The Social Readjustment Scale, developed by psychologists T. H. Holmes and R. H. Rahe, measures the intensity of people's reaction to change and the level of stress related to it (see Key 2.4). Holmes and Rahe found that people experience both positive and negative events as stressors. For example, whereas some events like the death of a relative are clearly negative, other stressors, like moving to a new house or even taking a vacation, are generally positive.

At their worst, stress reactions can make you physically ill (Chapter 9 will examine stress-related health issues—situations in which stress goes beyond normal levels, causing physical and emotional problems). But stress can also supply the heightened readiness you need to do well on tests, finish assignments on time, prepare for a class presentation, or meet new people. Your goal is to find a manageable balance. Key 2.5, based on research conducted by Drs. Robert M. Yerkes and John E. Dodson, shows that stress can be helpful or harmful, depending on how much you experience.

Stress management strategies

Dealing with the stress of college life is, and will continue to be, one of your biggest challenges. But here's a piece of good news: Every goal-achievement and time-management strategy you have read in this chapter contributes to your ability to cope with stress. Remember that stress refers to how you react to pressure. When you set up effective plans to move toward goals, you reduce pressure. When you set a schedule that works for you and stick to it, you reduce pressure. Less pressure, less stress.

Use the Holmes-Rahe scale to find your "stress score."

To find your current "stress score," add the values of the events that you experienced in the past year. The higher the number, the greater the stress. Scoring over 300 points puts you at high risk for developing a stress-related health problem. A score between 150 and 299 reduces your risk by 30 percent, and a score under 150 means that you have only a small chance of a problem.

EVENT	VALUE	EVENT	VALUE
Death of spouse or partner	100	Son or daughter leaving home	29
Divorce	73	Trouble with in-laws	29
Marital separation	65	Outstanding personal achievement	28
Jail term	63	Spouse begins or stops work	26
Personal injury	53	Starting or finishing school	26
Marriage	50	Change in living conditions	25
Fired from work	47	Revision of personal habits	24
Marital reconciliation	45	Trouble with boss	23
Retirement	45	Change in work hours, conditions	20
Changes in family member's health	44	Change in residence	20
Pregnancy	40	Change in schools	20
Sex difficulties	39	Change in recreational habits	19
Addition to family	39	Change in religious activities	19
Business readjustment	39	Change in social activities	18
Change in financial status	38	Mortgage or loan under $10,000	17
Death of a close friend	37	Change in sleeping habits	16
Change to different line of work	36	Change in # of family gatherings	15
Change in # of marital arguments	35	Change in eating habits	15
Mortgage or loan over $10,000	31	Vacation	13
Foreclosure of mortgage or loan	30	Christmas season	12
Change in work responsibilities	29	Minor violation of the law	11

Source: Reprinted from *Journal of Psychosomatic Research, 11*(2), T. H. Holmes and R. H. Rahe, "The social readjustment rating scale," 1967, with permission from Elsevier Science Inc.

Here are some more specific practical strategies for coping with the day-to-day stress of being a college student.

- Eat right. The healthier you are, the stronger you are—and the more able you will be to weather tough situations like all-nighters, illnesses, and challenging academic work. Try to eat a balanced, low-fat diet and maintain a healthy weight.
- Exercise. Physical exercise will help you manage your stress. Find a type of exercise you like and make it a regular part of your life.
- Get sleep. Avoid the systemwide dysfunction that sleep deprivation can create. Figure out how much sleep you need and do your best to get it.
- Think positively. Try to think of all you have to do as challenges, not problems.

Stress levels can help or hinder performance.

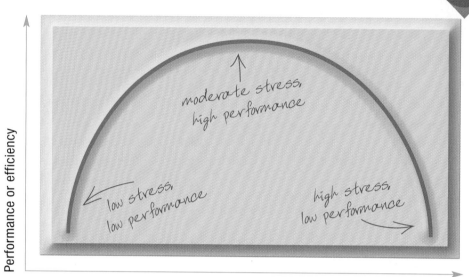

Performance or efficiency

moderate stress, high performance

low stress, low performance

high stress, low performance

Stress or anxiety

Source: From *Your Maximum Mind* by Herbert Benson, M.D., Copyright © 1987 by Random House, Inc. Used by permission of Time Books, a division of Random House.

Extracurricular activities can provide relaxation and stress relief, as these students have found in their work with the Dynamics, an a cappella group at Skidmore College.

- **Seek balance.** A balanced life includes time by yourself—for your thoughts, hopes, and plans—and time for relaxation, in whatever form you choose.

- **Address issues.** Try not to let things lie too long. Analyze stressful situations and use problem-solving strategies (see Chapter 4) to decide on a specific plan of action.

- **Set boundaries and learn to say no.** Try to delegate. Review obligations regularly; if you evaluate that something has become a burden, then consider dropping it from your roster of activities.

- **Surround yourself with people who are good for you.** Focus on friends who are good listeners and who will support you when things get rough. Friendship and humor go a long way toward reducing stress.

Remember: *Any step toward a goal is a stress-management strategy because it reduces pressure.* In that sense, this entire book is a stress-management strategy. Every useful tool, from test-taking hints to job-hunting strategies, will help you reduce the pressure and cover the distance toward your dreams.

In Hebrew, this word, pronounced "chai," means "life," representing all aspects of life—spiritual, emotional, family, educational, and career. Individual Hebrew characters have number values. Because the characters in the word *chai* add up to 18, the number 18 has come to be associated with good luck. The word *chai* is often worn as a good luck charm. The phrase *l'chaim* means "to life" and good luck.

As you plan your goals, think about the role luck may play in your success. If you work hard and are open to new opportunities, you may find yourself in the right place at the right time to benefit from a "lucky break." Because you are prepared, you may find a teacher who is so impressed by your tenacity and focus that she offers to become your mentor. Or, after you graduate, you may meet someone with a business opportunity that is a perfect match for your skills, and you are hired on the spot. All your hard work in the direction of your goal will prepare you to take advantage of lucky breaks that come your way.

Developing Successful Intelligence

PUTTING IT ALL TOGETHER

The Wheel of Life. This exercise uses a wheel—an image that has been used for centuries to promote understanding of the self and the world—to help you think about your strength and weakness in eight important goal areas. Assess your level of proficiency in self-knowledge, study skills, personal life goals, finances, health and stress management, relationships, career, and time management by filling out the wheel as directed in Key 2.6 on p. 51.

Let this self-assessment help you make decisions about how you approach the material in this course. If you need work on study skills, for example, then focus specifically on the reading, note-taking, and test-taking chapters. At the end of the book you will have a chance to revisit the Wheel. If you work hard in this course, you should sense improvement in your weaker goal areas over the course of the semester. Plus, you will have developed your ability to evaluate and manage yourself—a skill that is crucial to your success in school and at work.

Team Building

COLLABORATIVE SOLUTIONS

Multiple paths to a goal. In a group of three or four, brainstorm goals that focus on building a life skill—for example, leadership, teamwork, learning a foreign language. Write your ideas on a piece of paper. From that list, pick out one goal to explore together.

Each group member takes two minutes alone to think about this goal in terms of the first goal-achievement step on page 36—defining a strategy. In other words, answer the question: "How would I do it?" Each person writes down all of the paths they can think of.

Build self-knowledge with the Wheel of Life.

Rate yourself in each area of the wheel on a scale of 1 to 10, 1 being least developed (near the center of the wheel) and 10 being most developed (the outer edge of the wheel). In each area, at the level of the number you choose, draw a curved line and fill in the wedge below that line. Be honest—this is for your benefit only. Finally, look at what your wheel says about the balance in your life. If this were a real wheel, how well would it roll?

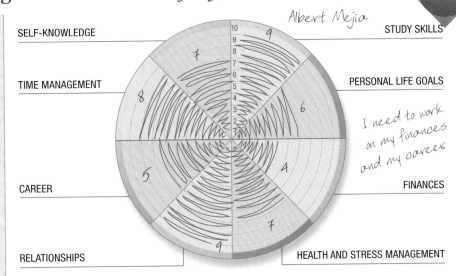

Sample Wheel

Albert Mejia

I need to work on my finances and my career.

SELF-KNOWLEDGE
(learning styles, interests, abilities)

STUDY SKILLS
(reading, note taking, writing, test taking)

TIME MANAGEMENT

PERSONAL LIFE GOALS

Where do you need to improve?

CAREER

FINANCES

RELATIONSHIPS
(family, friends, significant other)

HEALTH AND STRESS MANAGEMENT

Source: Based on "The Wheel of Life" model developed by the Coaches Training Institute. © Co-Active Space 2000.

key
2.6

Friday		Saturday		Sunday		Notes
TIME	ACTIVITY	TIME	ACTIVITY	TIME	ACTIVITY	
6:00 A.M.		6:00 A.M.		6:00 A.M.		
6:30 A.M.		6:30 A.M.		6:30 A.M.		
7:00 A.M.		7:00 A.M.		7:00 A.M.		
7:30 A.M.		7:30 A.M.		7:30 A.M.		
8:00 A.M.		8:00 A.M.		8:00 A.M.		
8:30 A.M.		8:30 A.M.		8:30 A.M.		
9:00 A.M.		9:00 A.M.		9:00 A.M.		
9:30 A.M.		9:30 A.M.		9:30 A.M.		
10:00 A.M.		10:00 A.M.		10:00 A.M.		
10:30 A.M.		10:30 A.M.		10:30 A.M.		
11:00 A.M.		11:00 A.M.		11:00 A.M.		
11:30 A.M.		11:30 A.M.		11:30 A.M.		
12:00 P.M.		12:00 P.M.		12:00 P.M.		
12:30 P.M.		12:30 P.M.		12:30 P.M.		
1:00 P.M.		1:00 P.M.		1:00 P.M.		
1:30 P.M.		1:30 P.M.		1:30 P.M.		
2:00 P.M.		2:00 P.M.		2:00 P.M.		
2:30 P.M.		2:30 P.M.		2:30 P.M.		
3:00 P.M.		3:00 P.M.		3:00 P.M.		
3:30 P.M.		3:30 P.M.		3:30 P.M.		
4:00 P.M.		4:00 P.M.		4:00 P.M.		
4:30 P.M.		4:30 P.M.		4:30 P.M.		
5:00 P.M.		5:00 P.M.		5:00 P.M.		
5:30 P.M.		5:30 P.M.		5:30 P.M.		
6:00 P.M.		6:00 P.M.		6:00 P.M.		
6:30 P.M.		6:30 P.M.		6:30 P.M.		
7:00 P.M.		7:00 P.M.		7:00 P.M.		
7:30 P.M.		7:30 P.M.		7:30 P.M.		
8:00 P.M.		8:00 P.M.		8:00 P.M.		
8:30 P.M.		8:30 P.M.		8:30 P.M.		
9:00 P.M.		9:00 P.M.		9:00 P.M.		
9:30 P.M.		9:30 P.M.		9:30 P.M.		
10:00 P.M.		10:00 P.M.		10:00 P.M.		
10:30 P.M.		10:30 P.M.		10:30 P.M.		
11:00 P.M.		11:00 P.M.		11:00 P.M.		
11:30 P.M.		11:30 P.M.		11:30 P.M.		
12–6 A.M.		12–6 A.M.		12–6 A.M.		

After a week, go through the chart below and add up how many hours you spent on the activities for which you previously estimated your hours. Tally the hours in the boxes in the following table using straight tally marks; round off to half hours and use a short tally mark for each half hour. In the third column, total the hours for each activity. Leave the "Ideal Time in Hours" column blank for now.

Activity	Time Tallied Over One-Week Period	Total Time in Hours	Ideal Time in Hours
Example: Class	IIII IIII IIII II	16.5	
Class			
Work			
Studying			
Sleeping			
Eating			
Family time/child care			
Commuting/traveling			
Chores and personal business			
Friends and important relationships			
Telephone time			
Leisure/entertainment			
Spiritual life			
Other			

Add the totals in the third column to find your grand total. Compare your grand total to your estimated grand total; compare your actual activity hour totals to your estimated activity hour totals. Use a separate sheet of paper to answer the following questions:

• What matches and what doesn't? Describe the most interesting similarities and differences.

• Where do you waste the most time? What do you think that is costing you?

Now evaluate what kinds of changes might improve your ability to achieve goals. Analyze what you do daily, weekly, and monthly. Go back to the chart above and fill in the "Ideal Time in Hours" column. Consider the difference between actual hours and ideal hours. Ask questions:

- On what activities do you think you should spend more or less time?
- What are you willing to do to change, and why?

Finally, write a short paragraph describing two key time-management changes in detail. Describe what goal you are aiming for, and map out how you plan to put the changes into action.

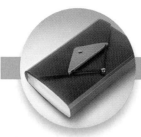

Career Portfolio

PLAN FOR SUCCESS

Complete the following in your electronic portfolio or on separate sheets of paper.

Career goals—knowledge and skills. No matter what career goals you ultimately pursue, certain knowledge and skills are useful in any career area. Consider this list of the general skills employers look for in people they hire:

Acceptance	Critical thinking	Leadership
Communication	Flexibility	Positive attitude
Continual learning	Goal setting	Teamwork
Creativity	Integrity	

Choose and circle three of these that you want to focus on developing this year.

Map out a plan for your progress by indicating a series of smaller goals—from short-term to long-term—that will lead you toward developing these skills. For each of the three skills, write what you hope to accomplish in the next year, the next six months, and the next month. For example:

Skill: Leadership

Next month: I will volunteer to lead a session with my Economics study group.

In six months: I will look into leadership positions on the college newspaper.

By the end of the year: I will have joined the newspaper team and expressed my interest in a leadership position.

SUGGESTED READINGS

Allen, David. *Getting Things Done: The Art of Stress-Free Productivity.* New York: Penguin Books, 2003.

Burka, Jane B., Ph.D. and Lenora M. Yuen, Ph.D. *Procrastination.* Reading, MA: Perseus Books, 1983.

Covey, Stephen. *The Seven Habits of Highly Effective People.* New York: Simon & Schuster, 1995.

Emmett, Rita. *The Procrastinator's Handbook: Mastering the Art of Doing It Now.* New York: Walker & Co., 2000.

Gleeson, Kerry. *The Personal Efficiency Program: How to Get Organized to Do More Work in Less Time,* 2nd ed. New York: John Wiley & Sons, 2000.

Lakein, Alan. *How to Get Control of Your Time and Your Life.* New York: New American Library, 1996.

Leyden-Rubenstein, Lori. *The Stress Management Handbook.* New York: McGraw-Hill, 1999.

Sapadin, Linda and Jack Maguire. *Beat Procrastination and Make the Grade: The Six Styles of Procrastination and How Students Can Overcome Them.* New York: Penguin USA, 1999.

Timm, Paul R. *Successful Self-Management: A Psychologically Sound Approach to Personal Effectiveness.* Los Altos, CA: Crisp Publications, 1996.

Mind Tools (section on time management): www.mind tools.com/pages/main/newMN_HTE.htm

Top Achievement—goal-setting and self-improvement resources: www.topachievement.com

About.com stress-management resources: http://stress.about.com/

Troubled With—information on stress management: www.troubledwith.com

ENDNOTES

1. Student essay submitted by the First Year Experience students of Patty Parma, Palo Alto College, San Antonio, Texas, January 2004.

2. *A Report from the Center for Academic Integrity*, Center for Academic Integrity, Kenan Institute for Ethics, Duke University, October 1999 [on-line]. Available:www.academicintegrity.org (March 2001).

3. Background information for information on cultural diversity from Afsaneh Nahavandi and Ali Malekzadeh, *Organizational Behavior: The Person-Organization Fit*. Upper Saddle River, NJ: Prentice Hall, 1999.

4. Louis E. Boone, David L. Kurtz, and Judy R. Block, *Contemporary Business Communication*, 2nd ed. Upper Saddle River, NJ: Prentice Hall, 1997, pp. 68–72.

5. Louis E. Boone and David L. Kurtz, *Contemporary Business Communication*. Englewood Cliffs, NJ: Prentice Hall, 1994, p. 643.

6. "What's an Ordinary Day Like When You're in College?" New Mexico State University Web site, June 1999 [on-line]. Available: www.nmsu.edu/aggieland/students/faq_ordinary.html (March 2004).

7. Paul Timm, *Successful Self-Management: A Psychologically Sound Approach to Personal Effectiveness*. Los Altos, CA: Crisp Publications, 1987, pp. 22–41.

8. Welch Suggs, "How Gears Turn at a Sports Factory: Running Ohio State's $79-million Athletics Program Is a Major Endeavor, with Huge Payoffs and Costs," *The Chronicle of Higher Education*, November 29, 2002 [on-line]. Available: http://chronicle.com/weekly/v49/il4/14a03201.htm (March 2004).

9. Jeffrey R. Young, "'Homework? What Homework?' Students Seem to be Spending Less Time Studying than They Used To," *The Chronicle of Higher Education*, December 6, 2002 [on-line]. Available: http://chronicle.com/weekly/v49/i15/15a03501.htm (March 2004).

10. William E. Sydnor, "Procrastination," from the California Polytechnic State University Study Skills Library [on-line]. Based on *Overcoming Procrastination* by Albert Ellis. Available: www.sas.calpoly.edu/asc/ssl/procrastination.html (May 2003). Used with permission.

11. Jane B. Burka, Ph.D. and Lenora M. Yuen, Ph.D., *Procrastination*. Reading, MA: Perseus Books, 1983, pp. 21–22.

12. Ibid.

13. The following articles were used as sources in this section: Glenn C. Altschuler, "Adapting to College Life in an Era of Heightened Stress," *New York Times*, Education Life, Section 4A, August 6, 2000, p. 12; Carol Hymowitz and Rachel Emma Silverman, "Can Workplace Stress Get Worse?" *Wall Street Journal*, January 16, 2001, p. B1; Robert M. Sapolsky, "Best Ways to Reduce Everyday Levels of Stress . . . Bad Ol' Stress," *Bottom Line Personal*, January 15, 2000, p. 13; Kate Slaboch, "Stress and the College Student: A Debate" [on-line]. Available: www.jour.unr.edu/outpost/voices/voi.slaboch.stress.htm (April 4, 2001); University of South Florida, The Counseling Center for Human Development, "Coping with Stress in College" [on-line]. Available: http://usfweb.usf.edu/counsel/self-hlp/stress.htm (April 4, 2001); Jodi Wilgoren, "Survey Shows High Stress Levels in College Freshmen," *New York Times*, January 23, 2000, p. NA.

3

IN THIS CHAPTER ...

*you will explore answers
to the following questions:*

Learning Styles, Majors, and Careers

KNOWING YOUR TALENTS AND FINDING YOUR DIRECTION

As a college student, you are investing valuable resources—time, effort, and money—in your education. Learning is the return on your investment. How well you learn, and therefore how good a return you receive, depends in part on knowing yourself in two ways: knowing *how* you learn and knowing what you want to *do* with what you learn.

This chapter focuses first on helping you identify your learning styles, because when you understand how you learn, you will be a more effective student. Then you will read about majors and careers, because knowing where you want your education to take you will motivate you toward a goal.

On the following page, read how student Michael Nolan is trying to find a major that reflects his talents and passions.

- How can you discover your learning styles?
- What are the benefits of knowing how you learn?
- How can you choose a major?
- How can Multiple Intelligences help you explore majors and careers?

How can I find the right major for me?

I have loved sports as long as I can remember. I love the strategy, the thought, and the decisions involved as much as I do the athletics. In fact, to me, the creation of a winning team from a jumble of talented players is often more interesting than the game itself.

Because of this, the business of sports is fascinating to me. One problem is that it's hard to get experience in as competitive a field as sports business. Also, there aren't a lot of sports business programs in the country, particularly at schools that interest me and have strong sports programs. Ideally, I'd also like to have a major that could be used elsewhere, in case I can't find a job in sports.

How can I find a major that appeals to my interests and that leads to a good career? How can I make sure that I like my chosen occupation and test its compatibility with me at school? And how can I learn what classes I should take to learn the most about sports business and excel in my field?

Michael Nolan
Oregon State University,
Corvallis, Oregon

I encourage you to take internships in your field . . .

From early childhood, I wanted to be a scientist. I lived for the day when I'd be able to go to a real university and do real research in a real lab and contribute to the growing body of scientific knowledge. So, when one of my professors asked me to work for him on some antibiotics research at the end of my freshman year, I was ecstatic. After years of anticipation, I'd finally get to do what I'd dreamed of.

And I found that I hated it. Most of what I did was repetitive, such as reacting the product, identifying the product, purifying the product—all in long, laborious tasks for which I couldn't see the end result. Worse, even if what I was working on did turn into a lifesaving antibiotic, it would likely take decades before anyone could use it. I found I just didn't have the patience for research. I don't like long hours of repetitive lab work and I don't want to wait for decades for a theory to become useful.

So, I discovered engineering. And I found a career that seems perfect for me, even though I couldn't have imagined myself as an engineer when I began college. Yet, the irony is that I discovered that I love engineering and don't adore scientific research only because I did an internship.

Had I not decided to do research in college, I'd probably be looking for a good Ph.D. program now, rather than doing something I love. I still like research and I still love reading about what's on the cutting edge of technology, but I also realize that a life of pure research isn't for me. That's probably the most important thing that I learned from my internship. I encourage you to take internships in your field because it was a lot better for me to learn that I didn't like lab work in college than it would have been several years into my first job.

Julia Nolan
University of California,
Davis, California

How can you *discover* your learning styles?

Your style of taking in and remembering information is as unique as you are. Have you ever thought in detail about what that style is? Doing just that—working to understand your learning strengths and preferences and the primary ways in which you interact with others—will help you achieve your personal best in school and beyond.

This chapter presents two assessments designed to help you figure out how you learn and interact. The first—*Multiple Pathways to Learning*—focuses on learning strengths and preferences and is based on Professor Howard Gardner's Multiple Intelligences Theory. The second—the *Personality Spectrum*—is based on the Myers-Briggs Type Inventory® (MBTI) and helps you evaluate how you react to people and situations.

The value of learning styles assessments

Everyone has some things that they do well and other things that they find difficult. To be a successfully intelligent learner, you need to maximize your strengths and compensate for your weaknesses. The first step toward that goal is knowing what those strengths and weaknesses *are*—and that's what these assessments will help you discover. With the information you gain from the Multiple Pathways to Learning and the Personality Spectrum, you can choose your own best ways to study, manage time, remember material, and much more.

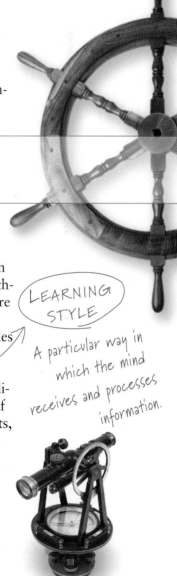

> To be what we are, and to become what we are capable of becoming, is the only end of life.
>
> **ROBERT LOUIS STEVENSON**

Knowing how you learn will help you set specific goals for positive change. For example, instead of saying, "I'm no good at math," you can strengthen your math skills with what you've learned from Multiple Pathways to Learning. You might draw diagrams of math problems if you are a visual learner or talk out problems with a study partner if you are an interpersonal learner. (You will learn about these and other learning styles later in the chapter.) The better you know yourself, the better you are able to handle different learning situations and challenges.

LEARNING STYLE

A particular way in which the mind receives and processes information.

Gaining an understanding of learning style will also enhance your ability to see and appreciate how people differ, because learning style is part of the diversity that lies within. When you sit in a classroom with 30 students, you can be sure that each person is learning the material in a unique way. The more you know about how others approach learning, the more you can use that understanding to improve communication and teamwork.

Putting assessment results in perspective

First, remember that any assessment is simply a snapshot, a look at who you are at a given moment. Your answers can, and will, change as you and the circumstances around you change. These assessments help you look at the present—and plan for the future—by asking questions: Who am I right now? How does this compare with who I want to be?

Second, there are no "right" answers, no "best" set of scores. Think of your responses in the same way you would if you were trying on a new set of eyeglasses to correct blurred vision. The glasses will not create new paths and possibilities, but they will help you see more clearly the ones that already exist.

Following each assessment is information about the typical traits of, and appropriate study strategies for, each intelligence or personality spectrum dimension. As you will see from your scores, you have abilities in all areas, though some are more developed than others. Therefore, you will find useful suggestions under all the headings. Try different techniques and keep what works for you.

Assess your Multiple Intelligences

In 1983, Howard Gardner, a Harvard University professor, changed the way people perceive (intelligence) and learning with his theory of Multiple Intelligences. Gardner believes that there are at least eight intelligences possessed by all people, and that every person has developed some intelligences more fully than others (see Key 3.1 for descriptions). According to

INTELLIGENCE

As defined by H. Gardner, an ability to solve problems or fashion products that are useful in a particular cultural setting or community.

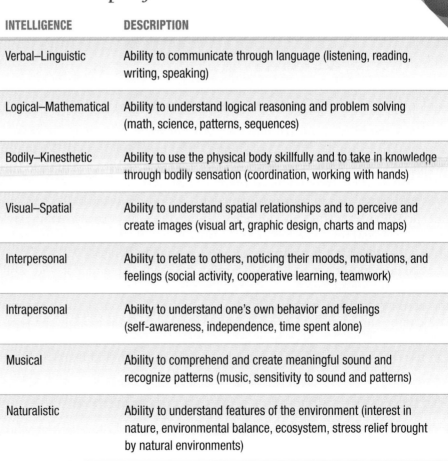

Each intelligence is linked to specific abilities.

key 3.1

INTELLIGENCE	DESCRIPTION
Verbal–Linguistic	Ability to communicate through language (listening, reading, writing, speaking)
Logical–Mathematical	Ability to understand logical reasoning and problem solving (math, science, patterns, sequences)
Bodily–Kinesthetic	Ability to use the physical body skillfully and to take in knowledge through bodily sensation (coordination, working with hands)
Visual–Spatial	Ability to understand spatial relationships and to perceive and create images (visual art, graphic design, charts and maps)
Interpersonal	Ability to relate to others, noticing their moods, motivations, and feelings (social activity, cooperative learning, teamwork)
Intrapersonal	Ability to understand one's own behavior and feelings (self-awareness, independence, time spent alone)
Musical	Ability to comprehend and create meaningful sound and recognize patterns (music, sensitivity to sound and patterns)
Naturalistic	Ability to understand features of the environment (interest in nature, environmental balance, ecosystem, stress relief brought by natural environments)

this theory, when you find a task or subject easy, you are probably using a more fully developed intelligence. When you have trouble, you may be using a less developed intelligence.[1]

Gardner believes that the way you learn is a unique blend of intelligences, resulting from your distinctive abilities, challenges, experiences, and training. In addition, ability in the intelligences may develop or recede as your life changes. Gardner thinks that the traditional view of intelligence, based on mathematical, logical, and verbal measurements, doesn't reflect the entire spectrum of human ability:

> I believe that we should . . . look . . . at more naturalistic sources of information about how peoples around the world develop skills important to their way of life. Think, for example, of sailors in the South Seas, who find their way around hundreds, or even thousands, of islands by looking at the constellations of stars in the sky, feeling the way a boat passes over the water, and noticing a few scattered landmarks. A word for intelligence in a society of these sailors would probably refer to that kind of navigational ability.[2]

The Multiple Pathways to Learning assessment helps you determine the levels to which your eight intelligences are developed. Key 3.2, immediately following the assessment, describes specific skills associated with the eight intelligences as well as study techniques that maximize each. Finally, the Multiple Intelligence Strategies grids in Chapters 5 through 9 will demonstrate how to apply your learning styles knowledge to key college success skills.

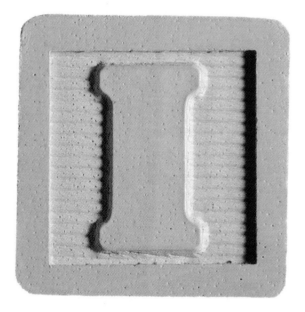

MULTIPLE PATHWAYS TO LEARNING

Each intelligence has a set of numbered statements. Consider each statement on its own. Then, on a scale from 1 to 4, rate how closely it matches who you are right now and write that number on the line next to the statement. Finally, total each set of six questions.

rarely — **1** sometimes — **2** usually — **3** always — **4**

1. _____ I enjoy physical activities.
2. _____ I am uncomfortable sitting still.
3. _____ I prefer to learn through doing.
4. _____ When sitting I move my legs or hands.
5. _____ I enjoy working with my hands.
6. _____ I like to pace when I'm thinking or studying.

_____ TOTAL for **BODILY–KINESTHETIC**

1. _____ I enjoy telling stories.
2. _____ I like to write.
3. _____ I like to read.
4. _____ I express myself clearly.
5. _____ I am good at negotiating.
6. _____ I like to discuss topics that interest me.

_____ TOTAL for **VERBAL–LINGUISTIC**

1. _____ I use maps easily.
2. _____ I draw pictures/diagrams when explaining ideas.
3. _____ I can assemble items easily from diagrams.
4. _____ I enjoy drawing or photography.
5. _____ I do not like to read long paragraphs.
6. _____ I prefer a drawn map over written directions.

_____ TOTAL for **VISUAL–SPATIAL**

1. _____ I like math in school.
2. _____ I like science.
3. _____ I problem-solve well.
4. _____ I question how things work.
5. _____ I enjoy planning or designing something new.
6. _____ I am able to fix things.

_____ TOTAL for **LOGICAL–MATHEMATICAL**

1. _____ I listen to music.
2. _____ I move my fingers or feet when I hear music.
3. _____ I have good rhythm.
4. _____ I like to sing along with music.
5. _____ People have said I have musical talent.
6. _____ I like to express my ideas through music.

_____ TOTAL for **MUSICAL**

1. _____ I need quiet time to think.
2. _____ I think about issues before I want to talk.
3. _____ I am interested in self-improvement.
4. _____ I understand my thoughts and feelings.
5. _____ I know what I want out of life.
6. _____ I prefer to work on projects alone.

_____ TOTAL for **INTRAPERSONAL**

1. _____ I like doing a project with other people.
2. _____ People come to me to help settle conflicts.
3. _____ I like to spend time with friends.
4. _____ I am good at understanding people.
5. _____ I am good at making people feel comfortable.
6. _____ I enjoy helping others.

_____ TOTAL for **INTERPERSONAL**

1. _____ I enjoy nature whenever possible.
2. _____ I think about having a career involving nature.
3. _____ I enjoy studying plants, animals, or oceans.
4. _____ I avoid being indoors except when I sleep.
5. _____ As a child I played with bugs and leaves.
6. _____ When I feel stressed I want to be out in nature.

_____ TOTAL for **NATURALISTIC**

Developed by Joyce Bishop, Ph.D., and based upon Howard Gardner's *Frames of Mind: The Theory of Multiple Intelligences*.[3]

SCORING GRID FOR MULTIPLE PATHWAYS TO LEARNING

For each intelligence, shade the box in the row that corresponds with the range where your score falls. For example, if you scored 17 in Bodily–Kinesthetic intelligence, you would shade the middle box in that row; if you scored a 13 in Visual–Spatial, you would shade the last box in that row. When you have shaded one box for each row, you will see a "map" of your range of development at a glance.

A score of 20–24 indicates a high level of development in that particular type of intelligence, 14–19 a moderate level, and below 14 an underdeveloped intelligence.

	20-24 (Highly Developed)	14-19 (Moderately Developed)	Below 14 (Underdeveloped)
Bodily–Kinesthetic			
Visual–Spatial			
Verbal–Linguistic			
Logical–Mathematical			
Musical			
Interpersonal			
Intrapersonal			
Naturalistic			

How to put your Multiple Intelligences to work for you.

ABILITIES AND SKILLS ASSOCIATED WITH EACH INTELLIGENCE

Verbal–Linguistic
- Analyzing own use of language
- Remembering terms easily
- Explaining, teaching, learning, using humor
- Understanding syntax and word meaning
- Convincing someone to do something

Musical–Rhythmic
- Sensing tonal qualities
- Creating/enjoying melodies, rhythms
- Being sensitive to sounds and rhythms
- Using "schemas" to hear music
- Understanding the structure of music

Logical–Mathematical
- Recognizing abstract patterns
- Reasoning inductively and deductively
- Discerning relationships and connections
- Performing complex calculations
- Reasoning scientifically

Visual–Spatial
- Perceiving and forming objects accurately
- Recognizing relationships between objects
- Representing something graphically
- Manipulating images
- Finding one's way in space

Bodily–Kinesthetic
- Connecting mind and body
- Controlling movement
- Improving body functions
- Expanding body awareness to all senses
- Coordinating body movement

Intrapersonal
- Evaluating own thinking
- Being aware of and expressing feelings
- Understanding self in relation to others
- Thinking and reasoning on higher levels

Interpersonal
- Seeing things from others' perspectives
- Cooperating within a group
- Communicating verbally and nonverbally
- Creating and maintaining relationships

Naturalistic
- Deep understanding of nature
- Appreciation of the delicate balance in nature

STUDY TECHNIQUES TO MAXIMIZE EACH INTELLIGENCE

Verbal–Linguistic
- Read text; highlight no more than 10%
- Rewrite notes
- Outline chapters
- Teach someone else
- Recite information or write scripts/debates

Musical–Rhythmic
- Create rhythms out of words
- Beat out rhythms with hand or stick
- Play instrumental music/write raps
- Put new material to songs you already know
- Take music breaks

Logical–Mathematical
- Organize material logically
- Explain material sequentially to someone
- Develop systems and find patterns
- Write outlines and develop charts and graphs
- Analyze information

Visual–Spatial
- Develop graphic organizers for new material
- Draw mind maps
- Develop charts and graphs
- Use color in notes to organize
- Visualize material (method of loci)

Bodily–Kinesthetic
- Move or rap while you learn; pace and recite
- Use "method of loci" or manipulatives
- Move fingers under words while reading
- Create "living sculptures"
- Act out scripts of material, design games

Intrapersonal
- Reflect on personal meaning of information
- Visualize information/keep a journal
- Study in quiet settings
- Imagine experiments

Interpersonal
- Study in a group
- Discuss information
- Use flash cards with others
- Teach someone else

Naturalistic
- Connect with nature whenever possible
- Form study groups of people with like interests

Adapted from Lazear, *Seven Pathways of Learning,* 1994.

Assess your personality with the Personality Spectrum

Personality assessments help you understand how you respond to the world around you—including information, thoughts, feelings, people, and events. The assessment used in this chapter is based on one of the most widely used personality inventories in the world—the Myers-Briggs Type Inventory, developed by Katharine Briggs and her daughter, Isabel Briggs Myers. It also relies upon the work of David Keirsey and Marilyn Bates, who combined the 16 Myers-Briggs types into four temperaments and developed an assessment called the Keirsey Sorter based on those temperaments.

The Personality Spectrum assessment adapts and simplifies their material into four personality types—Thinker, Organizer, Giver, and Adventurer—and was developed by Dr. Joyce Bishop. The Personality Spectrum helps you identify the kinds of interactions that are most, and least, comfortable for you. Key 3.3, on page 70, shows techniques that improve performance, learning strategies, and ways of relating to others for each personality type.

Three students engage verbal, bodily-kinesthetic, and interpersonal learning skills as they perform a skit about the mythological god Dionysus for a course on classic Greek mythology.

PERSONALITY SPECTRUM

STEP 1. Rank order all 4 responses to each question from most like you (4) to least like you (1) so that for each question you use the numbers 1, 2, 3, and 4 one time each. Place numbers in the boxes next to the responses.

4 most like me   **3** more like me   **2** less like me   **1** least like me

1. I like instructors who
   - a. ☐ tell me exactly what is expected of me.
   - b. ☐ make learning active and exciting.
   - c. ☐ maintain a safe and supportive classroom.
   - d. ☐ challenge me to think at higher levels.

2. I learn best when the material is
   - a. ☐ well organized.
   - b. ☐ something I can do hands-on.
   - c. ☐ about understanding and improving the human condition.
   - d. ☐ intellectually challenging.

3. A high priority in my life is to
   - a. ☐ keep my commitments.
   - b. ☐ experience as much of life as possible.
   - c. ☐ make a difference in the lives of others.
   - d. ☐ understand how things work.

4. Other people think of me as
   - a. ☐ dependable and loyal.
   - b. ☐ dynamic and creative.
   - c. ☐ caring and honest.
   - d. ☐ intelligent and inventive.

5. When I experience stress I would most likely
   - a. ☐ do something to help me feel more in control of my life.
   - b. ☐ do something physical and daring.
   - c. ☐ talk with a friend.
   - d. ☐ go off by myself and think about my situation.

6. I would probably not be close friends with someone who is
   - a. ☐ irresponsible.
   - b. ☐ unwilling to try new things.
   - c. ☐ selfish and unkind to others.
   - d. ☐ an illogical thinker.

7. My vacations could be described as
   - a. ☐ traditional.
   - b. ☐ adventuresome.
   - c. ☐ pleasing to others.
   - d. ☐ a new learning experience.

8. One word that best describes me is
   - a. ☐ sensible.
   - b. ☐ spontaneous.
   - c. ☐ giving.
   - d. ☐ analytical.

STEP 2. Add up the total points for each letter.

TOTAL FOR   **a.** ☐ Organizer   **b.** ☐ Adventurer   **c.** ☐ Giver   **d.** ☐ Thinker

STEP 3. Plot these numbers on the brain diagram on page 69.

SCORING DIAGRAM FOR PERSONALITY SPECTRUM

Write your scores from p. 68 in the four squares just outside the brain diagram—Thinker score at top left, Giver score at top right, Organizer score at bottom left, and Adventurer score at bottom right.

Each square has a line of numbers that go from the square to the center of the diagram. For each of your four scores, place a dot on the appropriate number in the line near that square. For example, if you scored 15 in the Giver spectrum, you would place a dot between the 14 and 16 in the upper right-hand line of numbers. If you scored a 26 in the Organizer spectrum, you would place a dot on the 26 in the lower left-hand line of numbers.

Connect the four dots to make a four-sided shape. If you like, shade the four sections inside the shape using four different colors.

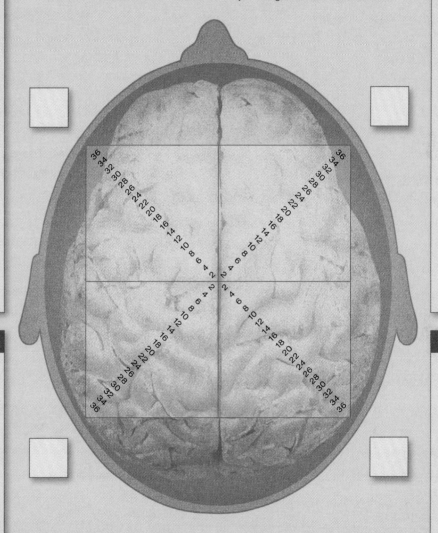

THINKER

Technical
Scientific
Mathematical
Dispassionate
Rational
Analytical
Logical
Problem Solving
Theoretical
Intellectual
Objective
Quantitative
Explicit
Realistic
Literal
Precise
Formal

GIVER

Interpersonal
Emotional
Caring
Sociable
Giving
Spiritual
Musical
Romantic
Feeling
Peacemaker
Trusting
Adaptable
Passionate
Harmonious
Idealistic
Talkative
Honest

ORGANIZER

Tactical
Planning
Detailed
Practical
Confident
Predictable
Controlled
Dependable
Systematic
Sequential
Structured
Administrative
Procedural
Organized
Conservative
Safekeeping
Disciplined

ADVENTURER

Active
Visual
Risking
Original
Artistic
Spatial
Skillful
Impulsive
Metaphoric
Experimental
Divergent
Fast-paced
Simultaneous
Competitive
Imaginative
Open-minded
Adventuresome

For the Personality Spectrum,
26–36 indicates a strong tendency in that dimension,
14–25 a moderate tendency,
and below 14 a minimal tendency.

*Source for brain diagram: Understanding Psychology, 3/e, by Morris, © 1996.
Adapted by permission of Prentice-Hall, Inc., Upper Saddle River, NJ.*

How to put your Personality Spectrum to work for you.

CHARACTERISTICS OF EACH PERSONALITY TYPE

Thinker

- Solving problems
- Developing models and systems
- Analytical and abstract thinking
- Exploring ideas and potentials
- Ingenuity
- Going beyond established boundaries
- Global thinking—seeking universal truth

Organizer

- Responsibility, reliability
- Operating successfully within social structures
- Sense of history, culture, and dignity
- Neatness and organization
- Loyalty
- Orientation to detail
- Comprehensive follow-through on tasks
- Efficiency
- Helping others

Giver

- Honesty, authenticity
- Successful, close relationships
- Making a difference in the world
- Cultivating potential of self and others
- Negotiation; promoting peace
- Openness
- Helping others

Adventurer

- High ability in a variety of fields
- Courage and daring
- Hands-on problem solving
- Living in the present
- Spontaneity and action
- Ability to negotiate
- Nontraditional style
- Flexibility
- Zest for life

STUDY TECHNIQUES TO MAXIMIZE PERSONALITY TYPES

Thinker

- Find time to reflect independently on new information
- Learn through problem solving
- Design new ways of approaching issues
- Convert material into logical charts
- Try to minimize repetitive tasks
- Look for opportunities to work independently

Organizer

- Try to have tasks defined in clear, concrete terms so that you know what is required
- Look for a well-structured, stable environment
- Request feedback
- Use a planner to schedule tasks and dates
- Organize material by rewriting and organizing class or text notes, making flash cards, or carefully highlighting

Giver

- Study with others
- Teach material to others
- Seek out tasks, groups, and subjects that involve helping people
- Find ways to express thoughts and feelings clearly and honestly
- Put energy into your most important relationships

Adventurer

- Look for environments that encourage nontraditional approaches
- Find hands-on ways to learn
- Seek people whom you find stimulating
- Use or develop games and puzzles to help memorize terms
- Fight boredom by asking to do something extra or perform a task in a more active way

Joyce Bishop, *Keys to Success,* © 2001

What are the benefits of knowing *how you learn*?

Generally, self-knowledge helps you make choices that boost your strong areas and help you to manage weaker ones. For example, understanding what you value can help you choose friends who cheer on your successes as well as friends who broaden your horizons with their different perspectives. Likewise for learning style: When you know your Multiple Intelligences and personality traits, you can choose strategies that will help you learn more, remember better, and use your knowledge more successfully—in any academic or workplace situation.

Study benefits

Knowing how you learn helps you choose study techniques that capitalize on your strengths. For example, if you learn successfully from a linear, logical presentation, you can look for order (for example, a chronology or a problem–solution structure) as you review notes. If you are a strong interpersonal learner, you can try to work in study groups whenever possible.

Learning style also points you toward strategies that help with tasks and topics that don't come so easily. An Adventurer who does *not* respond well to linear information, for example, has two choices when faced with logical presentations. She can apply her strengths to the material—for example, she might find a hands-on approach. Or she can work on her ability to handle the material by developing study skills that work well for linear learners.

When you study with others, understanding of diverse learning styles will help you assign tasks effectively and learn more comprehensively. An interpersonal learner might take the lead in teaching material to others; an Organizer might be the schedule coordinator for the group; a musical learner might present information in a new way that helps to solidify concepts.

Classroom benefits

Your college instructors will most likely have a range of teaching styles (an instructor's teaching style often reflects his or her dominant learning style). Your particular learning style may work well with some instructors and be a mismatch with others. After several class meetings, you should be able to assess an instructor's teaching styles (see Key 3.4). Then you can use what you know to maximize styles that suit you and compensate for those that don't.

Although presentation styles vary, the standard lecture is still the norm in most classrooms. For this reason, the traditional college classroom is generally a happy home for the verbal or logical learner and the Thinker and Organizer. However, many students learn best when interacting more than a lecture allows. What can you do if your styles don't match up with those of your instructor?

TEACHING STYLE	WHAT TO EXPECT IN CLASS
LECTURE, VERBAL FOCUS	Instructor speaks to the class for the entire period, with little class interaction. Lesson is taught primarily through words, either spoken or written on the board, overhead projector, handouts, or text.
GROUP DISCUSSION	Instructor presents material but encourages class discussion.
SMALL GROUPS	Instructor presents material and then breaks class into small groups for discussion or project work.
VISUAL FOCUS	Instructor uses visual elements such as diagrams, photographs, drawings, transparencies.
LOGICAL PRESENTATION	Instructor organizes material in a logical sequence, such as by time or importance.
RANDOM PRESENTATION	Instructor tackles topics in no particular order, and may jump around a lot or digress.

Play to your strengths. For example, an Organizer with an instructor who delivers material in a random way might rewrite notes in an outline format to bring structure to concepts and insert facts where they fit best. Likewise, a Giver taking a straight lecture course with no student-to-student contact might meet with a study group to go over the details and fill in factual gaps.

Work to build weaker areas. As a visual learner reviews notes from a structured lecture course, he could outline them, allot extra time to master the material, and work with a study group. A Thinker, studying for a test from notes delivered by an Adventurer instructor, could find hands-on ways to review the material (for example, for a science course, working in the lab).

Learning is not attained by chance, it must be sought for with ardor and attended to with diligence.

ABIGAIL ADAMS

Ask your instructor for additional help. If you are having trouble with coursework, communicate with your instructor through e-mail or face-to-face during office hours. This is especially important in large lectures where you are anonymous unless you speak up. The visual learner, for example, might ask the instructor to recommend graphs or figures that illustrate the lecture.

Instructors are unique. No instructor can give each of a diverse group of learners exactly what each one needs. The flexibility that you need to mesh your learning style with instructors' teaching styles is a tool for career and life success. Just as you can't hand-pick your instructors, you will rarely, if ever, be able to choose your supervisors or their work styles.

Workplace benefits

Knowing how you learn brings you these benefits in your career:

- **Better performance through self-awareness.** Since your learning styles are essentially the same as your working styles, knowing how you learn will help you identify career and work environments that suit you. Knowing your strengths will help you use and highlight them on the job. When a task involves one of your weaker skills, you can either take special care to accomplish it or suggest someone else who is a better fit.

- **Better teamwork.** The more attuned you are to abilities and personality traits, the better you will be at identifying the tasks you and others can best perform in team situations. For example, a Giver might enjoy helping new hires get used to the people and environment. Or a supervisor directing an intrapersonal learner might offer the chance to take material home to think about before a meeting.

- **Better career planning.** The more you know about how you learn and work, the more you will be able to focus on career paths that could work well for you. For the following student, strength in both logical–mathematical and interpersonal intelligence has guided him toward specific jobs and activities while in school and has helped him choose career goals:

A family joke around the Patterson household centers on the roots of eldest son Cody's love affair with mathematics. Like any young child, the story goes, Cody would grow impatient when forced to wait in line in a public place. In an attempt to distract her fidgeting son, his mother, Janalyn, would dig in her purse for her pocket calculator. Once in his hands, the calculator's blinking electronic numerals would mesmerize young Cody, and the wait was soon forgotten. . . . Patterson, 21, laughed as he recalled the hours spent punching buttons on that little gadget. "A lot of guys grew up with G.I. Joes and action figures," he said with a smile. "I grew up with calculators."

Whether or not his mother's calculator did indeed encourage a life dedicated to mathematical pursuits, there is no doubt that Patterson was born with a gift for numbers. He worked as a teaching assistant for an upper-level analysis course, a "math problem" writer for math competitions, and a help session leader for advanced math courses, and has served as a Math Camp counselor and vice president of the Pi Mu Epsilon math honor society. "I'd like to be a college teacher and help students like me who have had opportunities to hit the big time," Patterson said, "and find some other students who are trying to find their place in academics, get them interested in math, and make believers out of them."[4]

A better understanding of your learning strengths and preferences and personality traits will aid you in an upcoming educational challenge—choosing the right major.

How can you *choose a major?*

The major: It may not be around the corner, but it's probably not that far away. At some point in the next two years, after you complete your general education requirements, you will be asked to declare an academic major. Through this act you largely determine the courses you take, what you learn, with whom you spend your school time. Your major may also have a significant influence on your future career.

Taking a practical approach to declaring a major can help you avoid becoming overwhelmed by the task. Think of it as a long-term goal made up of multiple steps (short-term goals) that begin with knowing your learning styles, interests, and talents; exploring academic options; and establishing your academic schedule. You will be wise to start the process now, even though you probably don't need to decide right away—and even if, as is true of many students, you don't yet know what you want to study.

Short-term goal #1: Use learning styles assessments to identify interests and talents

Considering what you like and what you do well can lead to a fulfilling area of study. When you identify your interests and talents and choose a major that focuses on them, you are likely to have a positive attitude and perform at your highest level.

You may have sensed a career direction since you were young. This was the case with University of Illinois student Brian DeGraff, whose interests were mechanical: "I am amazed by how things work. The way a car can turn a tank of greasy, smelly, toxic liquid into my ride to school. People always say stop and smell the roses, but I'd rather stop and wonder why the roses smell. It was this passion that drove me to want to be an engineer; it's the best way I can imagine to spend my life figuring out how things work."[5]

Great minds have purposes; others have wishes.

WASHINGTON IRVING

To pinpoint the areas that spark your interest, use your Multiple Intelligences and Personality Spectrum assessment results to answer the following questions:

- What courses have I enjoyed the most in college and high school? What do these courses have in common?
- What subjects am I drawn to in my personal reading?
- What activities do I look forward to most?
- In what skills or academic areas do I perform best? Am I a "natural" in any area?
- What do people say I do well?
- What are my dominant learning styles?

Short-term goal #2:
Explore academic options

Next, find out about the academic choices available at your school. Plan to achieve the following minigoals in order to reach this short-term goal:

Learn what's possible. Consult your college catalog for guidelines on declaring (and changing) your major. Find answers to these questions:

- When do I have to declare a major? (generally at the end of the second year for four-year programs; earlier for associate or certificate programs)
- What are my options in majoring? (double majors, minors, interdisciplinary majors)
- What majors are offered at my school?

If a major looks interesting, explore it further by answering these questions:

- What minimum grade point average (GPA), if any, does the department require before it will accept me as a major?
- What GPA must I maintain in the courses included in the major?
- What preparatory courses (prerequisites) are required?
- What courses will I be required to take and in what sequence? How many credits do I need to graduate in the major?
- Will I have to write a thesis to graduate in this major?

Work closely with your advisor. Early on, begin discussing your major with your advisor; he or she can help you evaluate different options.

Visit the department. When considering a major, analyze your comfort with the academic department as well as with the material. When Ashiana Esmail decided to major in Ethnic Studies at the University of California at Berkeley, she did so in part because she wanted a close-knit department where faculty knew her and could be her advocates. Being involved like this "was better than an A+" in helping to build academic momentum, she explains.[6]

To learn more about the department, ask the department secretary for information. Then sit in on several classes to get a feel for the instructors and the work. Consider asking an instructor for an appointment to discuss the major.

Colleges offer different areas of study and types of classes. Listening to their instructor during a class on draft horses, these students learn from experiencing the horses firsthand.

Speak to people with experience in the major. Ask students who are a year or two ahead of you to describe their experiences with the courses, the workload, and the instructors.

Consider creative options for majoring. Think beyond the traditional majoring path, and investigate the possibilities at your school. One or more of the following may be open to you:

- Double majors. If, for example, you want to major in English and philosophy, ask your academic advisor if it is possible to meet the requirements for both departments.
- Interdisciplinary majors. If your preferred major isn't in the catalog, consult your advisor. Some schools allow students to design majors with guidance from advisors and instructors.
- Minors. A minor involves a concentration of departmental courses but has fewer requirements than a major. Many students choose a minor that is suited for a career. For example, a sociology major who wants to work in an inner-city hospital might consider a minor in Spanish.
- Majors involving courses outside your school. Some schools may offer study abroad programs (in which students spend a semester or a year at an affiliated college in a different country) or opportunities to take courses at nearby schools. Such courses might apply to a major that interests you.

Short-term goal #3: Establish your academic schedule

Effective time management will enable you to fulfill the requirements of your major and complete all additional credits.

Look at your time frame. How many years do you plan to study as an undergraduate or graduate student? Do you plan to attend graduate school? If so, do you plan to go there directly after graduation or take time off?

CURRICULUM

The particular set of courses required for a degree.

Set timing for short-term goals. Within your time frame, pinpoint when to accomplish the important short-term goals that lead to graduation. What are the deadlines for completing core requirements, declaring a major, writing a thesis? Although you won't need to plan out your entire college course load at the beginning of your first semester, drafting a tentative curriculum—both within and outside your major— can help clarify where you are heading.

Identify dates connected to your goal fulfillment. Pay attention to academic dates (you will find an academic calendar in each year's college catalog and on the college's Web site). Such dates include registration dates, final date to declare a major, final date to drop a course, and so forth. Plan ahead so you don't miss a deadline.

Be flexible as you come to a decision

As with any serious challenge that involves defining your path flexibility is essential. Many students change their minds as they consider majors; some declare a major and then change it one or more times before finding a good fit. Just act on any change right away—once you have considered it carefully—by informing your advisor, completing any required paperwork, and redesigning your schedule to reflect your new choices.

LINK YOUR INTERESTS TO INTRIGUING MAJORS

get analytical, creative, and practical!

Looking at a list of the majors your school offers, write down three that you want to consider.

1. _____
2. _____
3. _____

Now look at the list again. Other than what you wrote above, what majors catch your eye? Write down three intriguing majors—*without* thinking about what you would do with them or whether they are practical choices.

1. _____
2. _____
3. _____

Choose one major from the second list and explore it. Talk to your advisor about the major. Read about it in your college catalog. Consider a minor in the subject. Speak to an instructor in the department about related careers. You will have taken a casual interest and turned it into a viable academic option.

How can Multiple Intelligences help you *explore majors and careers*?

All that you have learned in this chapter about your learning styles and strengths has practical application as you begin thinking about your future at school and in the workplace. A strength in one or more intelligences may lead you to a major, an internship, and even a lifelong career.

Key 3.5 lists some possibilities for the eight intelligence types. This list is by no means complete. Rather, it represents only a fraction of the available opportunities. Use what you see here to inspire thought and spur investigation.

Career exploration strategies

Whatever your major, you will benefit from starting to think about careers early on. Use the following strategies to explore what's out there (later in the text, Chapter 9 will further examine the topic of career exploration).

Keep what you value in mind. Ask yourself what careers support the principles that guide your life. How important to you are service to others, financial security, a broad-based education, time for family?

Follow your passion. Find something you love doing more than anything else in the world, and then find a way to make money doing it. If you are sure of what you love to do but cannot pinpoint a career niche, open yourself to your instructors' advice.

MULTIPLE INTELLIGENCE	CONSIDER MAJORING IN . . .	THINK ABOUT AN INTERNSHIP AT A . . .	LOOK INTO A CAREER AS . . .
Bodily–Kinesthetic	Massage Therapy Physical Therapy Kinesiology Construction Engineering Chiropractics Sports Medicine Anatomy Dance Theater	Sports Physician's Office Athletic Club Physical Therapy Center Chiropractor's Office Construction Company Surveying Company Dance Studio Athletic Trainer Drafting Firm Theater Company	Carpenter Draftsman Recreational Therapist Physical Therapist Mechanical Engineer Massage Therapist Dancer or Acrobat Exercise Physiologist Actor
Intrapersonal	Psychology Sociology English Finance Liberal Arts Biology Computer Science Economics	Research and Development Firm Accounting Firm Computer Company Publishing House Pharmaceutical Company Engineering Firm Biology Lab	Research Scientist Motivational Speaker Engineer Physicist Sociologist Computer Scientist Economist Author Psychologist
Interpersonal	Psychology Sociology Education Real Estate Public Relations Nursing Business Hotel/Restaurant Management Rhetoric/Communications	Hotel or Restaurant Travel Agency Real Estate Agency Public Relations Firm Human Resources Customer Service Teaching Assistant Marketing/Sales Group Counseling Social Service	Social Worker PR Rep/Media Liaison Human Resources Travel Agent Sociologist Anthropologist Counselor Therapist Teacher Nurse
Naturalistic	Forestry Astronomy Geology Biology Zoology Atmospheric Sciences Oceanography Agriculture Animal Husbandry Environmental Law Physics	Museum National Park Oil Company Botanical Gardens Environmental Law Firm Outward Bound Adventure Travel Agency Zoo Camp Counselor Biological Research Firm	Forest Ranger Botanist or Herbalist Geologist Ecologist Marine Biologist Archaeologist Astronomer Adventure Travel Agent Wildlife Tour Guide Landscape Architect

(continued)

Continued.

MULTIPLE INTELLIGENCE	CONSIDER MAJORING IN . . .	THINK ABOUT AN INTERNSHIP AT A . . .	LOOK INTO A CAREER AS . . .
Musical	Music Musical History Musical Theory Performing Arts Composition Voice Liberal Arts Entertainment Law	Performance Hall Radio Station Record Label Ballet or Theater Company Recording Studio Children's Music Camp Orchestra or Opera Company Musical Talent Agency Entertainment Law Firm	Lyricist or Composer Singer or Musician Voice Coach Music Teacher or Critic Record Executive Conductor Radio DJ Sound Engineer Entertainment Lawyer
Logical–Mathematical	Math Accounting Physics Economics Medicine Banking/Finance Astronomy Computer Science Systems Theory Law Chemistry Engineering	Law Firm Health Care Office Real Estate Brokerage Accounting Firm Animal Hospital Science Lab Consulting Firm Pharmaceutical Firm Bank	Doctor, Dentist, or Veterinarian Accountant Pharmacist Chemist Physicist Systems Analyst Investment Banker Financial Analyst Computer Scientist
Verbal–Linguistic	Communications Marketing English/Literature Journalism Foreign Languages Linguistic Theory Political Science Advertising/PR	Newspaper/Magazine Network TV Affiliate Publishing House Law Firm PR/Marketing Firm Speech Therapist Ad Agency Training Company Human Resources Customer Service	Author Playwright Journalist TV/Radio Producer Literature Teacher Speech Pathologist Business Executive Copywriter or Editor
Visual–Spatial	Visual Arts Architecture Interior Design Multimedia Design Film Theory Photography Art History	Art Gallery Museum Photography Studio Design Firm Advertising Agency Theatrical Set Designer Multimedia Firm Architecture Firm Film Studio	Graphic Artist Photographer Architect Cinematographer Art Therapist Designer Cartoonist/Illustrator Art Museum Curator Art Teacher

Sonia Lopez did just that when she declared a major in engineering at Rensselaer Polytechnic Institute. Sonia randomly chose aerospace engineering as her specialty until a professor told her what she could accomplish as a civil engineer. "The professor said the U. S. would be completely different if it weren't for civil engineers, and that we'd have no public transportation or sanitation system without their work." The comment changed Sonia's thinking. Suddenly, "helping build the infrastructure of towns and designing buildings seemed a lot more important than building planes and motors."[7]

Use career resources. Visit your school's career center to read current media, take an assessment, or explore the career areas that currently have good prospects. Check out careers, industries, and companies on the Internet. Talk with people who have jobs that interest you.

Explore educational requirements of careers. How much your choice of a major matters may depend on the career. For example, pursuing a career in medicine usually requires majoring in the biological sciences. In contrast, aiming for a career in law gives you more flexibility (political science, philosophy, and English are just a few possibilities for pre-law students).

Try hands-on exploration. Extracurricular activities and volunteering opportunities might provide experiences that help you decide. For example, a student interested in teaching may volunteer as a camp counselor or an after-school tutor.

Sabiduría

In Spanish, the term *sabiduría* represents the two sides of learning: knowledge and wisdom. *Knowledge* involves gaining information, understanding concepts, building what you know about how the world works. *Wisdom* is the collected meaning and significance gained from knowledge. The learning and life experiences you gain in college will build your personal *sabiduría*, which, in turn, will help you make wise personal, educational, and career choices.

Think of this concept as you acquire knowledge in your classes. Try to transform the facts and concepts you study into the building blocks of wisdom.

PERSONAL TRIUMPH

DR. JOYCE BISHOP Professor of Psychology, Golden West College, Huntington Beach, CA

Dr. Bishop, the creator of the assessments in this chapter, has a passion for learning styles that was inspired by her ordeal as a college student with a learning disability. As it did with her, knowing your learning styles can help you surmount the obstacles that come your way. Read the account; then use a separate piece of paper to answer the questions on page 82.

I have learning problems understanding words I hear, which made listening to lectures in college very hard. No one would know I had this difficulty because I learned how to compensate for it. In fact, I didn't even know it until years later. This learning disability is called auditory discrimination.

College was very confusing for me. I did well in some classes and felt totally lost in others. The hardest were the lecture-based classes. When I wasn't familiar with the information or the words, I couldn't make sense of what I was hearing.

If I read the material ahead of time, I could make visual pictures in my mind that would help me absorb the material. I could also look up words and research concepts I didn't understand. Then the lectures made more sense.

I read lips and facial expressions well, so I did well in small classes where I could consistently see the teacher's face. The disadvantage for me in small classes was the noise. Because I heard voices around me as much as I heard the speaker, I had trouble blocking the extra noise. To make my lecture classes easier to understand, I would drag a tape recorder to class so that I could play back the lecture a number of times later. I found, however, that it didn't really help when I re-listened to the tapes. After that, I bargained with my classmates to borrow their notes in exchange for typing their term papers. Typing is bodily–kinesthetic and helped me to internalize what I was learning.

The only reason I got by in college was that I am strong in logical-mathematical intelligence. School is primarily taught in the verbal-linguistic and logical-mathematical learning styles. I am also a strong visual learner. Science classes were easiest for me because they are more visual. I switched from sociology to biology my freshman year; it was easier for me to remember the visual biology material as opposed to the more verbal liberal arts classes. Without my commitment to my education and my will to succeed, I probably would not have graduated.

Twelve years after graduating, I pursued my master's in public health. Part of why I waited so long was that I needed to heal from the trauma of my own learning process. My graduate classes were much more hands-on, but there was still a great deal of reading. One day my eye doctor expressed concern about the stress my school work was causing my eyes and suggested that I get tested for a learning problem. He sent me to a center that usually tests small children for learning disabilities. The person giving the test said words and I was to spell out the words with blocks. I couldn't get some of the words right. I would consistently confuse or mistake words with close sounds. It was determined that I processed language on a fourth-grade level, a condition that has not changed in my adult life.

"How far did you go through school?" asked the therapist conducting the test.

"How far do you think I went?" I asked.

After thinking for a moment, she answered, "The tenth grade." I shared that I was just completing my master's degree. Her eyes got big and she said: "You work really hard in school, don't you?"

At that moment my head flooded with memories of report cards saying "doesn't pay attention in class" and "isn't working up to potential." I started to cry. An explanation for what had brought years of pain and struggle had finally come to the surface.

Now that I know what the problem is, I use strategies that allow me to deal with the way I learn. This is why I am so passionate about the power of learning styles. We all have our strengths and weaknesses; the way we work to manage those weaknesses while maximizing our strengths makes all the difference.

Developing Successful Intelligence

PUTTING IT ALL TOGETHER

Learn from the experiences of others. Look back to Joyce Bishop's Personal Triumph on page 81. After you've read her story, relate her experience to your own life by completing the following:

Step 1. Think it through: *Analyze your experience and compare it to Joyce's.* What is a consistent challenge for you as a student, and how does this relate to Joyce's experience? How might this be explained by your learning styles? Do you have an "aha" experience story like Joyce's where you suddenly realized why you've struggled?

Step 2. Think out of the box: *Imagine ways of advising.* You are an advisor to a student identical to yourself. Be a harsh advisor—how would you criticize your performance as a student? Then be a wise advisor, focused on tapping into learning styles information—how would you identify challenges and suggest ways to handle them?

Step 3. Make it happen: *Head off your own challenges with practical strategies.* You have named a consistent challenge—and you have imagined what you would say as your own advisor. Now identify steps that will help you face your challenge (choosing particular courses, meeting with an advisor or instructor who can give you ideas, approaching work in particular ways).

Team Building

COLLABORATIVE SOLUTIONS

Ideas about personality types. Divide into groups according to the four types of the Personality Spectrum—Thinker-dominant students in one group, Organizer-dominant students in another, Giver-dominant students

in a third, and Adventurer-dominant students in the fourth. If you have scored the same in more than one of these types, join whatever group is smaller. With your group, brainstorm the following lists for your type:

1. the strengths of this type
2. the struggles it brings
3. the stressors (things that cause stress) for this type
4. career areas that tend to suit this type
5. career areas that are a challenge for this type
6. people who annoy this type the most (often because they are strong in areas where this type needs to grow)

If there is time, each group can present this information to the entire class; this will boost understanding and acceptance of diverse ways of relating to information and people.

Writing

DISCOVERY THROUGH JOURNALING

Record your thoughts on a separate piece of paper or in a journal.

Strengths and weaknesses. What have the personal assessments in this chapter taught you about your strengths? Choose what you consider your greatest strength and discuss how you plan to use it to your advantage this semester. What areas of weakness did the assessments highlight? Choose a weakness that has given you difficulty in school and brainstorm ways to compensate for it this semester. Finally, brainstorm ideas for how you will deal this semester with the kinds of people who challenge you the most.

Career Portfolio

PLAN FOR SUCCESS

Complete the following in your electronic portfolio, if you can use a graphics program, or on separate sheets of paper.

Self-portrait. Because self-knowledge helps you to make the best choices about your future, a self-portrait is an important step in your career exploration. Use this exercise to synthesize everything you have been exploring about yourself into one comprehensive "self-portrait." Design your protrait in "think link" style, using words and visual shapes to describe your dominant Multiple Intelligences and Personality Spectrum dimensions, values, abilities, career interests, and anything else that is an important part of who you are.

A think link is a visual construction of related ideas, similar to a map or web, that represents your thought process. Ideas are written inside geometric shapes, often boxes or circles, and related ideas and facts are attached to those ideas by lines that connect the shapes. See the note-taking section in Chapter 6 for more about think links.

Use the style shown in the example in Key 3.6 or create your own. For example, in this exercise you may want to create a "wheel" of ideas coming off your central shape, entitled "Me." Then, spreading out from each of those ideas (interests, learning style, etc.), draw lines connecting all of the thoughts that go along with that idea. Connected to "Interests," for example, might be "singing," "stock market," and "history."

You don't have to use the wheel image. You might want to design a treelike think link or a line of boxes with connecting thoughts written below the boxes, or anything else you like. Let your design reflect who you are, just as what you write does.

One example of a self-portrait.

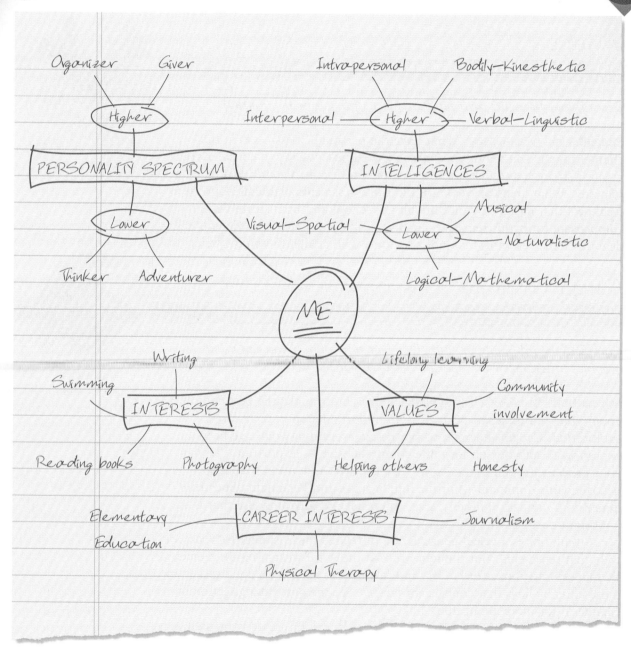

SUGGESTED READINGS

Cobb, Joyanne. *Learning How to Learn: A Guide for Getting into College with a Learning Disability, Staying in, and Staying Sane.* Washington, DC: Child Welfare League of America, 2001.

College Board, ed. *The College Board Index of Majors and Graduate Degrees 2001.* New York: College Entrance Examination Board, 2000.

Gardner, Howard. *Intelligence Reframed: Multiple Intelligences for the 21st Century.* New York: Basic Books, 2000.

Fogg, Neeta, et al. *The College Majors Handbook with Real Career Paths and Payoffs: The Actual Jobs,*

Earnings, and Trends for Graduates of 60 College Majors. Indianapolis, IN: Jist Works, 2004.

Keirsey, David. *Please Understand Me II: Temperament, Character, Intelligence.* Del Mar, CA: Prometheus Nemesis Book Company, 1998.

Pearman, Roger R. and Sarah C. Albritton. *I'm Not Crazy, I'm Just Not You: The Real Meaning of the 16 Personality Types.* Palo Alto, CA: Consulting Psychologists Press, 1997.

Phifer, Paul. *College Majors and Careers: A Resource Guide for Effective Life Planning,* 4th ed. Chicago: Ferguson Publishing, 1999.

INTERNET RESOURCES

Keirsey Sorter and other Myers-Briggs information: www.keirsey.com

Prentice Hall Student Success Supersite Majors Exploration: www.prenhall.com/success/MajorExp/index.html

ENDNOTES

1. Howard Gardner, *Multiple Intelligences: The Theory in Practice.* New York: HarperCollins, 1993, pp. 5–49.

2. Ibid, p. 7.

3. Developed by Joyce Bishop, Ph.D., Golden West College, Huntington Beach, CA. Based on Howard Gardner, *Frames of Mind: The Theory of Multiple Intelligences.* New York: HarperCollins, 1993.

4. Kara Bounds Socol, "Cody Patterson '03: Math Student Benefits from Private Gifts," Texas A&M website [on-line]. Available: http://giving.tamu.edu/content/impactofgiving/studentstories/studentget.php?get=6.

5. Students Speak: Excerpts from Your Educational Experience Essays, the University of Illinois,

October 2, 2001 [on-line]. Available: http://ae3.cen.uiuc.edu/stessay/StudentsSpeak (March 2004).

6. Terry Strathman, "L & S Colloquium on Undergraduate Education: What Do Students Want?," April 15, 2002 [on-line]. Available: http://ls.berkeley.edu/undergrad/colloquia/02–02.html (March 2004).

7. Elizabeth F. Farrell, "Engineering a Warmer Welcome for Female Students: The Discipline Tries to Stress Its Social Relevance, an Important Factor for Many Women," *The Chronicle of Higher Education,* February 22, 2002 [on-line]. Available: http://chronicle.com/weekly/v48/i24/24a03101.htm (March 2004).

Critical, Creative, and Practical Thinking

SOLVING PROBLEMS AND MAKING DECISIONS

To survive and to thrive in college and beyond, you will need to use your thinking power to do more than remember formulas for a test. When problems or decisions arise on the road toward goals large and small, how can you work through them successfully? The answer lies in how you combine your analytical, creative, and practical thinking skills—in other words, how you use your successful intelligence. As you remember from Chapter 1, successful intelligence is "the kind of intelligence used to achieve important goals."[1]

Thinking, like note taking or car repair, is a skill that can be developed with practice. This chapter will help you build your ability to analyze information, come up with creative ideas, and put a practical plan into action. With these skills you can become a better thinker, problem solver, and decision maker, able to reach the goals that mean the most to you.

On the next page, read how student Parisa Malekzadeh worries about her test-taking skills.

- What is successfully intelligent thinking?
- How can you improve your analytical thinking skills?
- How can you improve your creative thinking skills?
- How can you improve your practical thinking skills?
- How can you use your thinking skills to solve problems and make decisions?

How can I succeed in college if I don't test well?

Although it was not always easy and I did get a few less than perfect grades, I did well in a very academic high school. My grades were good and I was also involved and successful in extracurricular activities. As a senior, I was one of four student administrators in a highly successful freshman mentor program. I am a third-degree black belt in tae kwon do, a two-time Arizona State champ, and a certified instructor. My family, my high school teachers, and my martial arts students and their parents have told me that I am so much more mature than other people my age, and they all think I will do well in college.

But I am not so sure, and there are times when I really worry. I have difficulty with multiple-choice tests and I did not do well on the SAT and ACT or several other multiple-choice tests I took for AP and other advance exams. I worry that maybe I am just not smart enough. So much of college seems to be objective tests. I can certainly express myself well in essay and when I talk with people. I rarely lose an argument!

How can I do better on these tests? How important are they really? And how can I use what I already do well to succeed in college and after?

Parisa Malekzadeh University of Arizona, Major—Undeclared

Strive to improve your skills, and know that your other strengths will lead you to success.

To accomplish goals in life one must remain focused on the objectives and maintain perseverance at all times. As Samuel Johnson said, "Great works are performed, not by strength, but perseverance." You have already demonstrated that you possess these qualities by both your academic performance and the level of expertise that you have accomplished in tae kwon do. These qualities will prove more important to your success than your test scores alone.

Don't let your past difficulties with multiple-choice tests erode your confidence. I had a similar experience. At the time of my medical education in Argentina, all the tests that I took were oral. In order to continue my postgraduate education in this country, I had to pass the Educational Commission for Foreign Medical Graduates (ECFMG) examination, which is almost entirely multiple choice.

Because I knew the medical material, I prepared myself by learning how to properly answer multiple-choice questions. I reviewed and took many sample tests. I promptly realized that the majority of my wrong answers occurred because I was quickly glancing at the questions instead of reading them carefully. With a more focused approach, I passed the qualifying test and was able to continue my postgraduate training that eventually led to an academic career.

A similar approach has helped me when confronted by a medical diagnostic problem. Analyzing the key signs and symptoms of a medical condition, and then correlating them to clinical and laboratory findings, has allowed me, in the majority of instances, to arrive at the proper diagnosis and treatment. However, analysis is only part of what I do. My success as a physician has come from combining analytical work with creativity—to think through situations comprehensively—and practical ability—to discuss the diagnosis with the patient, apply the appropriate treatment, and monitor the results.

Yes, your testing and analytical skills are important. Work hard to improve them, but value and build your practical and creative skills just as much, knowing that the combination will help you reach your goals. Good luck with your college career!

Benjamin E. Victorica, MD Professor Emeritus, Pediatric Cardiology, University of Florida

What is *successfully intelligent* thinking?

Robert Sternberg uses this story to illustrate the impact of successful intelligence:

Two boys are walking in a forest. They are quite different. The first boy's teachers think he is smart, his parents think he is smart, and as a result, he thinks he is smart. He has good test scores, good grades, and other good paper credentials that will get him far in his scholastic life.

Few people consider the second boy smart. His test scores are nothing great, his grades aren't so good, and his other paper credentials are, in general, marginal. At best, people would call him shrewd or street smart.

As the two boys walk along in the forest, they encounter a problem—a huge, furious, hungry-looking grizzly bear, charging straight at them. The first boy, calculating that the grizzly bear will overtake them in 17.3 seconds, panics. In this state, he looks at the second boy, who is calmly taking off his hiking boots and putting on his jogging shoes.

The first boy says to the second boy, "You must be crazy. There is no way you are going to outrun that grizzly bear!"

The second boy replies, "That's true. But all I have to do is outrun you!"[2]

This story shows that successful problem solving and decision making require more than "book smarts." When confronted with a problem, using only analytical thinking put the first boy at a disadvantage. On the other hand, the second boy thought in different ways; he analyzed the situation, creatively considered the options, and took practical action. He asked and answered questions. He knew his purpose. And he lived to tell the tale.

Successfully intelligent thinking is balanced

Some tasks require only one thinking skill, or ability, at a time. You might use analytical thinking to complete a multiple-choice quiz, creative thinking to figure out how to get a paper done the same day you work a long shift, or practical thinking to put together a desk marked "some assembly required." However, when you need to solve a problem or make a decision, your analytical, creative, and practical thinking skills build upon one another to move you forward.[3] Envision it this way: Just as a pyramid needs three sides in order to stand, successful thinkers need all three thinking skills to develop the best solutions and decisions (see Key 4.1).

Each thinking skill adds an important dimension to accomplishing goals. Developing a balanced set of skills and knowing how and when to use each of them gives you more thinking power than having a strong aptitude in any one ability.[4] This kind of flexible thinking will help you connect your academic tasks to life goals—and show you where your hard work can take you (see Key 4.2).

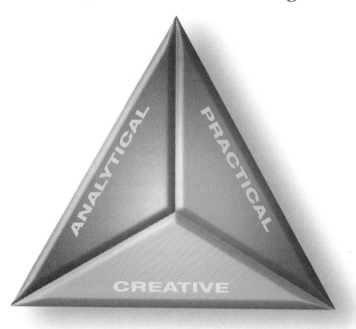

Successfully intelligent thinking means asking and answering questions

What is thinking? According to experts, it is what happens when you ask questions and move toward the answers.[5] "To think through or rethink anything," says Dr. Richard Paul, director of research at the Center for Critical Thinking and Moral Critique, "one must ask questions that stimulate our thought. Questions define tasks, express problems and delineate issues. . . . only students who have questions are really thinking and learning."[6]

As you answer questions, you transform raw data into information that you can use. A *Wall Street Journal* article entitled "The Best Innovations Are Those That Come from Smart Questions" relays the story of a cell biology student, William Hunter, whose professor told him that "the difference between good science and great science is the quality of the questions posed." Later, as a doctor and the president and CEO of a pharmaceutical company, Dr. Hunter asked questions about new ways to use drugs. His questions led to the development of a revolutionary product—a drug-coated coronary stent that prevents scar tissue from forming. Through seeking answers to probing questions, Dr. Hunter reached a significant goal.[7]

You use questions in order to analyze ("How bad is my money situation?"), come up with creative ideas ("What ways could I earn money?"), and apply practical solutions ("How can I get a job on campus?"). Later in the chapter, in the sections on analytical, creative, and practical thinking, you will find examples of the kinds of questions that drive each skill.

Like any aspect of thinking, questioning is not often a straightforward process. Sometimes the answer doesn't come right away. Often the answer leads to more—and more specific—questions.

DISCIPLINE	ANALYTICAL THINKING	CREATIVE THINKING	PRACTICAL THINKING
Behavioral Science	Comparing one theory of child development with another	Devising a new theory of child development	Applying child development theories to help parents and teachers understand and deal with children more effectively
Literature	Analyzing the development of the main character in a novel	Writing alternative endings to the novel	Using the experience of the main character to better understand and manage one's own life situations
History	Considering similarities and differences between World War I and World War II	Imagining yourself as a German citizen, dealing with economic depression after WWI	Seeing what WWI and WWII lessons can be applied to current Middle East conflicts
Sports	Analyzing the opposing team's strategy on the soccer field	Coming up with innovative ways to move the ball downfield	Using tactics to hide your strategy from an opposing team—or a competing company

Source: Adapted from Robert J. Sternberg, *Successful Intelligence*. Plume: New York, 1997, p. 149.

Successfully intelligent thinking requires knowing your purpose

In order to ask useful questions, you need to know *why* you are questioning. In other words, you need to define your purpose. A general question can be your starting point for defining your purposes: "What am I trying to accomplish, and why?" Then, within each stage of the process, you will find more specific purposes, or sub-goals, that help you generate analytical, creative, or practical questions along the way.

Successfully intelligent thinking is yours to build

You can improve, now and throughout your life, your ability to think. Studies have shown that the brain continues to develop throughout your life if you continue to learn new things.[8] Puzzle master Nob Yoshigahara has said, "As jogging is to the body, thinking is to the brain. The more we do it, the better we become."[9]

The mini-assessments within this chapter will help you to get an idea of how you perceive yourself as an analytical, creative, and practical thinker. Every other chapter's set of *Get Analytical, Get Creative,* and *Get Practical* exercises then helps you to build your skills in those areas. Finally, the *Developing Successful Intelligence: Putting It All Together* exercises at the ends of chapters encourage you to both build and combine your skills. *Your work throughout the book is geared toward building your successful intelligence.*

Begin by exploring the analytical thinking skills that you'll need in order to solve problems and make decisions effectively.

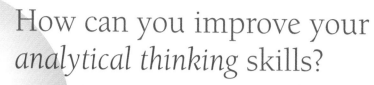

How can you improve your *analytical thinking skills?*

Analytical thinking—also known as critical thinking—is the process of gathering information, analyzing it in different ways, and evaluating it for the purposes of gaining understanding, solving a problem, or making a decision. It is as essential for real-life problems and decisions as it is for thinking through the hypothetical questions on your chemistry homework.

The first step in analytical thinking, as with all aspects of successful intelligence, is to define your purpose. What do you want to analyze, and why? Perhaps you need to analyze the plot of a novel in order to determine its structure; maybe you want to analyze your schedule in order to figure out whether you are arranging your time and responsibilities effectively.

Once you define your purpose, the rest of the analytical process involves gathering the necessary information, analyzing and clarifying the ideas, and evaluating what you've found.

Gather information

Information is the raw material for thinking. Choosing what to gather requires a careful analysis of how much information you need, how much time to spend gathering it, and whether the information is relevant. Say, for instance, that your assignment is to write a paper on one style of American jazz music. If you gathered every available resource on the topic, it might be next semester before you got to the writing stage.

Here's how you might use analysis to effectively gather information for that paper:

- Reviewing the assignment, you learn that the paper should be 10 pages and cover at least three influential musicians.
- At the library and on-line, you find lots of what appears to be relevant information.
- You choose a jazz movement, find five or six comprehensive pieces on it, and then select three in-depth sources on each of three musicians.

In this way you achieve a sub-goal—a selection of useful materials— on the way to your larger goal of writing a well-crafted paper.

Analyze and clarify information

Once you've gathered the information, the next step is to analyze it to determine whether the information is reliable and useful in helping you answer your questions.

Break information into parts

When analyzing information, you break information into parts and examine the parts so that you can see how they relate to each other and to information you already know. The following strategies help you break information down into pieces and set aside what is unclear, unrelated, or unimportant, resulting in a deeper and more reliable understanding.

Separate the ideas. If you are reading about the rise of the Bebop movement, you might name events that influenced it, key musicians, facts about the sound, and ideas behind it.

Compare and contrast. Look at how things are similar to, or different from, each other. You might explore how three Bebop musicians are similar in style. You might look at how they differ in what they want to communicate with their music.

Examine cause and effect. Look at the possible reasons why something happened (possible causes) and its consequences (effects, both positive and negative). You might examine the causes that led up to the Bebop sound as well as its effects on other non-jazz musical styles.

An important caution: Analyze carefully to seek out *true causes*—some apparent causes may not be actual causes (often called "false causes"). For example, events in the musical world and general society took place when the first musicians were developing the Bebop style. Some may have led directly to the new style; some may simply have occurred at the same time.

Look for themes, patterns, and categories. Note connections that arise out of how bits of information relate to one another. A theme of freedom vs. structure, for example, might emerge out of an examination of Bebop vs. swing jazz. A pattern of behavior might develop as you look at how different musicians broke off from the swing movement. Musicians with different styles might fall into the Bebop category based on their artistic goals.

> Too often we enjoy the comfort of opinion without the discomfort of thought.

JOHN F. KENNEDY

Once the ideas are broken down, you can examine whether examples support ideas, separate fact from opinion, consider perspective, and investigate hidden assumptions.

Examine whether examples support ideas

When you encounter an idea or claim, examine how it is supported with examples or evidence (facts, expert opinion, research findings, personal experience, and so on). Ideas that aren't backed up with solid evidence or made concrete with examples are not useful. Be critical of the information you gather; don't take it at face value.

For example, an advertisement for a weight-loss pill, claiming that it allows users to drop a pound a day, quotes "Anne" who says that she lost 30 pounds in 30 days. The word of one person, who may or may not be telling the truth, is not adequate support. On the other hand, a claim that water once existed on Mars, backed up by measurements and photography from one of the Mars Exploration Rovers, may prove more reliable.

Distinguish fact from opinion

A *statement of fact* is information presented as objectively real and verifiable ("It's raining outside right now"). In constrast, a *statement of opinion* is a belief, conclusion, or judgment that is inherently difficult, and sometimes impossible, to verify ("This is the most miserable rainstorm ever"). Key 4.3 defines important characteristics of fact and opinion. Even though facts may seem more solid, you can also make use of opinions if you determine that they are backed up with facts. However, it is important to examine opinions for their underlying perspectives and assumptions.

Shifting your perspective helps you accept and understand different ways of living and interacting. Two students communicate via sign language while walking on campus.

Examine perspectives and assumptions

Perspective is a characteristic way of thinking about people, situations, events, and ideas. Perspectives can be broad, such as a generally optimistic or pessimistic view of life. Or they can be more focused, such as an attitude about whether students should commute or live on campus.

Perspectives are associated with *assumptions*—judgments, generalizations, or biases influenced by experience and values. For example, the perspective that there are many different successful ways to be a family leads to assumptions such as "Single-parent homes can provide nurturing environments" and "Same-sex couples can rear well-adjusted children." Having a particular experience with single-parent homes or same-sex couples can build or reinforce a perspective.

Assumptions often hide within questions and statements, blocking you from considering information in different ways. Take this classic puzzler as an example: "Which came first, the chicken or the egg?" Thinking about this question, most people assume that the egg is a chicken egg. If you think past that assumption and come up with a new idea—such as, the egg is a dinosaur egg—then the obvious answer is that the egg came first!

Examining perspectives and assumptions is important for two reasons. First, they often affect your perception of the validity of materials you read and research. Second, your own perspectives and assumptions can cloud your interpretation of the information you encounter.

Perspectives and assumptions in information

BIASED

Leaning in a particular direction; influenced by a point of view.

Being able to determine the perspectives that underlie materials will help you separate (biased) from unbiased information. For example, the conclusions in two articles on federal versus state government control of education may differ radically if one appears in a politically conservative publication and one appears in a neutral publication.

Examine how fact and opinion differ.

OPINIONS INCLUDE STATEMENTS THAT . . .	FACTS INCLUDE STATEMENTS THAT . . .
. . . show evaluation. Any statement of value indicates an opinion. Words such as *bad, good, pointless,* and *beneficial* indicate value judgments. Example: "Jimmy Carter is the most successful peace negotiator to sit in the White House."	*. . . deal with actual people, places, objects, or events.* Example: "In 1978, Jimmy Carter's 13-day summit meeting with Egyptian President Anwar Sadat and Israeli Prime Minister Menachem Begin led to a treaty between the two countries."
. . . use abstract words. Words that are complicated to define, like *misery* or *success,* usually indicate a personal opinion. Example: "The charity event was a smashing success."	*. . . use concrete words or measurable statistics.* Example: "The charity event raised $5,862."
. . . predict future events. Statements that examine future occurrences are often opinions. Example: "Mr. Barrett's course is going to set a new enrollment record this year."	*. . . describe current events in exact terms.* Example: "Mr. Barrett's course has 378 students enrolled this semester."
. . . use emotional words. Emotions are by nature unverifiable. Chances are that statements using such words as *delightful* or *miserable* express an opinion. Example: "That class is a miserable experience."	*. . . avoid emotional words and focus on the verifiable.* Example: "Citing dissatisfaction with the instruction, 7 out of the 25 students in that class withdrew in September."
. . . use absolutes. Absolute *qualifiers,* such as *all, none, never,* and *always,* often point to an opinion. Example: "All students need to have a job while in school."	*. . . avoid absolutes.* Example: "Some students need to have a job while in school."

Source: Adapted from Ben E. Johnson, *Stirring Up Thinking.* New York: Houghton Mifflin, 1998, pp. 268–270.

Assumptions often affect the validity of materials you read and research. A historical Revolutionary War document that originated in the colonies, for example, may assume that the rebellion against the British was entirely justified and leave out information to the contrary. Clearly understanding such a document means separating the assumptions from the facts.

Personal perspectives and assumptions

Your own preferences, values, and prejudices—which influence your perspective—can affect how accurately you view information. A student who thinks that the death penalty is wrong, for example, may have a hard time analyzing the facts and arguments in an article that supports it. Or, in a research situation, he might use only materials that agree with his perspective.

Consider the perspectives and assumptions that might follow from your values. Then, when you have to analyze information, try to set them aside. "Anticipate your reactions and prejudices and then

Experience helps develop practical thinking skills

You gain much of your ability to think practically—your common sense—from personal experience, rather than from formal lessons. This knowledge is an important tool in achieving goals.[25]

What you learn from experience answers "how" questions—how to talk, how to behave, how to proceed.[26] For example, after completing a few papers for a particular course, you may pick up cues about how to impress that instructor. Following a couple of conflicts with a partner, you may learn how to avoid sore spots when the conversation heats up. See Key 4.8 for ways in which this kind of knowledge can be shown in "if-then" statements.

There are two keys to making practical knowledge work for you. First, make an active choice to learn from experience—to pay attention to how things work at school, in personal relationships, and at work. Second, make sure you apply what you learn, assuring that you will not have to learn the same lessons over and over again. As Sternberg says, "What matters most is not how much experience you have had but rather how much you have profited from it—in other words, how well you apply what you have learned."[27]

One way to map out what you learn from experience.

Goal: You want to talk to the soccer coach about your status on the team.

IF the team has had a good practice and IF you've played well during the scrimmage and IF the coach isn't rushing off somewhere, THEN grab a moment with him right after practice ends.

IF the team is having a tough time and IF you've been sidelined and IF the coach is in a rush and stressed, THEN drop in on his office hours tomorrow.

Practical thinking means action

Learning different ways to take action and stay in motion builds your practical thinking ability. Strategies you learn throughout this course will keep you moving toward your goals:[28]

- **Stay motivated.** Use techniques from Chapter 1 to persevere when you face a problem. Get started on achieving results instead of dwelling on exactly how to start. Translate thoughts into concrete actions instead of getting bogged down in "analysis paralysis."

- **Make the most of your personal strengths.** What you've learned in Chapter 2 will help you see what you do best—and use those strengths as you apply practical solutions.

- **When things go wrong, accept responsibility and reject self-pity.** You know from Chapter 1 that failure is an excellent teacher. Learn from what happened, act on what you have learned, and don't let self-pity stall your momentum.

- **Manage time and tasks effectively.** Use what you know from Chapter 2 to plan your time in a way that promotes goal accomplishment. Avoid the pitfalls of procrastination. Accurately gauge what you can handle—don't take on too many projects, or too few.

See Key 4.9 for some questions you can ask in order to apply practical thinking to your problems and decisions.

Ask questions like these to activate practical thinking.

key 4.9

To learn from experience, ask:	• What worked well, or not so well, about my approach? My timing? My tone? My wording?
	• What did others like or not like about what I did?
	• What did I learn from that experience, conversation, event?
	• How would I change things if I had to do it over again?
	• What do I know I would do again?
To apply what you learn, ask:	• What have I learned that would work here?
	• What have I seen others do, or heard about from them, that would be helpful here?
	• What does this situation have in common with past situations I've been involved in?
	• What has worked in similar situations in the past?
To boost your ability to take action, ask:	• How can I get motivated and remove limitations?
	• How can I, in this situation, make the most of what I do well?
	• If I fail, what can I learn from it?
	• What steps will get me to my goal, and what trade-offs are involved?
	• How can I manage my time more effectively?

get practical!

ASSESS PRACTICAL THINKING SKILLS

How do you perceive yourself as a practical thinker? For each statement, circle the number that feels right to you, from 1 for "least like me" to 5 for "most like me."

1. I can find a way around any obstacle. ① ② ③ ④ ⑤
2. People say I'm a "doer," the "go-to" person, "organized." ① ② ③ ④ ⑤
3. When I have a vision, I translate it into steps from A to B to C. ① ② ③ ④ ⑤
4. In a group setting, I like to set up the plan. ① ② ③ ④ ⑤
5. I don't like to leave loose ends dangling—I'm a finisher. ① ② ③ ④ ⑤

Total your answers here: _____

If your total ranges from 5–12, you consider your practical thinking skills to be *weak*.

If your total ranges from 13–19, you consider your practical thinking skills to be *average*.

If your total ranges from 20–25, you consider your practical thinking skills to be *strong*.

CREATIVE

Your skills at a glance: In the sections of the triangle, write your assessment scores from *Get Analytical (p. 96)*, *Get Creative (p. 103)*, and *Get Practical (above)*. Looking at the scores together will give you an idea of how you perceive your skills in all three aspects of successful intelligence, and will help you think about where you may want to build strength.

How can you put *analytical, creative, and practical thinking together* to solve a problem or make a decision?

You have developed your understanding of what it means to think analytically, creatively, and practically. You have explored your perception of where your strengths and weaknesses lie. Now you will see how to put analytical, creative, and practical thinking together to solve problems and make decisions successfully—at school, in the workplace, or in your personal life.

Problem solving and decision making follow similar paths. Both require you to identify and analyze a situation, generate possibilities, choose one, follow through on it, and evaluate its success. Key 4.10 gives an overview of the paths, indicating how you think at each step.

How do you choose which path to follow? Understanding the differences will help. First of all, problem solving generally requires more focus on coming up with possible solutions; when you face a decision, your choices are often determined. Second, problem solving aims to remove or counteract negative effects; decision making aims to fulfill a need. See Key 4.11 for some examples. Remember, too, that whereas all problem solving requires you to make a decision—when you decide on a solution—only some decision making requires you to solve a problem.

Solve problems and make decisions using successful intelligence.

PROBLEM SOLVING	THINKING SKILL	DECISION MAKING
Define the problem—recognize that something needs to change, identify what's happening, look for true causes	STEP 1 DEFINE	Define the decision—identify your goal (your need) and then construct a decision that will help you get it
Analyze the problem—gather information, break it down into pieces, verify facts, look at perspectives and assumptions, evaluate information	STEP 2 ANALYZE	Examine needs and motives—consider the layers of needs carefully, and be honest about what you really want
Generate possible solutions—use creative strategies to think of ways you could address the causes of this problem	STEP 3 CREATE	Name and/or generate different options—use creative questions to come up with choices that would fulfill your needs
Evaluate solutions—look carefully at potential pros and cons of each, and choose what seems best	STEP 4 ANALYZE (EVALUATE)	Evaluate options—look carefully at potential pros and cons of each, and choose what seems best
Put the solution to work—persevere, focus on results, and believe in yourself as you go for your goal	STEP 5 TAKE PRACTICAL ACTION	Act on your decision—go down the path and use practical strategies to stay on target
Evaluate how well the solution worked—look at the effects of what you did	STEP 6 ANALYZE (RE-EVALUATE)	Evaluate the success of your decision—look at whether it accomplished what you had hoped
In the future, apply what you've learned—use this solution, or a better one, when a similar situation comes up again	STEP 7 TAKE PRACTICAL ACTION	In the future, apply what you've learned—make this choice, or a better one, when a similar decision comes up again

Examine how problems and decisions differ.

SITUATION	YOU HAVE A PROBLEM IF . . .	YOU NEED TO MAKE A DECISION IF . . .
Planning summer activities	Your low GPA means you need to attend summer school—and you've already accepted a summer job.	You've been accepted into two summer abroad internship programs.
Declaring a major	It's time to declare but you don't have all the prerequisites for the major you want.	There are three majors that appeal to you and you qualify for them all.
Handling relationships with instructors	You are having trouble following the lecture style of a particular instructor.	Your psychology survey course has seven sections taught by different instructors; you have to choose one.

Solving a problem

A problem exists when a situation has negative effects. Recognizing that there is a problem—being aware of those effects—is essential before you can begin to solve it. In other words, your first move is to go from the effects—"I'm unhappy/uneasy/angry"—to determining why: "My schedule is overwhelming me." "I'm over my head in this course." "My credit card debt is out of control." Then you begin the problem-solving process in earnest.

What happens if you *don't* act in a successfully intelligent way? Take, for example, a student having an issue with an instructor. He may get into an argument with the instructor during class time. He may stop showing up to class. He may not make an effort with assignments. All of these choices will most likely have bad consequences for him.

Now look at how this student might work through this problem using his analytical, creative, and practical thinking skills. Key 4.12 shows how his effort can pay off.

As you go through the problem-solving process, keep these tips in mind.

Use probing questions to define problems. Focus on causes. If you are not happy in a class, for example, you could ask questions like these:

- What do I think about when I feel unhappy?
- Do my feelings involve my instructor? My classmates?
- Is the subject matter difficult? The volume of work too much?

Chances are that how you answer one or more of these questions may lead to a clear definition—and ultimately to the right solution.

Analyze carefully. Gather all the information you can, so that you can consider the situation comprehensively. Consider what you can learn from how the problem is similar to, or different from, other problems. Clarify facts. Note your own perspective, and ask others for theirs. Make sure you are not looking at the problem through the lens of an assumption.

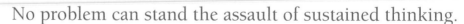

No problem can stand the assault of sustained thinking.

VOLTAIRE

Generate possible solutions based on causes, not effects. Addressing a cause provides a lasting solution, whereas "fixing" an effect cannot. Say your shoulder hurts when you use your computer. Getting a friend to massage it is a nice but temporary solution, because the pain returns whenever you go back to work. Changing the height of your keyboard and mouse is a better idea, because it eliminates the cause of your pain.

Making a decision

Psychologists who have studied decision making have learned that many random factors influence the choices people make. For example, you may choose a major, not because you love the subject, but because you think

Working through a problem relating to an instructor.

DEFINE PROBLEM HERE:

I don't like my Freshman Composition instructor

ANALYZE THE PROBLEM

We have different views and personality types—
I don't feel respected or heard.
I'm not interested in being there and my grades are suffering
from my lack of motivation.

Use boxes below to list possible solutions:

POTENTIAL POSITIVE EFFECTS	SOLUTION #1	POTENTIAL NEGATIVE EFFECTS
List for each solution:	Drop the course	*List for each solution:*
Don't have to deal with that		Grade gets entered on my transcript
instructor		I'll have to take the course
Less stress		eventually; it's required for
		my major

	SOLUTION #2	
Getting credit for the course	Put up with it until the end of the semester	Stress every time I'm there
Feeling like I've honored a		Lowered motivation
commitment		Probably not such a good final grade

	SOLUTION #3	
A chance to express myself	Schedule meetings with advisor and instructor	Have to face instructor one-on-one
Could get good advice		Might just make things worse
An opportunity to ask direct		
questions of the instructor		

Now choose the solution you think is best—circle it and make it happen.

ACTUAL POSITIVE EFFECTS	PRACTICAL ACTION	ACTUAL NEGATIVE EFFECTS
List for chosen solution:	I scheduled and attended meetings with both advisor and instructor, and opted to stick with the course.	*List for chosen solution:*
Got some helpful advice from advisor		The discussion was difficult and
Talking in person with the instructor		sometimes tense
actually promoted a fairly honest		I still don't know how much learning
discussion		I'll retain from this course
I won't have to take the course again		

FINAL EVALUATION: Was it a good or bad solution?

The solution has improved things. I'll finish the course, and even though the instructor and I aren't the best of friends, we have a mutual understanding now. I feel more respected and more willing to put my time into the course.

your parents will approve of it. The goal is to make well-considered decisions despite factors that may derail your thinking.

What happens when you make important decisions quickly, without using your analytical, creative, and practical thinking skills? Consider a student trying to decide whether to transfer schools. If she stays at her current school because a good friend says, "You can't leave me!" or transfers because she doesn't like her living situation, she may question her choice later—most likely because she didn't consider cause and effect carefully when deciding.

Now look at how this student might make a successfully intelligent decision. Key 4.13 shows how she worked through the analytical, creative, and practical parts of the process.

As you use the steps in Key 4.13 to make a decision, remember these hints.

Look at the given options—then try to think of more. Some decisions have a given set of options. For example, your school may allow you to major, double major, or major and minor. However, when you are making your decision, you may be able to brainstorm with an advisor to come up with more options—such as an interdisciplinary major you create on your own.

Think about how your decision affects others. For example, the student thinking about a transfer considers the impact on friends and family. What she concludes about that impact may inform when she transfers and even the school she chooses.

Gather perspectives. Talk with others who have made similar decisions. There are more ways of doing things than one brain can possibly imagine on its own.

Look at the long-term effects. For important decisions, do a short-term evaluation and another evaluation after a period of time. See whether your decision has sent you down a path that has continued to bring positive effects.

Keeping your balance

No one has equal strengths in analytical, creative, and practical thinking. Adjusting your expectations to match what you can accomplish is a key principle of successful intelligence. It requires that you

- use what you've learned in this chapter and the rest of the text to maximize your analytical, creative, and practical abilities.
- reflect on what you do well, and focus on strengthening weaker skills.
- combine all three thinking skills to accomplish your goals, knowing when and how to apply your analytical, creative, and practical abilities.
- believe in your skills as a thinker.

"Successfully intelligent people," says Sternberg, "defy negative expectations, even when these expectations arise from low scores on IQ

Making a decision about whether to transfer schools.

DEFINE THE DECISION	EXAMINE NEEDS AND MOTIVES
Whether or not to transfer schools	I attend a small private college. My father has changed jobs and can no longer afford my tuition. My goal is to become a physical therapist, so I need a school with a full physical therapy program. My family needs to cut costs. I need to transfer credits.

Use boxes below to list possible choices:

POTENTIAL POSITIVE EFFECTS	CHOICE #1	POTENTIAL NEGATIVE EFFECTS
List for each solution:	Continue at the current college	*List for each solution:*
No need to adjust to a new place or new people		Need to finance most of my tuition and costs on my own
Ability to continue course work as planned		Difficult to find time for a job
		Might not qualify for aid

POTENTIAL POSITIVE EFFECTS	CHOICE #2	POTENTIAL NEGATIVE EFFECTS
Opportunity to connect with some high school friends	Transfer to a state college	Need to earn some money or get financial aid
Cheaper tuition and room costs		Physical therapy program is small and not very strong
Credits will transfer		

POTENTIAL POSITIVE EFFECTS	CHOICE #3	POTENTIAL NEGATIVE EFFECTS
Many physical therapy courses available	Transfer to the community college	No personal contacts there that I know of
School is close so I could live at home and save room costs		Less independence if I live at home
Reasonable tuition; credits will transfer		No bachelor's degree available

Now choose the one you think is best—circle it and make it happen.

ACTUAL POSITIVE EFFECTS	PRACTICAL ACTION	ACTUAL NEGATIVE EFFECTS
List for chosen solution:	Go to community college for two years; then transfer to a four-year school to get a B.A. and complete physical therapy course work.	*List for chosen solution:*
Money saved,		Loss of some independence
Opportunity to spend time on studies rather than on working to earn tuition money		Less contact with friends
Availability of classes I need		

FINAL EVALUATION: Was it a good or bad choice?
I'm satisfied with the decision. It can be hard being at home at times, but my parents are adjusting to my independence and I'm trying to respect their concerns. With fewer social distractions, I'm really getting my work done. Plus the financial aspect of the decision is ideal.

or similar tests. They do not let other people's assessments stop them from achieving their goals. They find their path and then pursue it, realizing that there will be obstacles along the way and that surmounting these obstacles is part of the challenge."[29] Let the obstacles come, as they will for everyone, in all aspects of life. You can face and overcome them with the power of your successfully intelligent thinking.

Κριvειv

The word "critical" is derived from the Greek word *krinein*, which means to separate in order to choose or select. Successful intelligence requires that you separate, evaluate, and select ideas and information as you think through problematic situations. Says Sternberg, "It is more important to know when and how to use these aspects of successful intelligence than just to have them."[30]

Think of this concept as you use your analytical, creative, and practical thinking skills to solve problems, make decisions, innovate, and question. Consider information carefully, and separate out and select the best approaches. Successful intelligence gives you the power to choose how to respond to information, people, and events in ways that help you reach your goals.

BUILDING SKILLS

FOR COLLEGE, CAREER, AND LIFE SUCCESS

Developing Successful Intelligence

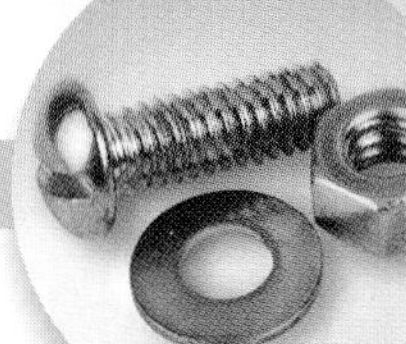

PUTTING IT ALL TOGETHER

Make an important decision. Put the decision-making process to work on something that matters to you. You will apply your analytical, creative, and practical thinking skills. Use a separate sheet of paper for steps 2 and 3.

Step 1. Analyze: *Define the decision.* Write an important long-term goal that you have, and define the decision that will help you fulfill it. Example: "My goal is to become a nurse. My decision: What to specialize in."

Step 2. Analyze: *Examine needs and concerns.* What do you want? What are your needs, and how do your values come into play? What needs of others will you need to take into account? What roadblocks might be involved? List everything you come up with. For example, the prospective nurse might list needs like: "I need to feel that I'm helping people. I intend to help with the nursing shortage. I need to make a good living."

Step 3. Be creative: *Generate options.* Ask questions to imagine what's possible. Where might you work? What might be the schedule and pace? Who might work with you? What would you see, smell, and hear on your job? What would you do every day? List, too, all of the options you know of. The prospective nurse, for example, might list ER, pediatrics, surgery, oncology, geriatrics, and so on. Brainstorm other options that might not seem so obvious.

Step 4. Analyze: *Evaluate options.* Think about how well your options will fulfill your needs. For two of your options, write potential positive and negative effects (pros and cons) of each.

Option 1:

Potential pros:

Potential cons:

Option 2:

Potential pros:

Potential cons:

Step 5. Get practical: *Imagine acting on your decision.* Describe one practical course of action, based on your thinking so far, that you might follow. List the specific steps you would take. For example, the prospective nurse might list actions that help him determine what type of nursing suits him best, such as interning, summer jobs, academic goals, and talking to working nurses.

Finally, over time, plan to put your decision into action. Eventually you will need to complete the two final steps of the process. Step 6 is to evaluate the decision: How did it work out? Analyze whether you, and others, got what you needed. Step 7 is to practically apply what you've learned from the decision to other decisions you make in the future.

Team Building

COLLABORATIVE SOLUTIONS

Powerful group problem solving. On a 3 × 5 card or a plain sheet of paper, each student in the class writes a school-related problem—this could be a fear, a challenge, a sticky situation, or a roadblock. Students hand these in without names. The instructor writes the list up on the board.

Divide into groups of two to four. Each group chooses one problem to work on (try not to have two groups working on the same problem). Use the empty problem-solving flow chart (Key 4.14) on p. 116 to fill in your work.

Step 1. Analyze: *Define the problem.* As a group, look at the negative effects and state your problem specifically. Then, explore and write down the causes.

Step 2. Analyze: *Examine the problem.* Pick it apart to see what's happening. Gather information from all group members, verify facts, go beyond assumptions.

Step 3. Create: *Generate possible solutions.* From the most likely causes of the problem, derive possible solutions. Record all the ideas that group members offer. After 10 minutes or so, each group member should choose one possible solution to evaluate independently.

Step 4. Analyze: *Evaluate each solution.* In thinking independently through the assigned solution, each group member should (a) weigh the positive and negative effects, (b) consider similar problems, and (c) describe how the solution affects the causes of the problem. Evaluate your assigned solution. Is it a good one? Will it work?

Step 5. Get practical: *Choose a solution.* Group members then come together, share observations and recommendations, and then take a vote: Which solution is the best? You may have a tie or may want to combine two different solutions. Try to find the solution that works for most of the group. Then, together, come up with a plan for how you would put your solution to work.

Step 6. Analyze: *Evaluate your solution.* As a group, share and discuss what you had individually imagined the positive and negative effects of this solution would be. Try to come to an agreement on how you think the solution would work out.

Writing

DISCOVERY THROUGH JOURNALING

Record your thoughts on a separate piece of paper or in a journal.

Wiser choices. Think about a choice you made that, looking back, you wish you had handled differently. First, describe what the decision was, what option you chose, and what the consequences were. Then, write about what you would do if you could make the decision again. What did you learn from your experience that you can apply to other decisions? How could being analytical, creative, and practical have helped you reach a more effective outcome?

Career Portfolio

PLAN FOR SUCCESS

Generating ideas for internships. People often put more time and effort into deciding what cell phone to buy than they do with life-altering decisions like how to prepare for career success. Pursuing internships is part of a comprehensive career decision-making process. It's a practical

Work through a problem using this flow chart.

DEFINE PROBLEM HERE:	ANALYZE THE PROBLEM

Use boxes below to list possible solutions:

POTENTIAL POSITIVE EFFECTS	SOLUTION #1	POTENTIAL NEGATIVE EFFECTS
List for each solution:		*List for each solution:*

SOLUTION #2

SOLUTION #3

Now choose the solution you think is best—circle it and make it happen.

ACTUAL POSITIVE EFFECTS	PRACTICAL ACTION	ACTUAL NEGATIVE EFFECTS
List for chosen solution:		*List for chosen solution:*

FINAL EVALUATION: Was it a good or bad solution?

way to get experience, learn what you like and don't like, and make valuable connections.

Fill in the following:

Career areas that I'm considering. Why?

1. _____ *Because:* _____

2. _____ *Because:* _____

3. _____ *Because:* _____

People whom I want to interview about their fields/professions. Why?

1. _____ *Because:* _____

2. _____ *Because:* _____

3. _____ *Because:* _____

Next, take practical steps to investigate internships. Talk to the people you listed. Contact companies you would like to work for and see what internship opportunities are available. Talk with someone in your school's career office. If a company doesn't offer internships, ask them if you might be the pioneer intern.

Finally, after you have gathered some useful information, use a separate sheet of paper to creatively envision your internship experience. Describe it: What would it look like? What would you do each day? Each week? Where would you go? With whom would you work? What would you contribute with your gifts and talents? Make it happen with your successful intelligence.

SUGGESTED READINGS

Cameron, Julia with Mark Bryan. *The Artist's Way: A Spiritual Path to Higher Creativity*, 10th ed. New York: G.P. Putnam's Sons, 2002.

deBono, Edward. *Lateral Thinking: Creativity Step by Step*. New York: Perennial Library, 1990.

Goleman, Daniel. *Emotional Intelligence: Why It Can Matter More Than IQ*. New York: Bantam, 1995.

Moscovich, Ivan. *1000 Playthinks*. New York: Workman Publishing, 2001.

Noone, Donald J., Ph.D. *Creative Problem Solving*. New York: Barron's, 1998.

Sark. *Make Your Creative Dreams Real: A Plan for Procrastinators, Perfectionists, Busy People, and People Who Would Rather Sleep All Day*. New York: Fireside Press, 2004.

von Oech, Roger. *A Kick in the Seat of the Pants*. New York: Harper & Row Publishers, 1986.

von Oech, Roger. *A Whack on the Side of the Head*. New York: Warner Books, 1998.

INTERNET RESOURCES

Creativity at Work (resources for workplace creativity): www.creativityatwork.com

Creativity for Life (tips and strategies for creativity): www.creativityforlife.com

Roger von Oech's Creative Think Web site: www.creative-think.com

1. Robert J. Sternberg, *Successful Intelligence*. New York: Plume, 1997, p. 12.

2. Ibid, p. 127.

3. Matt Thomas, "What Is Higher-Order Thinking and Critical/Creative/Constructive Thinking?" The Center for Studies in Higher-Order Literacy [on-line]. Available: http://members.aol.com/MattT10574/Higher OrderLiteracy.htm#What (April 2004).

4. Sternberg, p. 128.

5. Vincent Ruggiero, *The Art of Thinking*, 2001, quoted in "Critical Thinking," Oregon State University [on-line]. Available: http//success.oregonstate.edu/study/learning.cfm (April 2004).

6. Richard Paul, "The Role of Questions in Thinking, Teaching, and Learning," The Center for Thinking and Learning, 1995 [on-line]. Available: www.criticalthinking.org/University/univclass/roleofquest.html (April 2004).

7. "The Best Innovations Are Those That Come from Smart Questions," *Wall Street Journal*, April 12, 2004, B1.

8. Lawrence F. Lowery, "The Biological Basis of Thinking and Learning," 1998, Full Option Science System at the University of California at Berkeley [on-line]. Available: http://lhsfoss.org/newsletters/archive/pdfs/FOSS_BBTL.pdf (April 2004).

9. Ivan Moscovich, *1000 Playthinks*. New York: Workman Publishing, p. 7.

10. Colby Glass, "Strategies for Critical Thinking," March 1999 [on-line]. Available: www.accd.edu/pac/philosop/phil1301/ctstrategies.htm (April 2004).

11. Sternberg, p. 49.

12. Charles Cave, "Definitions of Creativity," August 1999 [on-line]. Available: http://members.ozemail.com.au/~caveman/Creative/Basics/definitions.htm (April 2003).

13. Elizabeth F. Farrell, "Engineering a Warmer Welcome for Female Students: The Dicipline Tries to Stress its Social Relevance, an Important Factor for Many Women," *The Chronicle of Higher Education*, February 22, 2002 [on-line]. Available: http://chronicle.com/weekly/v48/i24/24a03101.htm (March 2004).

14. Roger von Oech, *A Kick in the Seat of the Pants*. New York: Harper & Row Publishers, 1986, pp. 5–21.

15. Dennis Coon, *Introduction to Psychology: Exploration and Application*, 6th ed. St. Paul: West Publishing Company, 1992, p. 295.

16. Roger von Oech, *A Whack on the Side of the Head*. New York: Warner Books, 1990, pp. 11–168.

17. J. R. Hayes, *Cognitive Psychology: Thinking and Creating*. Homewood, IL: Dorsey, 1978.

18. Sternberg, p. 219.

19. Adapted from T. Z. Tardif and R. J. Sternberg, "What Do We Know About Creativity?" in *The Nature of Creativity*, ed. R. J. Sternberg, 1988. London: Cambridge University Press.

20. Sternberg, p. 212.

21. Hayes.

22. Sternberg, p. 202.

23. "The Best Innovations Are Those That Come from Smart Questions," *Wall Street Journal*, April 12, 2004, B1.

24. Sternberg, pp. 229–230.

25. Sternberg, p. 236.

26. Robert J. Sternberg and Elena L. Grigorenko, "Practical Intelligence and the Principal," Yale University: Publication Series No. 2, 2001, p. 5.

27. Sternberg, p. 241.

28. Sternberg, pp. 251–269.

29. Sternberg, p. 19.

30. Sternberg, p. 128.

5

IN THIS CHAPTER . . .

*you will explore answers
to the following questions:*

Reading and Studying
FOCUSING ON CONTENT

Your ability to read—and to understand, analyze, and use what you read—is the cornerstone of college learning. However, your background as a reader may not have prepared you for the amount and the complexity of the reading you will be assigned in college. It isn't just students with learning disabilities who face challenges. Almost all students need to adjust their habits in order to handle the increased demands of a college reading load.

Taking a step-by-step approach linked to analytical, creative, and practical thinking techniques will help you get what you need from the materials you read and study. This chapter introduces you to strategies to increase your speed, efficiency, and depth of understanding. When you use these strategies to learn more and retain more of what you learn, every hour you spend with your books will be more valuable.

On the next page, read how student Darrin Estepp is looking for ways to learn successfully while coping with learning disabilities.

- What will help you understand what you read?
- How can you set the stage for reading?
- How can SQ3R help you own what you read?
- How can you respond critically to what you read?
- How and why should you study with others?

How can I cope with learning disabilities in order to improve my reading and studying?

In elementary school I needed extra help with reading. By high school, I was having a hard time keeping up, and a test I took showed I had dyslexia. Study assistance helped, but I attended high school for an extra year to improve my record. Then I enrolled in community college and worked part-time as a nursing home cook. I transferred to Ohio State after two years. Recently I was also diagnosed with attention deficit hyperactivity disorder (ADHD).

I learn best by hearing, seeing, and doing all at once. If I just hear something, it doesn't sink in very well. It seems no matter how hard I try it's never enough. I keep hanging in there though. Eventually I would like to help others in my career—I can see myself being on the lookout for the early signs of disabilities like mine. What suggestions do you have for how I can cope with my learning disabilities?

Darrin Estepp
Ohio State University,
Columbus, Ohio

One thing I learned in college was that there is more than one way to succeed.

My reading-related disability was discovered in the fourth grade. I remember dreading to read out loud to my class; students would laugh. One thing I learned in college was that there is more than one way to succeed, even if I couldn't keep up with the reading. First, I attended every single class without exception. Second, if I got behind in my note taking (and I often did), I would borrow a friend's notes and rewrite mine, combining the two versions. Third, I made friends with my teachers, and they would help me during their office hours.

One incident showed me that anything was possible. A friend worked for a newspaper and asked me to write a story. I laughed—I said I could barely spell my name, never mind write an article. He said, "Come on, computers have spell checkers," which are a big help. I labored through it; my friend loved the writing (though he did say that I had used some very creative grammar), and it appeared as a two-part story in the travel section. I have since had 17 articles published.

It never gets easy—but one route to success is to do something you love. I write travel stories because I love traveling and sharing stories. I am now a film maker, and I am studying film in graduate school so I can someday teach it. Darrin, you already know the skills you need to achieve your goals, though maybe they are deep in your subconscious mind. I was 27 years old before I knew what I really wanted to do. Just keep following your passions, never give up, figure out what you need to do to achieve your goals, and know that there is more than one path to your destination.

Morgan Paar
Graduate Student, Academy of Art College
San Francisco, California

What will *help you understand* what you read?

Reading is an analytical process that requires you, the reader, to make meaning from written words. You do this by connecting what you know to what you read. Your understanding is affected by your familiarity with a subject, your cultural background and life experiences, and even the way you interpret words and phrases. Because these factors are different for every person, your reading experiences are uniquely your own.

Reading comprehension refers to your ability to understand what you read. True comprehension goes beyond parroting facts and figures to being able to apply concepts to new ideas and situations. Improving your reading comprehension is especially important in college because assignments are generally longer and more difficult, and you usually have to complete them on your own. In addition, what you learn from introductory-level texts is the foundation for your understanding of advanced course material. Following are general comprehension boosters to keep in mind as you work through this chapter and tackle early-semester reading assignments.

Read as much as you can. More than any other factor, what you already know influences comprehension by giving you a frame of reference for what you read.

Think analytically. Ask yourself questions: Do I understand the sentence, paragraph, or chapter I just read? Are the ideas and supporting examples clear? Could I explain the material to someone else? Could I apply the concepts to another topic or situation?

BE THE AUTHOR OF YOUR LIFE

get creative!

Think about a book that made a difference for you.

Henry David Thoreau, a nineteenth-century American author, poet, and philosopher, made the following observation: "How many a man has dated a new era in his life from the reading of a book." What do you think Thoreau meant by this statement?

_____

_____

Think of a book that influenced your education—or life—and describe why it is important.

_____

_____

If you could write a book that would help others succeed in college, what would be the book's message? Why do you think your book would be important for others to read?

_____

_____

_____

_____

Build vocabulary. The larger your vocabulary, the more material you will understand without checking a dictionary or guessing.

Look for order and meaning in seemingly chaotic reading materials. The information in this chapter on the SQ3R reading technique contains patterns that will help you learn new material.

Think positively. Instead of telling yourself that you cannot understand, tell yourself: *I can learn this material. I am able to complete every reading assignment.*

How can you *set the stage* for reading?

On any given day during college, you may face reading assignments like these:

- a textbook chapter on the history of South African apartheid (World History)
- an original research study on the relationship between sleep deprivation and the development of memory problems (Psychology)
- chapters 4 to 6 in John Steinbeck's classic novel *The Grapes of Wrath* (American Literature)
- a technical manual on the design of computer antivirus programs (Computer Science—Software Design)

This material is rigorous by anyone's standards. In fact, many students are surprised at how much reading there is in college, and that they may be expected to learn material that is never covered in class.

To get through it all—and master what you read—you need a systematic approach that taps into your analytic and practical thinking skills. Without one, you may have trouble allocating your time and energy appropriately to each of your classes. Some material may make sense to you fairly quickly; some may require much more time and focus. A class may demand a lot of you one week and very little the next. With the following strategies you can begin to gather the tools you need for reading success.

Take an active approach to difficult texts

Generally, the further you advance in your education, the more likely you are to encounter unfamiliar concepts and terms. This happens often when assignments involve *primary sources*—original documents rather than another writer's interpretation of these documents—or when they are from academic journals and scientific studies that don't define terms or supply examples. Primary sources include historical documents, works of literature (novels, poems, and plays), scientific studies including lab reports and accounts of experiments, and journal articles.

The following strategies may help you approach difficult material actively and positively:

Approach reading assignments with an open mind. Avoid prejudging material as impossible or boring before you start.

Know that some texts require extra work and concentration. Set a goal to make your way through the material and learn. Do whatever it takes. Consult resources—instructors, students, reference materials—for help.

Own frequently used reference materials. Purchase a dictionary, a writer's style handbook, an atlas, and references in your major. "If you find yourself going to the library to look up the same reference again and again, consider purchasing that book for your personal library," advises library expert Sherwood Harris.[1]

Choose the right setting

Finding the best places and times to study will maximize your focus and discipline. Here are some suggestions:

Select the right location. Many students study at a library desk. Others prefer an easy chair or even the floor. Choose a spot that's comfortable but not so cushy that you fall asleep. Make sure you have adequate lighting and aren't too hot or cold. If you prefer to read alone, find an out-of-the-way spot at the library or an after-class hour in an empty classroom where interruptions are less likely. Even if you don't mind activity nearby, try to minimize distractions.

> Reading is a means of thinking with another person's mind; it forces you to stretch your own.
>
> **CHARLES SCRIBNER JR.**

Select the right time. Choose a time when you feel alert and focused. If possible, complete assignments just before or after the related class. Eventually, you will associate preferred places and times with focused reading. Recall from Chapter 2 what you learned about creating a schedule that suits your natural body rhythms—your goal is to study when your energy is high. Though night owls may be productive after ten o'clock at night, morning people will be fuzzy during late-night sessions.

Deal with internal distractions. Internal distractions—personal worries, anticipation of upcoming events, or even hunger—can get in the way of work. Try taking a break to tend to an issue that's bothering you, or use exercise, music, or silence to relax and refocus. If you're hungry, get a snack and come back to work.

Students with young children have an added factor when deciding when, where, and how to study. Key 5.1 explores ways that these students can maximize their study efforts.

Keep them up to date on your schedule.	**Explain what your education entails.**
Let them know when you have a big test or project due and when you are under less pressure, and what they can expect of you in each case.	Tell them how it will improve your life and theirs. This applies, of course, to older children who can understand the situation and compare it with their own schooling.

Find help.	**Keep them active while you study.**
Ask a relative or friend to watch your children or arrange for a child to visit a friend. Consider trading babysitting hours with another parent, hiring a sitter to come to your home, or using a day-care center.	Give them games, books, or toys. If there are special activities that you like to limit, such as watching videos or TV, save them for your study time.

Offset study time with family time and rewards.
Children may let you get your work done if they have something to look forward to, such as a movie night or a trip for ice cream.

Study on the phone.
You might be able to have a study session with a fellow student over the phone while your child is sleeping or playing quietly.

SPECIAL NOTES FOR INFANTS

Study at night if your baby goes to sleep early, or in the morning if your baby sleeps late.	Study during nap times if you aren't too tired yourself.	Lay your notes out and recite information to the baby. The baby will appreciate the attention, and you will get work done.	Put baby in a safe and fun place while you study, such as a playpen, motorized swing, or jumping seat.

Define your purpose for reading

It's study time and you are about to crack open a book. Before you start, define your purpose by asking yourself: "Why am I reading this?" You might answer by completing this sentence: "In reading this material, I intend to define/learn/answer/achieve . . ."

Defining your purpose helps you choose reading strategies and decide how much time and effort to spend. You will approach each of the four following purposes in different ways. Keep in mind that you may have one or more purposes for any "reading event."

Purpose 1: Read for understanding. Studying involves reading to comprehend general ideas and specific facts or examples. Facts and examples help explain or support ideas, and ideas provide a framework for remembering facts and examples.

- **General ideas.** Reading for general ideas requires rapid reading of headings, subheadings, and summary statements to gain an overview—in other words, skimming the material (see page 132).
- **Specific facts or examples.** At times, your focus may be on specific pieces of information—names and dates, chronologies, etc. At other times, your search may center on examples that support general ideas—for example, the causes of economic recession. In both cases, scanning will help you rapidly find information (see page 133).

Purpose 2: Read to evaluate analytically. Analytical evaluation involves considering ideas and asking questions that test the writer's argument and assumptions. Analytical reading brings an understanding of the material that goes beyond basic information recall (see pages 140–142 for more on analytical reading).

Purpose 3: Read for practical application. When you read a computer manual or an instruction sheet for conducting a chemistry experiment, your goal is to learn how to do something. Reading and action usually go hand in hand.

Comparing notes to textbook chapters is an important part of reviewing and retaining material.

Purpose 4: Read for pleasure. Some materials are read for entertainment, such as *Sports Illustrated* magazine, the latest John Grisham courtroom thriller, or a Jane Austen novel.

Use special strategies with math and science texts

Different subjects present different reading challenges. Subjects vary—a Calculus text and a World Religions text have little in common—and your learning styles and preferences may make you more comfortable with some subjects than others. Math and science readings present unique challenges to many students. Try some of the following analytical, creative, and practical thinking techniques to meet the challenge:

- **Interact with the material critically as you go.** Math and science texts move sequentially (later chapters build on concepts introduced in previous chapters) and are often problem-and-solution based. Keep a pad nearby to solve problems and take notes. Draw sketches to help visualize material. Try not to move on until you understand the example and how it relates to the central ideas. Write down questions to ask your instructor or classmates.
- **Note formulas.** Make sure you understand the principle behind every formula—why it works—before memorizing it. Read the assigned material to prepare for homework.

FORMULA

A general fact, rule, or principle usually expressed in mathematical symbols.

Reading ◄

Use selected reading techniques in Multiple Intelligence areas to strengthen your ability to read for meaning and retention.

INTELLIGENCE	SUGGESTED STRATEGIES	WHAT WORKS FOR YOU? WRITE NEW IDEAS HERE
Verbal–Linguistic	<ul><li>Mark up your text with marginal notes while you read.</li><li>When tackling a chapter, use every stage of SQ3R, taking advantage of each writing opportunity (writing Q stage questions, writing summaries, and so on).</li></ul>	
Logical–Mathematical	<ul><li>Read material in sequence.</li><li>Think about the logical connections between what you are reading and the world at large; consider similarities, differences, and cause-and-effect relationships.</li></ul>	
Bodily–Kinesthetic	<ul><li>Take physical breaks during reading sessions—walk, stretch, exercise.</li><li>Pace while reciting important ideas.</li></ul>	
Visual–Spatial	<ul><li>As you read, take particular note of photos, tables, figures, and other visual aids.</li><li>Make charts, diagrams, or think links illustrating difficult concepts you encounter in your reading.</li></ul>	
Interpersonal	<ul><li>With a friend, have a joint reading session. One should read a section silently and then summarize aloud the important concepts for the other. Reverse the roles of summarizer and listener for each section.</li><li>Discuss reading material and clarify important concepts in a study group.</li></ul>	
Intrapersonal	<ul><li>Read in a solitary setting and allow time for reflection.</li><li>Think about how a particular reading assignment makes you feel, and evaluate your reaction by considering the material in light of what you already know.</li></ul>	
Musical	<ul><li>Play music while you read.</li><li>Recite important concepts in your reading to rhythms or write a song to depict those concepts.</li></ul>	
Naturalistic	<ul><li>Read and study in a natural environment.</li><li>Before reading indoors, imagine your favorite place in nature in order to create a relaxed frame of mind.</li></ul>	

- **Use memory techniques.** Science textbooks are packed with specialized vocabulary that you will be expected to know. Mnemonic devices, flash cards, and rehearsing aloud or silently aid memorization (for more on memory techniques, see Chapter 6). Selective highlighting and summarizing your readings in table format will also help.

Develop strategies to manage learning disabilities

Students with reading-related learning disabilities may need to engage their practical thinking skills to manage reading assignments. Roxanne Ruzic of CAST explored the strategies used by LD students at an urban college in the Northeast. For two students, here is what worked:

- Danielle received an A in her Art History survey course, in part because she chose some courses with heavy reading requirements and some with light requirements. This allowed her to complete all her assignments on time. In addition, she frequently sought instructors' advice about what they wanted her to learn from assigned texts and used tutors whenever she needed extra help.

- Chloe received an A in her Introduction to Psychology course, in part because she met twice weekly with a tutor who helped her prioritize her reading assignments and keep on top of her work. She also learned to tailor the amount of time she spent on different text sections to the importance of the sections on upcoming tests. Finally, when she felt comfortable with text concepts, she read them quickly or skipped them entirely, but when she had trouble with the material, she did extra reading or sought help.[2]

If you have a learning disability, think of these students as you investigate the services your college offers through reading centers and tutoring programs. Remember: The ability to succeed is often linked to the willingness to ask for help.

Build reading speed

Although comprehension is more important than reading quickly, a reasonable increase in reading speed saves time and effort. Though the average American adult reads between 150 and 350 words per minute, faster readers are capable of speeds up to 1,000 words per minute.[3] Raising your reading speed above 350 words per minute involves "skimming" and "scanning." The following suggestions also increase speed without sacrificing comprehension:

- Try to read groups of words rather than single words.
- Avoid pointing your finger to guide your reading; use an index card to move quickly down the page.
- When reading narrow columns, focus your eyes in the middle of the column. With practice, you'll be able to read the entire column width as you read down the page.

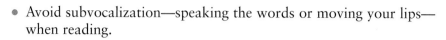

- Avoid subvocalization—speaking the words or moving your lips—when reading.

A key component to building speed is practice and more practice, says reading expert Steve Moidel. To achieve your goal of reading between 500 and 1,000 words per minute, Moidel suggests that you start practicing at three times the rate you want to achieve, a rate that is much faster than you can comprehend.[4] For example, if your goal is 500 words per minute, speed up to 1,500 words per minute. Reading at such an accelerated rate pushes your eyes and mind to adjust to the faster pace. When you slow down to 500 words per minute—a pace you can actually manage—your rate will feel comfortable even though it is much faster than your original speed. Self-paced computer software is available to help you gain speed.

Expand your vocabulary

A strong vocabulary increases speed and comprehension. The best way to build your vocabulary is to learn new and unfamiliar words as you encounter them. This involves the following steps.

Analyze word parts

Often, if you understand part of a word, you can figure out the entire word. This is true because many English words are made up of a combination of Greek and Latin prefixes, roots, and suffixes. *Prefixes* are word parts that are added to the beginning of a root. *Suffixes* are added to the end of the root.

ROOT

The central part or basis of a word, around which prefixes and suffixes can be added to produce different words.

Key 5.2 contains some common prefixes, roots, and suffixes. Knowing these verbal building blocks can dramatically increase your vocabulary. Key 5.3 shows how one root can be the stem of many words.

Using prefixes, roots, and suffixes, you can piece together the meaning of new words. For example, the word *prologue* is made up of the prefix *pro* (before) and the root *logue* (to speak). Thus, prologue refers to words spoken or written before the main text.

Use words in context

Although a definition tells you what a word means, it may not include a *context*—the part of a statement that surrounds a word and affects its meaning. Using a word in context after defining it helps anchor the information in memory. Here are strategies for using context to solidify new vocabulary words.

- Use a new word in a sentence immediately after reading a definition, while the meaning is fresh.
- Reread, a few times, the sentence where you originally saw the word to make sure that you understand how the word is used.
- Use the word over the next few days whenever it may apply. Try it while talking with friends, writing e-mails or notes, or in your own thoughts.

Knowing common prefixes, roots, and suffixes expands your vocabulary.

PREFIX	PRIMARY MEANING	EXAMPLE
a-, ab-	from	abstain, avert
con-, cor-, com-	with, together	convene, correlate, compare
il-	not	illegal, illegible
sub-, sup-	under	subordinate, suppose

ROOT	PRIMARY MEANING	EXAMPLE
-chron-	time	synchronize
-ann-	year	biannual
-sper-	hope	desperate
-voc-	speak, talk	convocation

SUFFIX	PRIMARY MEANING	EXAMPLE
-able	able	recyclable
-meter	measure	thermometer
-ness	state of	carelessness
-y	inclined to	sleepy

Knowing a single root can help you build different words.

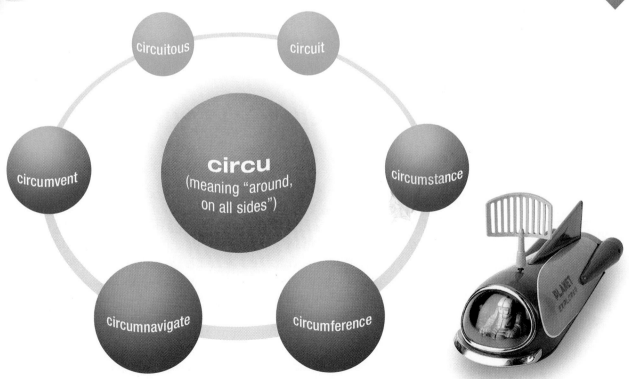

circuitous

circuit

circu (meaning "around, on all sides")

Circumvent

circumstance

Circumnavigate

circumference

- Solidify your understanding by going back to sentences you previously didn't "get." For example, most children learn the Pledge of Allegiance by rote without understanding what *allegiance* means. When they finally learn the definition, the Pledge itself will help them connect "allegiance" with the concept of loyalty.

- Talk about it. If after looking up a word you still have trouble with its meaning, ask an instructor or a friend to help you figure it out.

Use a dictionary

Dictionaries provide broad information such as word origin, pronunciation, parts of speech, and multiple meanings. Get a good quality college dictionary, and consult it when you encounter unfamiliar words. Many textbooks include a *glossary* that defines terms found in the text. Electronic dictionaries are handy, although definitions are less complete. Dictionaries are also available on the Internet.

You may not always have time to use the following suggestions, but when you can, they will help you make the most of your dictionary.

- Read every meaning of a word, not just the first. Think critically about which meaning suits the context, then choose the one that is the best fit.

- Use the definition. Imagine, for example, that you read the following sentence and do not know the word *indoctrinated*:
  The cult indoctrinated its members to reject society's values.
  In the dictionary, you find several definitions, including "brainwashed" and "instructed." You decide that the one closest to the correct meaning is "brainwashed." With this term, the sentence reads:
  The cult brainwashed its members to reject society's values.

You have laid the groundwork for effective studying. You are now ready for the SQ3R process, which will give you tools for learning and mastering textbook material. As you will see next, SQ3R engages all three aspects of successful intelligence—analytical, creative, and practical.

How can SQ3R *help you own* what you read?

SKIMMING

Rapid, superficial reading of material that involves glancing through to determine central ideas and main elements.

Even with all the time and energy you spend reading textbook chapters, there's no guarantee that you'll understand and remember what you read. The SQ3R study method will help you grasp ideas quickly, remember more, and review effectively for tests. SQ3R stands for *survey, question, read, recite,* and *review*—all steps in the studying process. Developed about 60 years ago by Francis Robinson, the technique is still used today because it works.[5]

Moving through the stages of SQ3R requires that you know how to skim and scan. Skimming involves the rapid reading of chapter elements, including introductions, conclusions, and summaries; the first and last lines of paragraphs; boldfaced or italicized terms; and pictures, charts, and diagrams. The goal of skimming is a quick construction of the main ideas. In contrast, (scanning) involves the careful search for specific ideas and facts. You might use scanning during the review phase of SQ3R to locate particular information (such as a chemistry formula).

SQ3R is a studying framework, not a rigid system. You can follow the steps exactly as they are described or adjust them according to your preferences. You may decide, for example, to survey chapter elements in a different order than your classmates or to write different questions or favor different review strategies. Explore the strategies, evaluate what works, and then make the system your own. Although SQ3R will help you as you study almost every subject, it is not suited for literature.

SCANNING

Reading material in an investigative way to search for specific information.

Survey

Surveying involves previewing, or pre-reading, material before you actually study it. Compare it to looking at a map before a trip; taking a few minutes to analyze the route may save hours when you are on the road. You are combining your analytical and practical thinking skills to assess the material as quickly as possible.

When you survey, pay attention to the following text-wide and chapter-by-chapter elements:

Front matter. Before you even get to page 1, most textbooks have a table of contents, a preface, and other materials. The table of contents tells you about coverage, topic order, and features. The preface, in particular, can point out the book's unique approach. For example, the preface for the American history text *Out of Many* states that it highlights "the experiences of diverse communities of Americans in the unfolding story of our country."[6] In other words, cultural diversity is a central theme.

Chapter elements. Chapters generally include devices that help you learn material. Among these are:

- chapter title, which establishes the topic and perhaps the author's perspective on the topic
- chapter introduction, outline, list of objectives, or list of key topics
- headings, tables and figures, quotes, marginal notes, and photographs, which help you understand the structure and identify important concepts within the chapter
- special chapter features, often presented in boxes set off from the main text, that point to text-wide themes
- particular styles or arrangements of type (boldface, italics, underline, larger fonts, bullet points, boxed text) that call attention to important words and concepts
- chapter summary, which reviews the concepts that were presented
- review questions and exercises, which help you review and think critically about the material

Skimming these elements before reading the chapter will lead you to identify what is important.

Back matter. Some texts include a glossary at the back of the book, an index to help you locate topics, and a bibliography that lists additional readings.

Key 5.4 shows the many devices that texts employ. Think about how many of these devices you already use and which you will start using to boost comprehension.

Question

Your next step in the SQ3R process is to examine the chapter headings and, on a separate page or in the book margins, to *write questions* linked to them. If your reading material has no headings, develop questions as you read. These questions help you build comprehension and relate new ideas to what you already know. You can take questions from the textbook or from your lecture notes, or come up with them when you survey, based on the ideas you think are most important.

Key 5.5 shows how this works. The column on the left contains primary- and secondary-level headings from a section of *Out of Many*. The column on the right rephrases these headings in question form.

There is no "correct" set of questions. In fact, given the same headings, you could write many different questions. As you develop the type of probing questions discussed in Chapter 4—questions that delve into the material and help you learn—you are engaging your creative and analytical abilities.

Survey with text and chapter previewing devices.

key
5.4

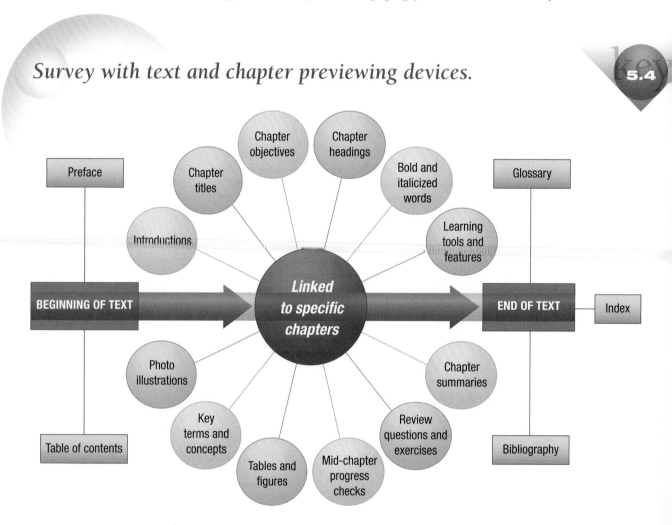

Use headings to form questions.

The Meaning of Freedom	What did freedom mean for both slaves and citizens in the United States?
Moving About	Where did African Americans go after they were freed from slavery?
The African American Family	How did freedom change the structure of the African American family?
African American Churches and Schools	What effect did freedom have on the formation of African American churches and schools?
Land and Labor after Slavery	How was land farmed and maintained after slaves were freed?
The Origins of African American Politics	How did the end of slavery bring about the beginning of African American political life?

Read

Your questions give you a starting point for *reading*, the first R in SQ3R. Learning from textbooks requires that you read actively. Active reading means engaging with the material through questioning, writing, note taking, and other activities. As you can see in Key 5.6, the activities of SQ3R promote active reading. Following are some analytical, creative, and practical strategies that encourage active involvement.

Focus on your Q-stage questions. Read the material with the purpose of answering each question. As you discover ideas and examples that relate to your question, write them down or note them in the text.

Take notes on important concepts. As you read, record keywords, phrases, and concepts in your notebook. Some students divide the notebook page into two columns, writing questions on the left and answers on the right. This method is called the Cornell note-taking system (see Chapter 6).

Mark up your textbook. Writing notes in the text margins and circling or highlighting key ideas will help you make sense of the material. Key 5.7 shows effective highlighting and marginal notes on the page of a marketing text. Owning your own texts and marking them up is an invaluable learning tool.

Selective highlighting may help you pinpoint material to review before an exam, although excessive highlighting may actually interfere with comprehension. Here are tips on striking a balance:

- Mark the text after you read the material once through. If you do it on the first reading, you may mark less important passages.

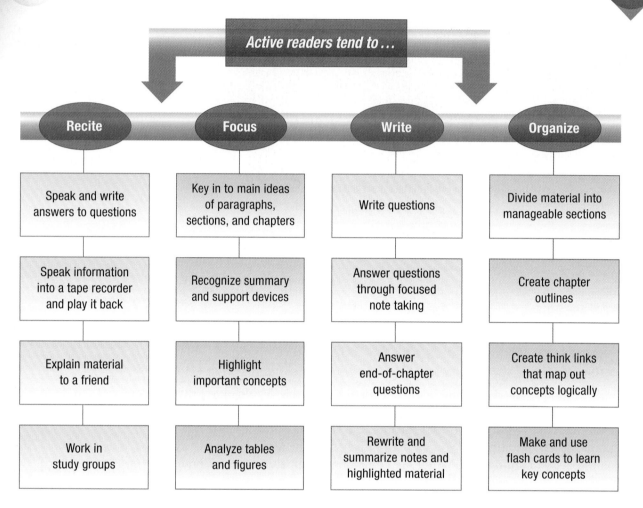

- Highlight key terms and concepts. Mark the examples that explain and support important ideas.
- Avoid overmarking. A phrase or two in any paragraph is usually enough, since too much underlining may overwhelm your eyes. Set off long passages with brackets rather than marking every line.
- Don't confuse highlighting for learning. You will not learn what you highlight unless you interact with it through careful review—questioning, writing, and reciting.

Divide your reading into digestible segments. If you are losing the thread of the ideas, try smaller segments or take a break. Try to avoid reading according to the clock—such as, "I'll read for 30 minutes and then quit"—or you may short-circuit your understanding by stopping in the middle of a key explanation.

Find the main idea. A crucial analytical skill in textbook reading is the ability to find the main idea—the thoughts that are at the heart of the writing, the ideas that create its essential meaning. Comprehension depends on your

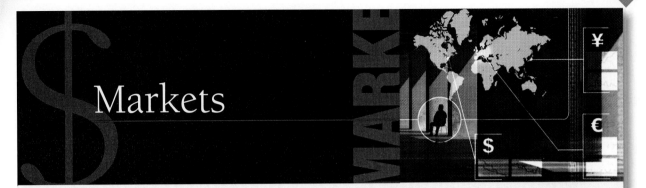

Markets

The term *market* has acquired many meanings over the years. In its original meaning, a market is a physical place where buyers and sellers gather to exchange goods and services. Medieval towns had market squares where sellers brought their goods and buyers shopped for goods. In today's cities, buying and selling occur in shopping areas rather than markets. To an economist, a market describes all the buyers and sellers who transact over some good or service. Thus, the soft-drink market consists of sellers such as Coca-Cola and PepsiCo, and of all the consumers who buy soft drinks. To a marketer, a market is the set of all actual and potential buyers of a product or service.

Organizations that sell to consumer and business markets recognize that they cannot appeal to all buyers in those markets, or at least not to all buyers in the same way. Buyers are too numerous, too widely scattered, and too varied in their needs and buying practices. And different companies vary widely in their abilities to serve different segments of the market. Rather than trying to compete in an entire market, sometimes against superior competitors, each company must identify the parts of the market that it can serve best.

> *Definition of a market*
>
> *Companies can't appeal to everyone*

Sellers have not always practiced this philosophy. Their thinking has passed through three stages:

- *Mass marketing.* In mass marketing, the seller mass produces, mass distributes, and mass promotes one product to all buyers. At one time, Coca-Cola produced only one drink for the whole market, hoping it would appeal to everyone. The argument for mass marketing is that it should lead to the lowest costs and prices and create the largest potential market.

  > *One-size-fits-all approach*

- *Product-variety marketing.* Here, the seller produces two or more products that have different features, styles, quality, sizes, and so on. Later, Coca-Cola produced several soft drinks packaged in different sizes and containers that were designed to offer variety to buyers rather than to appeal to different market segments. The argument for product-variety marketing is that consumers have different tastes that change over time. Consumers seek variety and change.

  > *Offer variety to buyers*

- *Target marketing.* Here, the seller identifies market segments, selects one or more of them, and develops products and marketing mixes tailored to each. For example, Coca-Cola now produces soft drinks for the sugared-cola segment (Coca-Cola Classic and Cherry Coke), the diet segment (Diet Coke and Tab), the no-caffeine segment (Caffeine-Free Coke), and the noncola segment (Minute Maid sodas).

  > *A tailored approach to specific market segments*

Today's companies are moving away from mass marketing and product-variety marketing toward target marketing. Target marketing can better help sellers find their marketing opportunities. Sellers can develop the right product for each target market and adjust their prices, distribution channels, and advertising to reach the target market efficiently. Instead of scattering their marketing efforts (the "shotgun" approach), they can focus on the buyers who have greater purchase interest (the "rifle" approach).

> *Current approach is usually TARGET MARKETING*

87

ability to recognize main ideas and to link the author's other thoughts to them. Here are places you are likely to find these core ideas:

- in a topic sentence at the beginning of the paragraph, stating the topic of the paragraph and what about that topic the author wants to communicate, followed by sentences adding support
- at the end of the paragraph, following supporting details that lead up to it
- buried in the middle of the paragraph, sandwiched between supporting details
- in a compilation of ideas from various sentences, each of which contains a critical element. It is up to the reader to piece these elements together to create the essence of meaning
- never explicitly stated, but implied by the information presented in the paragraph

How, then, do you decide just what is the main idea? Ophelia H. Hancock, a specialist in improving reading skills for college students, suggests a three-step approach:[7]

1. **Search for the topic of the paragraph.** The topic of the paragraph is not the same thing as the main idea. Rather, it is the broad subject being discussed—for example, former President John F. Kennedy, hate crimes on campus, or the Internet.

2. **Identify the aspect of the topic that is the paragraph's focus.** If the general topic is former President John F. Kennedy, the writer may choose to focus on any of thousands of aspects of that topic, such as his health problems, his civil rights policies, or his effectiveness as a public speaker.

3. **Find what the author wants you to know about the specific aspect being discussed, which is the main idea.** The main idea of a paragraph dealing with President Kennedy as a public speaker may be this: *President Kennedy was a gifted, charismatic speaker who used his humor, charm, and intelligence to make the presidency accessible to all Americans during regularly televised presidential news conferences.*

Recite

Once you finish reading a topic, stop and answer the questions you raised in the Q stage of SQ3R. Engage your practical thinking skills to choose the best way to do this. You may decide to *recite* each answer aloud, silently speak the answers to yourself, tell or teach the answers to

Knowledge is power they say. Knowledge is not only power, it is good fun.

E. M. FORSTER

another person, or write your ideas and answers in brief notes. Writing is often the most effective way to solidify what you have read because writing from memory checks your understanding.

FIND THE MAIN IDEA

Develop your ability to analyze the parts of a paragraph.

Use the three-step approach described on page 138 to find the main idea of the following paragraph:

> Tone relates not so much to what you say as to how you say it. The tone of your writing has a major impact on what you are trying to communicate to your audience. Tone involves your choice of words interacting with your message. Have you ever reacted to someone's understanding of what you wrote with "That's not what I meant to say"? Your tone can be what has thrown your readers off track, although you can only be misunderstood if your writing is unclear or imprecise.[8]

- What is the topic of this paragraph?

_____

_____

- What aspect of tone is being discussed?

_____

_____

- What main idea is being communicated?

_____

_____

Now choose a meaty paragraph from one of the texts you are currently studying, and use the same questions to find the paragraph's main idea. How do these questions help you focus on the paragraph's most important points?

Keep your learning styles in mind when you explore different strategies (see Chapter 3). For example, an intrapersonal learner may prefer writing, whereas an interpersonal learner might want to recite answers aloud to a classmate. A logical–mathematical learner may benefit from organizing material into detailed outlines, whereas a musical learner might want to chant information aloud to a rhythm.

After you finish one section, read the next. *Repeat the question–read–recite cycle until you complete the entire chapter.* If you find yourself fumbling for thoughts, you may not yet "own" the ideas. Reread the section that's giving you trouble until you master its contents. Understanding each section as you go is crucial because the material in one section often forms a foundation for the next.

Review

Review soon after you finish a chapter. Reviewing immediately and periodically in the days and weeks after you read solidifies understanding. Chances are good that if you close the book after you read, you will forget most of the material. Here are reviewing techniques that engage all three components of successful intelligence. Try many, and use what works best for you.

- Skim and reread your notes. Then try summarizing them from memory.
- Answer the text's end-of-chapter review, discussion, and application questions.
- Quiz yourself, using the questions you raised in the Q stage. If you can't answer any of your own or the text's questions, scan the text for answers.
- Create a chapter outline in standard outline or think link form.
- Reread the preface, headings, tables, and summary.
- Recite important concepts to yourself, or record important information on a cassette tape and play it in your car or on a portable cassette player.
- Make flash cards that have an idea or word on one side and examples, a definition, or other related information on the other. Test yourself.
- Review and summarize in writing the material you have highlighted or bracketed. Your goal is to create a summary that focuses on the central ideas, setting the stage for critical thinking.
- Think critically: Break ideas down into examples, consider similar or different concepts, recall important terms, evaluate ideas, and explore causes and effects.
- Discuss the concepts with a classmate or in a study group. Trying to teach study partners what you learned will pinpoint the material you know and what still needs work.

SUMMARY

A concise restatement of the material, in your own words, that covers the main points.

If a concept is still unclear, ask your instructor for help. Pinpoint the material you wish to discuss, schedule a meeting during office hours, and bring a list of questions.

Refreshing your knowledge is easier and faster than learning it the first time. Set up regular review sessions—for example, once a week. Reviewing in different ways increases the likelihood of retention.

How can you *respond critically* to what you read?

The fundamental purpose of all college reading is understanding. Think of your reading process as an archaeological dig. The first step is to excavate a site and uncover the artifacts—that's your initial survey and reading of the material. As important as the excavation is, the process is incomplete if you stop there. The second step is to investigate each item, evaluate what they all mean, and derive knowledge from what you discover. Critical reading allows you to complete that crucial second step.

Like critical thinking, critical reading is a part of analytical thinking (see Chapter 4). Instead of simply accepting what you read, seek understanding by questioning the material as you move from idea to idea. The best critical readers question every statement for accuracy, relevance, and logic. They also extend critical analysis to all media.

Use knowledge of fact and opinion to evaluate arguments

Critical readers evaluate arguments to determine whether they are accurate and logical. In this context, *argument* refers to a persuasive case—a set of connected ideas supported by examples—that a writer makes to prove or disprove a point.

It's easy—and common—to accept or reject an argument outright, according to whether it fits with your point of view. If you ask questions, however, you can determine the argument's validity and understand it in greater depth. Evaluating an argument involves

- evaluating the quality of the evidence.
- evaluating whether support fits the concept.
- evaluating the logical connections.

When quality evidence combines with appropriate support and tight logic, the argument is solid.

What is the quality of the evidence? Ask the following questions to evaluate the evidence:

- What is the source?
- Is the source reliable and free of bias?
- Who wrote this and with what intent?
- What assumptions underlie this material?
- Is the argument based on opinion?
- How does the evidence compare with evidence from other sources?

How well does the evidence support the idea? Ask these questions to determine whether the evidence fits the concept:

- Is there enough evidence to support the central idea?
- Do examples and ideas logically connect to one another?
- Is the evidence convincing? Do the examples build a strong case?
- What different and perhaps opposing arguments seem just as valid?

Approach every argument with healthy skepticism. Have an open mind in order to assess whether you are convinced or have serious questions. Use critical thinking to make an informed decision.

If, for example, you read an article with this premise: "The dissolution of the traditional family unit (working father, stay-at-home mother, dependent children) is contributing to society's problems," you might examine the facts and examples the writer uses to support this statement, looking carefully at the cause-and-effect structure of the argument. You might question the writer's sources. You might think of examples that support the statement. You might find examples that disprove this argument, such as statistics that show strong job numbers and college degree completion in areas where nontraditional family units are common. Finally, you might think of opposing arguments, including the ideas and examples to support those arguments.

Media literacy

Use your analytical thinking skills to analyze the information you receive through the (media,) including television, radio, film, the Internet, newspapers, magazines, and books. By improving your *media literacy*, you will approach every media message with a healthy skepticism that leads you to ask questions, look for evidence, recognize perspectives, and challenge assumptions. This approach will help you decide which information you can trust and use.

The Center for Media Literacy explains "Five Core Concepts of Media Literacy":[9]

1. **All media are constructions.** All media are carefully constructed presentations designed for particular effect—to encourage you to feel certain emotions, to develop particular opinions, or to buy advertised products.

2. **Media use unique "languages."** Creators of media carefully choose wording, music, colors, timing, and other factors to produce a desired effect.

3. **Different audiences understand the same media message differently.** Individuals understand media in the context of their unique experiences. Someone who has climbed a mountain, for example, will experience a Mount Everest documentary differently than someone who has not.

4. **Media have commercial interests.** Creators of media are driven by the intent to sell products, services, or ideas. Advertising is chosen to appeal to the most likely audience (for example, beer and automobile ads, directed at 20 to 30 year-old men, often appear during sporting events).

5. **Media have embedded values and points of view.** Any media product reflects the values and biases of the people who created it.

Critical reading of texts and the media takes time and focus. You can learn from others by working in pairs or groups whenever you can.

Why and how should you *study with others?*

Tap your practical thinking skills to set up or find a study partner or group. When you study with others, you benefit from shared knowledge, solidified knowledge, increased motivation, and increased teamwork ability.

- **Shared knowledge.** It takes less time for study group members to pass on their knowledge to each other than for each member to learn all the material alone.

The agencies of mass communication—television, film, journalism (magazines and newspapers), books, and the Internet.

- **Solidified knowledge.** When you discuss concepts or teach them to others, you reinforce what you know and strengthen your critical thinking. Part of the benefit comes from repeating information aloud, and part comes from how you think through information before you pass it on to someone else.

Knowledge is of two kinds. We know a subject ourselves, or we know where we can find information upon it.

SAMUEL JOHNSON

- **Increased motivation.** When you study by yourself, you are accountable to yourself alone. In a study group, however, others see your level of preparation, which may increase your motivation.
- **Increased teamwork ability.** The more experience you have with group dynamics, the more effective your teamwork will be.

A group of students taking the same course may get together once or twice a week or right before exams. Instructors sometimes initiate study groups for their students. Known as peer-assisted study sessions or supplemental instruction, these groups are common in math and science courses.

Roommates sometimes become study partners. When Lucila Crena, a freshman at Emory University and a native of Argentina, met her roommate Jolyn Taylor, she was fortunate enough to also find a partner who helped her focus. "I'm very easily distracted—she's definitely the more committed one," said Lucila. "With another student, I don't know that I would learn less, but it might be harder for me to actually do the work." The arrangement also benefited Jolyn, who turned to Lucila for help with Spanish.[10]

Group study can make a real difference if group members are dedicated. Choosing a leader, meeting at regular times, and setting goals all help groups accomplish their work.

Leaders and participants

Study groups and other teams rely on both leaders and participants to accomplish goals. Becoming aware of the roles each plays will increase your effectiveness.[11] Keep in mind that participants sometimes perform leadership tasks and vice versa. In addition, some teams shift leadership frequently during a project.

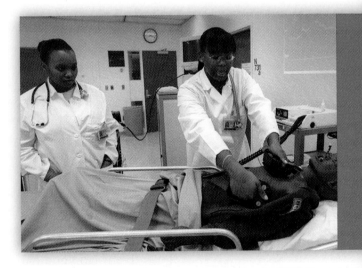

What you learn in your textbook is often enhanced and solidified by hands-on experience. These respiratory therapy students put their knowledge to work on a medical mannequin.

Being an effective participant

Some people are most comfortable when participating in a group that someone else leads. Participants are "part owners" of the team process with a responsibility for, and a stake in, the outcome. The following strategies will help you become more effective in this role.

get practical! FORM A STUDY GROUP

Form a study group for one of your courses.

Get a group together and use this form to decide on and record the details.

- Course name: _____

- Study group members (names, phone numbers, e-mail addresses):

  Member #1 _____

  Member #2 _____

  Member #3 _____

  Member #4 _____

  Member #5 _____

- Regular meeting time(s):

- Regular meeting place(s):

- Three strategies you plan to use to make the most of group time:

  Strategy #1: _____

  Strategy #2: _____

  Strategy #3: _____

- **Get involved.** Let people know your views on decisions.

- **Be organized.** The more focused your ideas, the more others will take them seriously.

- **Be willing to discuss.** Be open to different opinions. Always be respectful.

- **Keep your word.** Carry out whatever tasks you promise to do.

Being an effective leader

Some people prefer to initiate the action, make decisions, and control how things proceed. Leaders often have a "big-picture" perspective that allows them to envision and plan group projects. The following strategies help a leader succeed.

- **Define and limit projects.** The leader should define the group's purpose (Is it to brainstorm, to make decisions, or to collaborate on a project?) and limit tasks so that the effort remains focused.

- **Assign work and set a schedule.** A group functions best when everyone has an assigned task and when deadlines are clear.

- **Set meeting and project agendas.** The leader should, with advice from other members, establish and communicate goals and define how the work will proceed.

- **Focus progress.** It is the leader's job to keep everyone headed in the right direction.
- **Set the tone.** If the leader is fair, respectful, encouraging, and hard-working, group members are likely to follow the example.
- **Evaluate results.** The leader should determine whether the team is accomplishing its goals on schedule. If the team is not moving ahead, the leader should make changes.

Strategies for study group success

Every study group is unique. The way a group operates may depend on members' personalities, the subject being studied, and the group's size. No matter the particulars, the following general strategies will foster success.

- **Choose a leader for each meeting.** Rotating the leadership helps all members take ownership of the group.
- **Set long-term and short-term goals.** At your first meeting, determine what the group wants to accomplish over the semester. At the beginning of each meeting, have one person compile a list of questions to address.
- **Adjust to different personalities.** The art of getting along will serve you well no matter what you do.
- **Share the work.** The most important factor is a willingness to work, not a particular level of knowledge.
- **Set a regular meeting schedule.** Try every week, every two weeks, or whatever the group can manage.
- **Create study materials for one another.** Give each group member the task of finding a piece of information to compile, photocopy or e-mail, and review for other group members.
- **Help each other learn.** Have group members teach pieces of information, make up quizzes for each other, or go through flash cards together.
- **Pool your note-taking resources.** Compare notes with your group members and fill in any information you don't have. Try different note-taking styles (see Chapter 6 for more on note taking).
- **Be aware of cultural differences.** When members of a study group come from different countries, cultural values may impact how easily members get along. For example, whereas a student from a high-context culture such as Greece may want to begin every meeting with social talk, Americans and others from low-context cultures are likely to want to focus on assignments right away. Or students from a high-context culture like Japan may be uncomfortable talking about personal accomplishments in the way Americans do and, instead, want to emphasize what the group does together.

  Addressing the communication issues that result from these and other cultural differences requires group members to talk openly about what they observe and to work to accommodate each other's style. Making such adjustments will prepare you well for the twenty-first-century workplace. (For more on high-context and low-context cultures, see Chapter 2.)

читать

People who read Russian, Japanese, Greek, Arabic, or other languages process the symbols of their alphabets as easily as you process the letters on this page. If you read Russian, for example, you know that the word preceding this paragraph means "read." The brain's ability to process and group letters to form words, phrases, and sentences is the basis for reading and studying.

Think of the vast amounts of information your mind processes as you read and study your textbooks. Challenge yourself to raise the bar of achievement by reading often and using the strategies suggested in this chapter. You will understand more, remember more, and have more to use as you work toward goals in school and beyond.

BUILDING SKILLS

FOR COLLEGE, CAREER, AND LIFE SUCCESS

Developing Successful Intelligence

Studying a text page. The following page is from the chapter "Groups and Organizations" in the sixth edition of John J. Macionis's *Sociology*.[12] Apply SQ3R as you read the excerpt. Using what you learned in this chapter about study techniques, complete the questions that follow (some questions ask you to mark the page itself).

Step 1. Think it through: *Gather information and analyze it.* First gather: Skim the excerpt. Identify the headings on the page and the relationships among them. Mark primary-level headings with a #1, secondary headings with a #2, and tertiary (third-level) headings with a #3. Then analyze:

Which heading serves as an umbrella for the rest?

_____

What do the headings tell you about the content of the page?

_____

What are three concepts that seem important to remember?

*1.*_____

*2.*_____

*3.*_____

create your future

SOCIAL GROUPS

Virtually everyone moves through life with a sense of belonging; this is the experience of group life. A **social group** refers to *two or more people who identify and interact with one another.* Human beings continually come together to form couples, families, circles of friends, neighborhoods, churches, businesses, clubs, and numerous large organizations. Whatever the form, groups encompass people with shared experiences, loyalties, and interests. In short, while maintaining their individuality, the members of social groups also think of themselves as a special "we."

Groups, Categories, and Crowds

People often use the term "group" imprecisely. We now distinguish the group from the similar concepts of category and crowd.

Category. A *category* refers to people who have some status in common. Women, single fathers, military recruits, homeowners, and Roman Catholics are all examples of categories.

Why are categories not considered groups? Simply because, while the individuals involved are aware that they are not the only ones to hold that particular status, the vast majority are strangers to one another.

Crowd. A *crowd* refers to a temporary cluster of individuals who may or may not interact at all. Students sitting in a lecture hall do engage one another and share some common identity as college classmates; thus, such a crowd might be called a loosely formed group. By contrast, riders hurtling along on a subway train or

bathers enjoying a summer day at the beach pay little attention to one another and amount to an anonymous aggregate of people. In general, then, crowds are too transitory and impersonal to qualify as social groups.

The right circumstances, however, could turn a crowd into a group. People riding in a subway train that crashes under the city streets generally become keenly aware of their common plight and begin to help one another. Sometimes such extraordinary experiences become the basis for lasting relationships.

Primary and Secondary Groups

Acquaintances commonly greet one another with a smile and the simple phrase, "Hi! How are you?" The response is usually a well scripted, "Just fine, thanks, how about you?" This answer, of course, is often more formal than truthful. In most cases, providing a detailed account of how you are *really* doing would prompt the other person to beat a hasty and awkward exit.

Sociologists classify social groups by measuring them against two ideal types based on members' genuine level of personal concern. This variation is the key to distinguishing *primary* from *secondary* groups.

According to Charles Horton Cooley (1864–1929), a **primary group** is a *small social group whose members share personal and enduring relationships.* Bound together by primary relationships, individuals in primary groups typically spend a great deal of time together, engage in a wide range of common activities, and feel that they know one another well. Although not without periodic conflict, members of primary groups display sincere concern for each other's welfare. The family is every society's most important primary group.

Cooley characterized these personal and tightly integrated groups as *primary* because they are among the first groups we experience in life. In addition, the family and early play groups also hold primary importance in the socialization process, shaping attitudes, behavior, and social identity.

Source: Sociology 6/E by Macionis, © 1977. Reprinted by permission of Pearson Education, Inc., Upper Saddle River, NJ.

Step 2. Think out of the box: *Create useful study questions.* Based on the three concepts you pulled out, write three study questions that you can review with an instructor, a teaching assistant, or a fellow student.

1. _____

2. _____

3. _____

Step 3. Make it happen: *Read and remember.* Read the excerpt putting SQ3R to work. Using a marker pen, highlight key phrases and sentences. Write short marginal notes to help you review the material later. After reading this page thoroughly, write a short summary paragraph.

_____

_____

_____

Team Building

Organizing a study group. Organize a study group with three or four members of your class. At the group's first meeting:

- Set a specific goal for the group—to prepare for an upcoming test or project, for example—and create a weekly schedule. Write everything down and make sure everyone has a copy.

- Talk about the specific ways you will work together. Discuss which of the following methods you want to try in the group: pooling your notes, teaching each other difficult concepts; making up, administering, and grading quizzes for each other; creating study flash cards; using SQ3R to review required readings. Set specific guidelines for how group members will be held accountable.

As an initial group exercise, try the following:

- Review the study questions that you wrote for the *Sociology* excerpt. Each person should select one question to focus on while reading (no two people should have the same question). Group members should then reread the excerpt individually, thinking about their questions as they read and answering them in writing.

- When you finish reading critically, gather as a group. Each person should take a turn presenting the question, the response or answer that was derived through critical reading, and any other ideas that came up while reading. The other members of the group may then present any other ideas to add to the discussion. Continue until all group members have had a chance to present their concepts.

Over several weeks, try the group study methods you have chosen. Then evaluate the methods as a group, singling out the methods that most effectively helped group members master the course material. Finally, revise the group's methods if necessary, to focus on those most useful methods.

Writing

Record your thoughts on a separate piece of paper or in a journal.

Reading challenges. What course this semester presents your most difficult reading challenge? What makes it tough—the type of material you have to read, the amount, the level of difficulty? Thinking about the strategies in this chapter, create and describe a plan that addresses this challenge. What techniques might help, and how will you use them? What positive effects do you think they'll have?

Career Portfolio

Complete the following in your electronic portfolio or on separate sheets of paper.

Reading skills on the job. American society revolves around the written word. The focus on word processing and computerized documents has increased the need for literate employees. As a recent *Condition of Education* report states, literacy is "viewed as one of the fundamental tools necessary for successful economic performance in industrialized societies. Literacy is no longer defined merely as a basic threshold of reading ability, but rather as the ability to understand and use printed information in daily activities, at home, at work, and in the community."[13]

For each of the following skill areas listed, indicate all of the ways in which you use that skill on the job or know you will need to use it in your future career. Then, also for each skill, rate your ability on a scale from 1 to 10, with 10 being highest. Finally, on the same document or sheet of paper, highlight or circle the two skills that you think will be most important for your career as well as for your success as a learner in college.

- ability to define your reading purpose
- reading speed
- reading comprehension
- vocabulary building
- identification and use of text-surveying devices
- using analytical thinking skills when reading
- evaluating reading material with others
- ability to understand and use visual aids

For the two skill areas in which you rated yourself lowest, think about how you can improve your abilities. Make a problem-solving plan for each (you may want to use a flow chart like the one on page 116). Check your progress in one month and at the end of the semester.

SUGGESTED READINGS

Armstrong, William H. and M. Willard Lampe II. *Barron's Pocket Guide to Study Tips: How to Study Effectively and Get Better Grades*. New York: Barron's Educational Series, 2004.

Chesla, Elizabeth. *Reading Comprehension Success: In 20 Minutes a Day*, 2nd ed. Florence, KY: Thomson Delmar Learning, 2002.

Frank, Steven. *The Everything Study Book*. Holbrook, MA: Adams Media, 1997.

Labunski, Richard E. *The Educated Student: Getting the Most Out of Your College Years*. Versailles, KY: Marley and Beck, 2003.

Luckie, William R., Wood Smethurst, and Sarah Beth Huntley. *Study Power Workbook: Exercises in Study Skills to Improve Your Learning and Your Grades*. Cambridge, MA: Brookline Books, 1999.

Silver, Theodore. *The Princeton Review Study Smart: Hands-on, Nuts and Bolts Techniques for Earning Higher Grades*. New York: Villard Books, 1996.

INTERNET RESOURCES

Academictips.org (study tips and links): www.academictips.org/

How to Study (study advice with valuable links): www.howtostudy.com

Prentice Hall Student Success Supersite Study Skills: www.prenhall.com/success/

ENDNOTES

1. Sherwood Harris, *The New York Public Library Book of How and Where to Look It Up*. Englewood Cliffs, NJ: Prentice Hall, 1991, p. 13.

2. Roxanne Ruzic, CAST, "Lessons for Everyone: How Students with Reading-Related Learning Disabilities Survive and Excel in College Courses with Heavy Reading Requirements." Paper presented at the Annual Meeting of the American Educational Research Association, April 13, 2001 [on-line]. Available: www.cast.org/udl/index.cfm?i=1540 (February 2004).

3. Steve Moidel, *Speed Reading*. Hauppauge, NY: Barron's Educational Series, 1994, p. 18.

4. Ibid.

5. Francis P. Robinson, *Effective Behavior*. New York: Harper & Row, 1941.

6. John Mack Faragher, et al., *Out of Many*, 4th ed. Upper Saddle River, NJ: Prentice Hall, 2003, p. xxxvii.

7. Ophelia H. Hancock, *Reading Skills for College Students*, 5th ed. Upper Saddle River, NJ: Prentice Hall, 2001, pp. 54–59.

8. Excerpted from Lynn Quitman Troyka, *Simon & Schuster Handbook for Writers*, 5th ed. Upper Saddle River, NJ: Prentice Hall, 1999, p. 12.

9. Center for Media Literacy, 1998.

10. Eric Hoover, "Peer Factor: Do Smart Students Improve the Performance of Others?" *The Chronicle of Higher Education*, February 7, 2003 [on-line]. Available: http://chronicle.com/weekly/v49/i22/22a02901.htm (March 2004).

11. Louis E. Boone, David L. Kurtz, and Judy R. Block, *Contemporary Business Communication*. Englewood Cliffs, NJ: Prentice Hall, 1994, pp. 489–499.

12. John J. Macionis, *Sociology*, 6th ed. Upper Saddle River, NJ: Prentice Hall, 1997, p. 174.

13. U.S. Department of Education, National Center for Education Statistics, *The Condition of Education, 1996*, NCES 96–304, by Thomas M. Smith. Washington, DC: U.S. Government Printing Office, 1996, p. 84.

6

IN THIS CHAPTER . . .

you will explore answers
to the following questions:

Listening, Note Taking, and Memory

TAKING IN, RECORDING, AND REMEMBERING INFORMATION

College exposes you daily to all kinds of information—and your job as a student is to take it in, sort through it, and keep what is important. This chapter shows you how to do just that by building your listening (taking in information), note-taking (recording what's important), and memory skills (remembering information).

Compare these skills to using a camera: You start by locating an image through the viewfinder, then you carefully focus the lens (listening), record the image on film or a digital card (note taking), and produce a print (remembering). The whole process engages your analytical, creative, and practical abilities and helps you build knowledge you can use.

On the following page, read how student Shyama Parikh is working to improve her memory skills.

- How can you become a better listener?
- How can you make the most of note taking?
- Which note-taking system should you use?
- How can you write faster when taking notes?
- How does memory work?
- What memory strategies can improve recall?

How can I improve my memory?

Recently I took a memory test in one of my psychology classes. I discovered that I'm better at remembering a full definition to a word rather than reading the definition and remembering the word. Most of my classmates had the same results. This surprised all of us; it seems like it would be easier to recall a word than an entire definition, but that was not the case.

Sometimes I find memorization work difficult, even though I know I have the ability. For instance, I know I have the material written down in my notes, down to the exact page, but then on the test, I sometimes can't remember the answers. I find Biology especially hard for that reason; there's a lot more memorization because of all the diagrams and classification systems.

I'm aware of mnemonic devices and I try to incorporate those into my study time, but that doesn't always work. I know rereading and repetition probably reinforce what I've studied, but I don't always have enough time. I am involved in so many other activities on campus that it's hard to find the time to devote to retaining information for five classes. I think memorization for me is the first step in learning, so I need to learn more effective ways to memorize.

I've just been accepted to law school, and I'm concerned because it seems that law requires learning a lot of technical terms. Can you suggest ways for me to improve my memory?

Shyama Parikh
DePaul University, Chicago, Illinois

A combination of organization, reading comprehension, and reinforcement will help with your memory concerns.

First, an important point: The definitions exercise you took in your psychology class illustrates how meaning enhances memory. The reason you are more likely to remember a sentence of 30 words than a list of 15 random words is because the sentence is organized in such a way that it has meaning for you. Keep this point in mind.

When you study, understand how the material is organized. For example, if a chapter outline makes sense to you, then the material is more likely to make sense. Organization improves recall (that's why mnemonics help when memorizing unrelated items). Because understanding is just as important, though, you need to both organize *and* understand. For instance, if a system of categorizing biology terms makes sense to you, then you are more likely to understand and recall the terms. Mentally placing information in logical categories enhances memory. How do you know if you have memorized a list? Write it down to find out exactly what you do and do not know.

Reading comprehension is similar. To enhance your reading comprehension, preview the entire textbook or chapter before reading it. Read the table of contents, chapter titles, sections, and subsections. By understanding the organization of the textbook you can more actively make meaningful connections and, therefore, learn the details more efficiently.

The final technique is reinforcement. As you read a text, continually ask yourself whether the information makes sense. If not, try to figure out why you're stuck. For reinforcement of reading comprehension, pause at good stopping points and try taking notes from memory. Your notes are proof that you can recall and understand the material. This pause-and-reflect technique is critical for learning new material. Good luck!

Stephen Beck
Director, Learn-to-Learn Company
Winston-Salem, North Carolina

How can you become a better *listener?*

The act of hearing isn't the same as the act of (listening.) Hearing refers to sensing spoken messages from their source. Listening, however, involves a complex process of communication. Successful listening occurs when the listener understands the speaker's intended message. The good news is that listening is a teachable—and learnable—skill that engages analytical and practical abilities.

> LISTENING
>
> A process that involves sensing, interpreting, evaluating, and reacting to spoken messages.

Know the stages of listening

Listening is made up of four stages that happen instantaneously and build on one another: sensing, interpreting, evaluating, and reacting. You move through these stages without being aware as they take the message from the speaker to the listener and back to the speaker (see Key 6.1).

During the *sensation* stage, your ears pick up sound waves and transmit them to the brain. For example, you are sitting in class and hear your instructor say, "The only opportunity to make up last week's test is Tuesday at 5:00 P.M."

In the *interpretation* stage, listeners attach meaning to a message. This involves understanding what is being said and relating it to what you already know. You relate this message to your knowledge of the test, whether you need to make it up, and what you are doing on Tuesday at 5:00 P.M.

Understand the stages of listening.

key 6.1

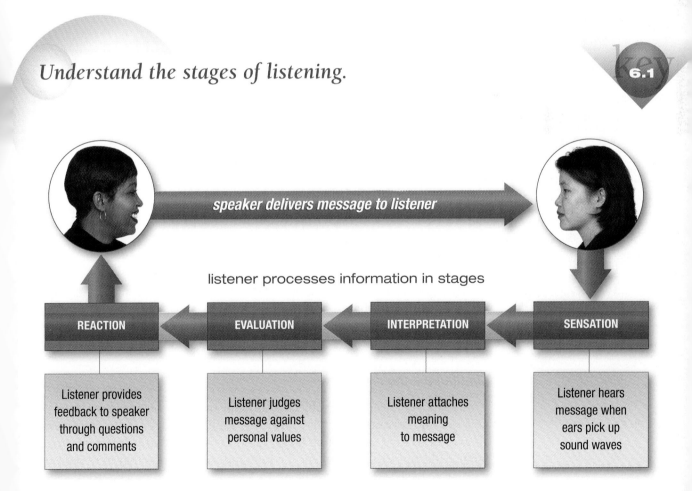

speaker delivers message to listener

listener processes information in stages

REACTION	EVALUATION	INTERPRETATION	SENSATION
Listener provides feedback to speaker through questions and comments	Listener judges message against personal values	Listener attaches meaning to message	Listener hears message when ears pick up sound waves

In the *evaluation* stage, you decide how you feel about the message, whether, for example, you like it or agree with it and how it relates to your needs and values. If the message goes against your values or does not fulfill your needs, you may reject it, stop listening, or argue in your mind with the speaker. In this example, if you do need to make up the test but have to work on Tuesday at 5:00 P.M., you may evaluate the message as less than satisfactory.

The final stage of listening is a *reaction* to the message in the form of direct feedback. In a classroom, direct feedback comes in the form of questions and comments. Your reaction, in this case, may be to ask the instructor if she can schedule another test time.

Improving your listening skills involves two primary goals: managing listening challenges (maximizing the sensation stage) and becoming an active listener (maximizing the interpretation and evaluation stages).

Manage listening challenges

Classic studies have shown that immediately after listening, students are likely to recall only half of what was said. This is partly due to such listening challenges as divided attention and distractions, the tendency to shut out the message, the inclination to rush to judgment, and partial hearing loss or learning disabilities.[1] Fortunately, you can minimize these challenges. Here are some ways to do it.

Divided attention and distractions

Internal and external distractions often divide your attention. *Internal distractions* include anything from hunger to headache to personal worries. Something the speaker says may also trigger a reaction that causes your mind to drift. In contrast, *external distractions* include anything from noises (whispering, police sirens) to excessive heat or cold to a wobbly seat. It is hard to listen when you are sweating, uncomfortable, or distracted by talkers.

Opportunities are often missed because we are broadcasting when we should be listening.

AUTHOR UNKNOWN

Use practical strategies to reduce distractions so that you can concentrate on what you're hearing. Sitting near the front of the room will help, as will moving away from chatting classmates. Work to concentrate when you're in class and save worrying about personal problems for later. Get enough sleep to stay alert, eat enough to avoid hunger, and dress comfortably.

Shutting out the message

If students perceive that a subject is difficult or uninteresting, they may tune out and miss material that forms the foundation for what comes next. To avoid this kind of listening lapse, remind yourself that instructors often use their lectures to supplement the text and then include that material on tests. If you pay attention to the entire lecture, you will be able to read over your notes later, compare your notes to the textbook, and use your analytical thinking skills to figure out how everything fits together.

If you experience a listening lapse, refocus your concentration quickly, instead of worrying about what you missed. Later, connect with a classmate to fill in the gaps in your notes.

The rush to judgment

It is common for people to stop listening when they hear something they don't like. Their focus turns to their personal reactions and away from the message. Students who disagree during a lecture often spend valuable class time figuring out how to word a question or comment in response.

Judgments may also involve reactions to the speakers themselves. If you do not like your instructors or if you have preconceived notions about their ideas or background, you may decide that you don't value what they have to say. Anyone whose words have ever been ignored because of race, ethnicity, gender, physical characteristics, or disability understands how prejudice can interfere with listening. Although it is human nature to stop listening, at times, in reaction to a speaker or message, this tendency can get in the way of your education.

Partial hearing loss and learning disabilities

If you have a hearing loss, seek out special services, including tutoring and equipment that can help you listen in class. For example, listening to a taped lecture at a higher-than-normal volume can help you hear things you missed in the classroom. Meeting with your instructor outside of class to clarify your notes may also help. It is also smart to sit near the front of the room.

Other disabilities, such as attention deficit disorder (ADD) or a problem with processing spoken language, can add to listening difficulties. People with these problems may have trouble paying attention or understanding what they hear. If you have a disability that creates a listening challenge, seek help through the counseling or student health center, an advisor, or an instructor.

Become an active listener

On the surface, listening seems like a passive activity: you sit back and take in information as someone else speaks. Effective listening, however, is an active process that involves setting a listening purpose, asking questions, paying attention to verbal signposts, and expecting the unexpected.

Set purposes for listening. Begin by establishing what you want to achieve, such as understanding the material better or mastering a specific task. Many instructors state their purpose at the beginning of the class. Writing it down will help you focus on the message.

Ask questions. A willingness to ask questions shows a desire to learn and is the mark of an active, analytical thinker and listener. Among the most important types of questions you will ask are *clarifying questions*, which state your understanding of what you heard and ask whether that understanding is correct.

Although questions and comments turn you into an active, analytical participant, they may sometimes distract you from the speaker. One practical way to avoid this is to jot down your questions quickly and come back to them during a discussion period. This strategy helps you relax and continue to listen.

Students from different cultures may take different approaches to questioning. American students are more likely to actively question instructors than students from Japan and other high-context cultures who tend to avoid confronting someone in authority. In addition, because students from high-context cultures are accustomed to hearing vague, indirect language designed to move them to form their own conclusions, they may be less likely to ask for clarification. (For more on high-context and low-context cultures, see Chapter 2.)

Pay attention to verbal signposts. Speakers' choice of words may tell you a lot about the information they consider important and help you predict test questions. For example, an idea described as "new and exciting" or "classic" is more likely to be on a test than one described as "interesting." Verbal signposts often involve transition words and phrases that help organize information, connect ideas, and indicate what is important and what is not. Listen for phrases like those in Key 6.2 and pay attention to the material that follows those phrases.

Expect the unexpected. Active listening requires opening your mind to diverse points of view and to the heated classroom debates that may result.

Effective listening skills prepare you to take effective notes—a necessary and powerful study tool.

> VERBAL SIGNPOSTS
>
> Spoken words or phrases that call attention to the information that follows.

CAUTION

Verbal signposts point out important information.

key 6.2

SIGNALS POINTING TO KEY CONCEPTS	SIGNALS OF SUPPORT
There are two reasons for this . . .	For example, . . .
A critical point in the process involves . . .	Specifically, . . .
Most important, . . .	For instance, . . .
The result is . . .	Similarly, . . .

SIGNALS POINTING TO DIFFERENCES	SIGNALS THAT SUMMARIZE
On the contrary, . . .	Finally, . . .
On the other hand, . . .	Recapping this idea, . . .
In contrast, . . .	In conclusion, . . .
However, . . .	As a result, . . .

DISCOVER YOURSELF AS A LISTENER

Take a look at your personal listening habits.

Complete the following:

- Analyze how present you are as a listener. Are you easily distracted, or can you focus well? Do you prefer to listen, or do you tend to talk?

  _____

  _____

- When you are listening, what tends to distract you?

  _____

  _____

- What happens to your listening skills when you become confused?

  _____

  _____

- How do you react when you strongly disagree with something your instructor says—when you are convinced that you are "right" and your instructor is "wrong"?

  _____

  _____

- Thinking about your answers and about your listening challenges, list two strategies from the chapter that can help you focus and improve your listening skills.

1. _____

   _____

2. _____

   _____

How can you make the most of *note taking?*

By encouraging you to decide what is worth remembering, the act of note taking gets you thinking analytically and practically. Note taking involves you in the learning process in many important ways:

- Having notes to read after class can help you process and learn information for tests.
- When you take notes, you listen better and become more involved in class.
- Notes help you think critically and organize ideas.

- When a lecture includes information not found in your text, you will have no way to study it without writing it down.
- Note taking is a lifetime skill that you will use at work and in your personal life.

He listens well who takes notes.

DANTE ALIGHIERI

Record information in class

Taking useful notes involves effort before class (preparation), during class (focus and note-taking strategies), and after class (reviewing and revising notes).

Preparing to take class notes

There are a number of ways to prepare for note-taking sessions:

Preview your reading material. *More than anything else you do, reading the assigned materials before class prepares you to understand the lecture and class discussion*. It also gives you the background to take effective notes. The class syllabus should tell you when specific reading assignments are due. If you have any questions, ask your instructor.

Gather your supplies. Use separate pieces of notebook paper for each class. Punch holes in handouts and insert them immediately into your binder following your notes for that day. If you take notes on a laptop, open the file containing your class notes right away.

Location, location, location. Find a seat where you can see and hear. Sitting near the front will minimize distractions. Be ready to write when the instructor begins speaking.

Choose the best note-taking system. Later in the chapter, you will learn about different note-taking systems. Take the following factors into account when choosing an appropriate system for any situation:

- The instructor's style (you'll be able to identify it after a few classes). Whereas one instructor may deliver organized lectures at a normal speaking rate, another may jump from topic to topic or talk very quickly.
- The course material. You may decide that an informal outline works best for a highly structured philosophy course, but that a think link is better for a looser sociology course. Try a note-taking system for a few classes, then make adjustments.
- Your learning style. Choose strategies that make the most of your strong points and help boost weaker areas. A visual–spatial learner might prefer think links or the Cornell system; a thinker type might stick to outlines; an interpersonal learner might use the Cornell system

and fill in the cue column in a study group setting (see Chapter 3 for a complete discussion of learning styles). You might even find that one system is best in class and another works best for review sessions.

Gather support. Set up a support system with two students in each class. Then, when you are absent, you can ask either one for the notes you missed.

Writing down important information helps to keep you involved. As they take notes, these community college students are staying connected to what's happening in class.

Record information effectively during class

Because no one has time to write everything down, the following practical strategies will help you record what you consider important for later study. This is not a list of "musts." Rather, it is a list of ideas to try as you work to find the right note-taking strategy for you.

- Date and identify each page.
- If your instructor jumps from topic to topic during a single class, it may help to start a new page of notes for each new topic.
- Record whatever an instructor emphasizes—key terms, definitions, ideas, and examples. (Key 6.3 shows methods an instructor might use to call attention to information.)
- Write down all questions raised by the instructor; these questions may appear on a test.
- Leave one or more blank spaces between points. This "white space" will help you review your notes, which will be in segments. (This suggestion does not apply to a think link.)
- Draw pictures and diagrams to illustrate ideas.
- Write quickly but legibly, perhaps using a form of personal shorthand. (See the section on shorthand on p. 171.) Remember that you can always make improvements and additions later.
- Mark important material with a star, underlining, a highlighter pen, a different color pen, or capital letters.
- If you don't understand a concept, leave a space and place a question mark in the margin. Then take advantage of your resources—ask the instructor to explain the concept after class, discuss it with a classmate, or consult your text—and fill in the blank when the idea is clear.
- Try to use the same system to indicate importance—such as indenting, spacing, or underlining—on each page. This will allow you to perceive key information with a minimum of effort.

How to pick up on instructor cues.

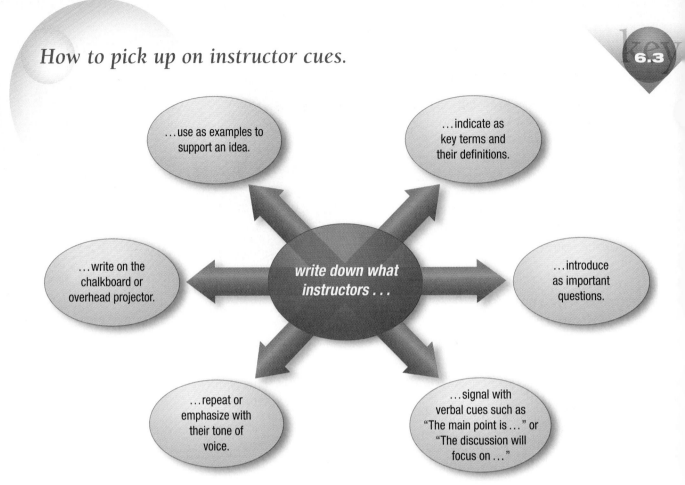

...use as examples to support an idea.

...indicate as key terms and their definitions.

...write on the chalkboard or overhead projector.

write down what instructors . . .

...introduce as important questions.

...repeat or emphasize with their tone of voice.

...signal with verbal cues such as "The main point is ..." or "The discussion will focus on ..."

Taking notes during class discussions

During discussion periods, one student may say something, then another, and finally the instructor may summarize the comments or link them together to make a point. Frequently, class discussion periods have tremendous value, but just as frequently information is presented in a disorganized, sometimes chaotic way. Here are suggestions for recording what you need to know during these discussions:

- Listen carefully to everyone. Jot down relevant points and ignore points that seem irrelevant.
- Listen for idea threads that weave through comments.
- Listen for ideas the instructor picks up on and emphasizes and for encouraging comments to students, such as "You make a great point," "I like your idea," and so on.
- Take notes when the instructor rephrases and clarifies a student's point.
- Try using a think link as your note-taking system, since discussions often take the form of brainstorming sessions. A think link will help you connect ideas that come at you from different perspectives and in different voices.
- Finally, if you are unsure, ask the instructor (during the discussion or in office hours) whether a student's statement is important.

FACE A NOTE-TAKING CHALLENGE

get practical!

Prepare to take notes in your toughest class.

In the spaces below, record the specific steps you will take to prepare to take notes in what you consider to be your most challenging course.

- Course name and date of class:

  _____

- List all the reading you must complete before your next class (include pages from text and supplemental sources):

  _____

  _____

- Where will you sit in class to focus your attention and minimize distractions?

  _____

- Which note-taking system is best suited for the class, and why?

  _____

  _____

- Write the names and e-mail addresses of two classmates whose notes you can borrow if you miss a class:

  _____

  _____

Review and revise your notes

Reviewing your notes helps solidify information in memory. Review also helps you link new information to information you already know, which is a key step in building new ideas. The review-and-revision stage of note taking should include time for planning, critical thinking, adding information from other sources, summarizing, and working with a study group.

Plan a review schedule

Review within a day of the lecture. You don't have to spend hours memorizing every word. Just set some time aside to reread your notes and perhaps write questions and comments on them. An hour between classes, for example, would be an ideal time for a quick review.

Review regularly. Try to schedule times during the week for reviewing notes from that week's class meetings. For example, if you know you are free from 2 P.M. to 5 P.M. every Tuesday and Thursday, plan to review notes from two courses on Tuesday and from two others on Thursday. Having a routine helps assure that you will look at material regularly.

MULTIPLE INTELLIGENCE STRATEGIES FOR
Note Taking

Note taking is a critical learning tool. The tips below will help you retain information for both the short and long term.

INTELLIGENCE	SUGGESTED STRATEGIES	WHAT WORKS FOR YOU? WRITE NEW IDEAS HERE
Verbal–Linguistic	• Rewrite important ideas and concepts in class notes from memory. • Write summaries of your notes in your own words.	
Logical–Mathematical	• Organize the main points of a lecture or reading using outline form. • Make charts and diagrams to clarify ideas and examples.	
Bodily–Kinesthetic	• Make note taking as physical as possible—use large pieces of paper and different colored pens. • When in class, choose a comfortable spot where you have room to spread out your materials and shift body position when you need to.	
Visual–Spatial	• Take notes using colored markers. • Rewrite lecture notes in think link format, focusing on the most important and difficult points from the lecture.	
Interpersonal	• Whenever possible, schedule a study group right after a lecture to discuss class notes. • Review class notes with a study buddy. See what you wrote that he or she missed and vice versa.	
Intrapersonal	• Schedule some quiet time as soon as possible after a lecture to reread and think about your notes. If no class is meeting in the same room after yours and you have free time, stay in the room and review there.	
Musical	• Play music while you read your notes. • Write a song that incorporates material from one class period's notes or one particular topic. Use the refrain to emphasize the most important concepts.	
Naturalistic	• Read or rewrite your notes outside. • Review notes while listening to a nature CD—running water, rain, forest sounds.	

Review with an eye toward tests. Step up your efforts before a test. Schedule longer review sessions, call a study group meeting, and review more frequently. Shorter sessions of intense review work interspersed with breaks may get more results than long hours of continuous studying. Some students find that recopying their notes, before an exam or earlier in the study process, helps them remember key concepts.

Revise using other sources and critical thinking

Adding text material, other required course readings, and Internet material to your notes is one of the best ways to link and apply new information to what you already know. Try using the following analytical, creative, and practical strategies to build understanding as you revise:

- Brainstorm and record examples from other sources that illustrate ideas in your notes.
- Pay attention to similarities between your text materials and class notes (ideas that appear in both are probably important to remember).
- Think of material from the readings that supports and clarifies ideas in your notes.
- Consider what in your class notes differs from your readings and why.
- Write down new ideas that occur to you as you review.
- Extend and apply the concepts from your notes and other sources to new situations.

When you use your notes to inspire successfully intelligent thinking, your grades may reflect your efforts.

Summarize

Summarizing your notes involves critically evaluating which ideas and examples are most important and then rewriting the material in a shortened form. You may prefer to summarize as you review, with the notes in front of you. If you are using the Cornell system (see page 166), you would summarize in the space at the bottom of the page.

Some students summarize from memory after review, to see how much they have retained. Others summarize as they read, then summarize from memory, and compare the two.

Work with study groups

When you work with a study group, you have the opportunity to review both your personal notes and those of your classmates. This can be an enormous help if, for example, you lost concentration during part of a lecture and your notes don't make sense. You and another student may even have notes that have radically different information. When this happens, try to reconstruct what the instructor said and, if necessary, bring in a third person to clear up the confusion. See Chapter 5 for more on effective studying in groups.

Which *note-taking system* should you use?

The most common note-taking systems include outlines, the Cornell system, and think links. Consider two factors when choosing which to use—what feels comfortable to you and what works best with course content. For example, someone who prefers the Cornell system might use it for European History but will switch to a think link for French.

Take notes in outline form

When a reading assignment or lecture seems well organized, you may choose to take notes in outline form. Outlining means constructing a line-by-line representation, with certain phrases set off by varying indentations, showing how concepts, facts, and examples are related.

Formal outlines indicate ideas and examples with Roman numerals, uppercase and lowercase letters, and numbers. In contrast, *informal outlines* show the same associations but replace the formality with a system of consistent indenting and dashes. Key 6.4 shows the difference between the two outline forms. Many students find informal outlines easier for in-class note taking. Key 6.5 shows how a student has used the structure of a formal outline to write notes on the topic of civil rights legislation.

Use the Cornell note-taking system

The Cornell note-taking system, also known as the T-note system, developed by Walter Pauk at Cornell University, consists of three sections on ordinary notepaper.[2]

- Section 1, the largest section on the right, is the *note-taking column*. Record your notes here in whatever form is most comfortable for you.
- Section 2, to the left of your notes, is the *cue column*. Leave it blank while you read or listen, then fill it in later as you review. You might fill it with comments that highlight main ideas, clarify meaning, suggest examples, or link ideas and examples. You can even draw diagrams. Many students use this column to raise questions that they will ask themselves when they study. By placing specific questions in the cue column, you can help yourself focus on critical details.
- Section 3, at the bottom of the page, is known as the *summary area*. Here you briefly summarize the notes on the page. Use this section during the review process to reinforce concepts and provide an overview of what the notes say.

Create this note-taking structure before class begins. Picture an upside-down letter T as you follow these directions:

- Start with a sheet of standard loose-leaf paper. Label it with the date and title of the lecture.

Choose between different outline structures.

FORMAL OUTLINE	INFORMAL OUTLINE
Topic	Topic
I. First Main Idea	First Main Idea
A. Major supporting fact	—Major supporting fact
B. Major supporting fact	—Major supporting fact
1. First reason or example	—First reason or example
2. Second reason or example	—Second reason or example
a. First supporting fact	—First supporting fact
b. Second supporting fact	—Second supporting fact
II. Second Main Idea	Second Main Idea
A. Major supporting fact	—Major supporting fact
1. First reason or example	—First reason or example
2. Second reason or example	—Second reason or example
B. Major supporting fact	—Major supporting fact

- To create the cue column, draw a vertical line about 2½ inches from the left side of the paper. End the line about 2 inches from the bottom of the sheet.

- To create the summary area, start at the point where the vertical line ends (about 2 inches from the bottom of the page) and draw a horizontal line that spans the entire paper.

Key 6.6 shows how a student used the Cornell system to take notes in a business course.

Create a think link

A think link, also known as a mind map or word web, is a visual form of note taking. When you draw a think link, you diagram ideas by using shapes and lines that link ideas and supporting details and examples. The visual design makes the connections easy to see, and the use of shapes and pictures extends the material beyond just words. Many learners respond well to the power of visualization. You can also use think links to brainstorm ideas for paper topics.

    To create a think link, start by circling or boxing your topic in the middle of a sheet of paper. Next, draw a line from the topic and write the name of one major idea at the end of the line. Circle that idea also. Then, jot down specific facts related to the idea, linking them to the idea with lines. Continue the process, connecting thoughts to one another by using circles, lines, and

VISUALIZATION

The interpretation of verbal ideas through the use of visual images.

CIVIL RIGHTS LEGISLATION: 1860–1968

I. Post-Civil War Era
   A. Fourteenth Amendment, 1868: equal protection of the law for all citizens
   B. Fifteenth Amendment, 1870: constitutional rights of citizens regardless of race, color, or previous servitude
II. Civil Rights Movement of the 1960s
   A. National Association for the Advancement of Colored People (NAACP)
      1. Established in 1910 by W.E.B. DuBois and others
      2. Legal Defense and Education fund fought school segregation
   B. Martin Luther King Jr., champion of nonviolent civil rights action
      1. Led bus boycott: 1955–1956
      2. Marched on Washington, D.C.: 1963
      3. Awarded NOBEL PEACE PRIZE: 1964
      4. Led voter registration drive in Selma, Alabama: 1965
   C. Civil Rights Act of 1964: prohibited discrimination in voting, education, employment, and public facilities
   D. Voting Rights Act of 1965: gave the government power to enforce desegregation
   E. Civil Rights Act of 1968: prohibited discrimination in the sale or rental of housing

The Cornell system adds note-taking flexibility.

October 3, 2005, p. 1

UNDERSTANDING EMPLOYEE MOTIVATION

Why do some workers have a better attitude toward their work than others?	Purpose of motivational theories — To explain role of human relations in motivating employee performance — Theories translate into how managers actually treat workers

Some managers view workers as lazy; others view them as motivated and productive.	2 specific theories
	— Human resources model, developed by Douglas McGregor, shows that managers have radically different beliefs about motivation.
	  — Theory X holds that people are naturally irresponsible and uncooperative
	  — Theory Y holds that people are naturally responsible and self-motivated

Maslow's Hierarchy
 	
self-actualization needs (challenging job)
esteem needs (job title)
social needs (friends at work)
security needs (health plan)
physiological needs (pay)
	— Maslow's Hierarchy of Needs says that people have needs in 5 different areas, which they attempt to satisfy in their work.
	  — Physiological need: need for survival, including food and shelter
	  — Security need: need for stability and protection
	  — Social need: need for friendship and companionship
	  — Esteem need: need for status and recognition
	  — Self-actualization need: need for self-fulfillment
	Needs at lower levels must be met before a person tries to satisfy needs at higher levels.
	— Developed by psychologist Abraham Maslow

Two motivational theories try to explain worker motivation. The human resources model includes Theory X and Theory Y. Maslow's Hierarchy of Needs suggests that people have needs in 5 different areas: physiological, security, social, esteem, and self-actualization.

words. Key 6.7 shows how a student used this particular think link structure to map out the sociology concept of social stratification. Other think link designs include stair steps showing connected ideas that build toward a conclusion or a tree shape with roots as causes and branches as effects.

A think link may be difficult to construct in class, especially if your instructor talks quickly. In this case, use another note-taking system during class. Then, create a think link as part of the review process.

No matter what note-taking system you choose, your success will depend on how well you use it. Mastering the practical skill of personal shorthand will help you make the most of your choice.

Think links provide a visual approach to note taking.

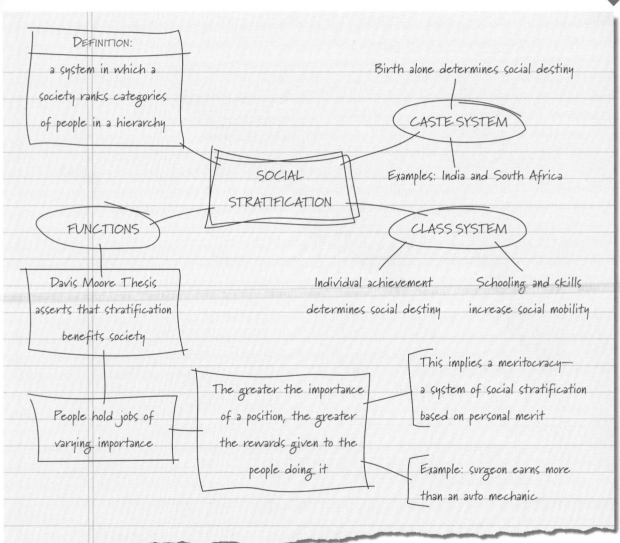

DEFINITION:
a system in which a society ranks categories of people in a hierarchy

Birth alone determines social destiny

CASTE SYSTEM

Examples: India and South Africa

SOCIAL STRATIFICATION

FUNCTIONS

CLASS SYSTEM

Individual achievement determines social destiny

Schooling and skills increase social mobility

Davis Moore Thesis asserts that stratification benefits society

People hold jobs of varying importance

The greater the importance of a position, the greater the rewards given to the people doing it

This implies a meritocracy—a system of social stratification based on personal merit

Example: surgeon earns more than an auto mechanic

How can you *write faster* when taking notes?

Using some form of personal (shorthand,) you can push your pen faster. Because you alone are the intended reader, you can misspell and abbreviate words in ways that only you understand.

To avoid forgetting what shorthand notations mean, review your notes while they are fresh in your mind. If anything confuses you, spell out words as you review.

Here are some suggestions that will help you master this important practical skill:

1. Use standard abbreviations in place of complete words.

w/	with		cf	compare, in comparison to
w/o	without		ff	following
→	means; resulting in		Q	question
←	as a result of		p.	page
↑	increasing		*	most important
↓	decreasing		<	less than
∴	therefore		>	more than
∵ or b/c	because		=	equals
≈	approximately		%	percent
+ or &	and		△	change
−	minus; negative		2	to; two; too
no. or #	number		vs	versus; against
i.e.	that is,		eg	for example
etc.	and so forth		c/o	care of
ng	no good		lb	pound

2. Shorten words by removing vowels from the middle of words.

   prps   =   purpose

3. Substitute word beginnings for entire words.

   assoc   =   associate; association

4. Form plurals by adding s to shortened words.

   prblms   =   problems

5. Make up your own symbols and use them consistently.

   b/4   =   before

6. Use standard or informal abbreviations for proper nouns such as places, people, companies, scientific substances, events, and so on.

   DC   =   Washington, D.C.

> **SHORTHAND**
> A system of rapid handwriting that employs symbols, abbreviations, and shortened words to represent words and phrases.

7. If you are repeatedly writing a word or phrase throughout a class, write it out once and then create an abbreviation. For example, if you are taking notes on Argentina's former first lady Eva Perón, you might start by writing *Eva Perón (EP)* and then use *EP* through the rest of your notes for that class.

Finally, throughout your note taking, remember that the primary goal is to generate materials that help you learn and remember information. If you find that your notes aren't comprehensible, legible, or focused, analyze the problem. Can't read your notes? You might have been sleepy. Confusing gaps in information? You might be distracted in class, have an instructor who jumps around in the lecture, or lack an understanding of the course material. Put your problem-solving skills to work and brainstorm solutions from the variety of strategies in this chapter. With effort, your notes will become a helpful learning tool in school and beyond.

Learning listening skills and finding a system for taking effective notes prepare you for one of the most important challenges you face in school—developing your memory so you can remember what you hear in class, study in your texts, and record in your notes.

How does *memory* work?

Your Accounting instructor is giving a test tomorrow on the double-entry accounting system. You feel confident because you spent hours last week memorizing your notes. Unfortunately, by the time you take the test, you remember very little. This is not surprising, since most forgetting occurs within minutes after memorization.

In a classic study conducted in 1885, researcher Herman Ebbinghaus memorized a list of meaningless three-letter words such as CEF and LAZ. He then examined how quickly he forgot them. Within one hour he forgot more than 50 percent of what he had learned; after two days, he knew fewer than 30 percent of the material. Although Ebbinghaus's recall of the nonsense syllables remained fairly stable after that, his experiment shows how fragile memory can be—even when you take the time and expend the energy to memorize information.[3]

How your brain remembers:
Short-term and long-term memory

Memories are stored in three different "storage banks" in your brain. The first, called sensory memory, is an exact copy of what you see and hear and lasts for a second or less. Certain information is then selected from sensory memory and moved into short-term memory, a temporary information storehouse that lasts no more than 10 to 20 seconds. You are consciously aware of material in short-term memory. Unimportant information is quickly dumped. Important information is transferred to long-term memory—the mind's more permanent storehouse.

Long-term memory involves four stages.

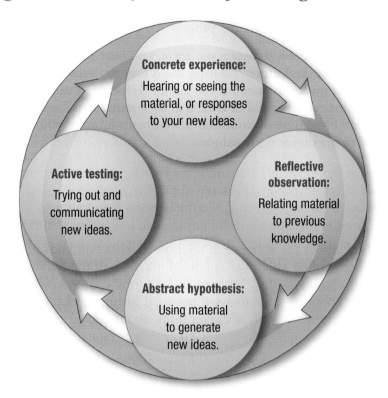

Concrete experience:
Hearing or seeing the material, or responses to your new ideas.

Reflective observation:
Relating material to previous knowledge.

Abstract hypothesis:
Using material to generate new ideas.

Active testing:
Trying out and communicating new ideas.

Although all three stages are important, targeting long-term memory will solidify learning the most. "Short-term—or working—memory is useful when we want to remember a phone number until we can dial," says biologist James Zull. "We use short-term memory for these momentary challenges, all the time, every day, but it is limited in capacity, tenacity, and time."[4] Zull explains that short-term memory can hold only small amounts of information for brief periods. In addition, it is unstable—a distraction can easily dislodge information.

Retaining information in long-term memory

In order to retain information in long-term memory, your brain moves through a four-stage process, which relates directly to the stages of the listening process described on pages 155–156. Key 6.8 illustrates the process.

1. Experiencing the material (concrete experience). Your brain takes in the information through one or more of your senses.

2. Relating the material to what you already know (reflexive observation). You reflect on the new information and connect it to previous knowledge.

3. Forming new ideas (abstract hypothesis). You come up with new insights from the combination of what you knew before and what you are learning now.

Practice the middle. When you are trying to learn something, you usually study some material first, attack other material in the middle of the session, and approach still other topics at the end. The weak link in your recall is likely to be the material you study midway. It pays to give this material special attention.

Create groupings. When items do not have to be remembered in any particular order, the act of grouping can help you recall them better. Say, for example, that you have to memorize these four 10-digit numbers:

9806875087   9876535703   7636983561   6724472879

It may look impossible. If you group the numbers to look like telephone numbers, however, the job may become more manageable:

(980) 687–5087   (987) 653–5703   (763) 698–3561   (672) 447–2879

In general, try to limit groups to 10 items or fewer. It's hard to memorize more at one time.

Use flash cards. Flash cards are a great visual memory tool. They give you short, repeated review sessions that provide immediate feedback, and they are portable, which gives you the flexibility to use them wherever you go. Use the front of a 3-by-5-inch index card to write a word, idea, or phrase you want to remember. Use the back for a definition, an explanation, and other key facts. Key 6.9 shows two flash cards used to study for a Psychology exam.

Here are some suggestions for making the most of your flash cards:

- Carry the cards with you and review them frequently.
- Shuffle the cards and learn the information in various orders.
- Test yourself in both directions. First, look at the terms and provide the definitions or explanations. Then turn the cards over and reverse the process.

Flash cards help you memorize important facts.

6.9

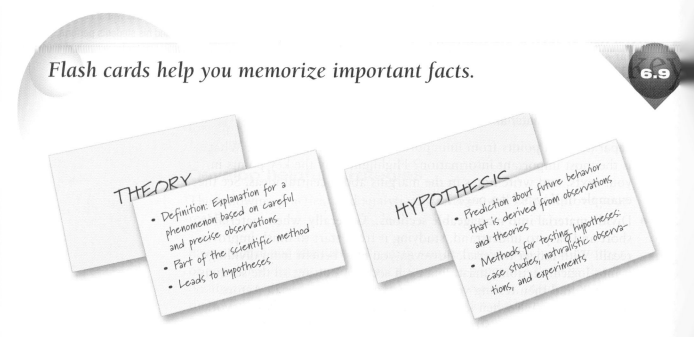

THEORY
- Definition: Explanation for a phenomenon based on careful and precise observations
- Part of the scientific method
- Leads to hypotheses

HYPOTHESIS
- Prediction about future behavior that is derived from observations and theories
- Methods for testing hypotheses: case studies, naturalistic observations, and experiments

Use a tape recorder. Use a tape recorder as an immediate feedback "audio flash card." Record short-answer study questions on tape, leave 10 to 15 seconds between questions to answer out loud, then record the correct answer after each pause. For example, a question for a writing class might be, "What are the three elements of effective writing? . . . (10–15 second pause) . . . topic, audience, and purpose."

Use mnemonic devices

Certain performers entertain their audiences by remembering the names of 100 strangers or flawlessly repeating 30 ten-digit phone numbers. Although these performers probably have superior memories, they also rely on memory techniques, known as mnemonic devices (pronounced neh-MAHN-ick), for assistance.

> MNEMONIC
> DEVICES
> Memory techniques
> that involve
> associating new
> information with
> information you
> already know.

Mnemonic devices depend on vivid associations (relating new information to other information). Instead of learning new facts by rote (repetitive practice), associations give you a "hook" on which to hang these facts and retrieve them later. Mnemonic devices make information familiar and meaningful through unusual, unforgettable mental associations and visual pictures. Forming mnemonics depends on activating your creative ability.

There are different kinds of mnemonic devices, including visual images and associations, acronyms, and songs and rhymes. Study how these devices work, then use your creative thinking skills to apply them to your own memory challenges.

Create visual images and associations

You are more likely to remember a piece of information if you link it to a visual image. The best mental images often involve bright colors, three dimensions, action scenes, inanimate objects with human traits, ridiculousness, and humor.

Turning information into mental pictures helps improve memory, especially for visual learners. To remember that the Spanish artist Picasso painted *The Three Women*, you might imagine the women in a circle dancing to a Spanish song with a pig and a donkey (pig-asso). The more outlandish the image the better, since these images are the most memorable.

> Memory is the stepping-stone to thinking, because without remembering facts, you cannot think, conceptualize, reason, make decisions, create, or contribute.
>
> **HARRY LORAYNE**

Use the mental walk strategy to remember items in a list

Using the mental walk strategy, you imagine that you store new ideas in familiar locations. Say, for example, that for Biology you have to remember the major endocrine glands. To do this, you can think of the route you take to the library. You pass the college theater, the science center, the bookstore, the cafeteria, the athletic center, and the social science building before reaching the library. At each spot along the route, you "place" the idea or concept you wish to learn. You then link the concept with a similar-sounding word that brings to mind a vivid image:

- At the campus theater, you imagine bumping into the actor Brad Pitt, who is holding two terriers (pituitary gland).
- At the science center, you visualize Mr. Universe with bulging thighs. When you are introduced, you learn that his name is Roy (thyroid gland).
- At the campus bookstore, you envision a second Mr. Universe with his thighs covered in mustard (thymus gland).
- In the cafeteria, you see an ad for Dean Al for president (adrenal gland).
- At the athletic center, you visualize a student throwing a ball into a pan and creatures applauding from the bleachers (pancreas).
- At the social science building, you imagine receiving a standing ovation (ovaries).
- And at the library, you visualize sitting at a table taking a test that is easy (testes).

Create acronyms

ACRONYM

A word formed from the first letters of a series of words, created in order to help you remember the series.

Another helpful association method involves the use of acronyms. In History class, you can remember the World War II Allies—Britain, the United States, and Russia—with the acronym BAR. This is an example of a word acronym, because the first letters of the items you wish to remember spell a word. The word (or words) spelled don't necessarily have to be real words. As you see in Key 6.10, the acronym Roy G. Biv will help you remember the colors of the spectrum.

An acronym will help you recall the colors of the spectrum. 6.10

red
orange
yellow
green
blue
indigo
violet

R O Y G. B I V

Other acronyms take the form of an entire sentence in which the first letter of each word in each sentence stands for the first letter of the memorized term. This is called a *list order acronym*. For example, when science students want to remember the list of planets in order of their distance from the sun (Mercury, Venus, Earth, Mars, Jupiter, Saturn, Uranus, Neptune, and Pluto), they can learn the sentence:

My very elegant mother just served us nine pickles.

Use songs or rhymes

Some of the classic mnemonic devices are rhyming poems that tend to stick in your mind. One you may have heard is the rule about the order of "i" and "e" in spelling:

I before E, except after C, or when sounded like "A" as in "neighbor" and "weigh." Four exceptions if you please: either, neither, seizure, seize.

Make up your own poems or songs, linking tunes or rhymes that are familiar to you with information you want to remember. When Susan W. Fisher teaches Introductory Biology at Ohio State University, she uses this "biorap," performed by class members, to help everyone remember part of DNA replication (the rap includes references to the football coach and student-government president):

A pairs with T and G pairs with C
It works 'cause the code's complementary
It lets you be you and me be me
From Coach Tressel to Eddie Pauline.

The chorus "*DNA makes protein*" is then repeated four times. Said junior David S. Waterman of this musical mnemonic, "Because the performances are entertaining, students are more apt to pay attention and remember what we see or hear."[5]

Improving your memory requires energy, time, and work. In school, it also helps to master SQ3R, the textbook study technique that was introduced in Chapter 5. By going through the steps in SQ3R and using the specific memory techniques described in this chapter, you will be able to learn more in less time—and remember what you learn long after exams are over.

BUILDING SKILLS

FOR COLLEGE, CAREER, AND LIFE SUCCESS

SUCCESSFUL INTELLIGENCE
PRACTICAL CREATIVE
ANALYTICAL
SUCCESSFUL INTELLIGENCE

Developing Successful Intelligence
PUTTING IT ALL TOGETHER

Learn from the experiences of others. Look back to Carol Comlish's Personal Triumph on p. 181. After you've read her story, relate her experience to your own life by completing the following:

Think it through: *Analyze your experience and compare it to Carol's.* What academic goal are you trying to reach now that will take you a long time, and how does this relate to Carol's experience? Why is this goal important to you? From your memory of reaching other important goals, what strategies will help you achieve it?

Think out of the box: *Let others inspire ideas.* Choose two people whom you respect. Put your listening skills to work: Spend a few minutes talking with each of them about your goal. Ask them about similar experiences they have had, and listen to the ideas that they used. From what you've heard, begin brainstorming ideas about how you will achieve your goal.

Make it happen: *Put a practical plan together.* Map out how you will achieve your goal. Create a mnemonic device that will help you remember your plan. Envision your success as you put your plan into action.

Team Building
COLLABORATIVE SOLUTIONS

Create a note-taking team. Although students often focus much more on taking notes in class than on taking notes while reading, reading notes are just as important to your understanding of the course material. In

create your future

your most demanding course, form a study group with two other people and choose a reading assignment—a text chapter, an article, or any other assigned reading—to work on together. Agree to read it and take notes independently before your next meeting. Each student should make photocopies of his or her notes for the other group members.

When you meet again, compare your notes, focusing on the following characteristics:

- Legibility (Can everyone read what is written?)
- Completeness (Did you all record the same information? If not, why not?)
- Organizational effectiveness (Does everyone get an idea of how ideas flow?)
- Value of the notes as a study aid (Will this help everyone remember the material?)

Based on what you've discussed with your group, come up with specific ways to improve your personal note-taking skills. You can also work with your study group to compare notes taken in a particular class period and work on improving in-class note-taking techniques.

Writing

DISCOVERY THROUGH JOURNALING

Record your thoughts on a separate piece of paper or in a journal.

How people retain information. How do you react to the following statement? "We retain 10 percent of what we read, 20 percent of what we hear, 30 percent of what we see, 50 percent of what we hear and see, 70 percent of what we say, 90 percent of what we say and do." How can you use this insight to improve your ability to retain information? What will you do differently as a result of this insight?

Career Portfolio

PLAN FOR SUCCESS

Matching career to curriculum. Your success in most career areas depends in part on your academic preparation. Some careers, such as medicine, require very specific curriculum choices (for example, specific biology and chemistry courses are required for medical school). Some careers require certain courses that teach basic competencies; for example, to be an accountant, you have to take accounting and bookkeeping. Other career areas, such as many business careers, don't have specific requirements, but employers often look for certain curriculum choices that indicate the mastery of particular skills and knowledge.

Put your listening and note-taking skills to work as you investigate your options. Choose a career area that interests you. Interview two people in that area—one from an academic setting (such as an instructor in a related subject area or an academic advisor) and one from the working world (such as a person working in that career or a career planning and placement office counselor). Choose a setting where you can listen well and take effective notes.

Ask your interviewees two questions: First, ask them about curriculum—what courses are required for this area, and what courses are beneficial but not required. Then ask them how you can stretch yourself outside of class in ways that will help you stand out—extracurricular activities, internships, leadership roles, part-time work, and any other helpful pursuits.

When you have completed your interviews, create two lists—one of recommended courses, marking the required ones with a star, and one of activities, internships, and any other recommendations.

SUGGESTED READINGS

Burley-Allen, Madelyn. *Listening: The Forgotten Skill: A Self-Teaching Guide*. New York: John Wiley & Sons, 1995.

DePorter, Bobbi and Mike Hernacki. *Quantum Notes: Whole-Brain Approaches to Note-Taking*. Chicago: Learning Forum, 2000.

Dunkel, Patricia A., Frank Pialorsi, and Joane Kozyrez. *Advanced Listening Comprehension: Developing Aural & Note-Taking Skills*, 3rd ed. Boston: Heinle & Heinle, 2004.

Higbee, Kenneth L. *Your Memory: How It Works and How to Improve It*. New York: Marlowe & Co., 2001.

Lebauer, R. Susan. *Learn to Listen, Listen to Learn: Academic Listening and Note-Taking*. Upper Saddle River, NJ: Prentice Hall, 2000.

Levin, Leonard. *Easy Script Express: Unique Speed Writing Methods to Take Fast Notes and Dictation*. Chicago: Legend Publishing, 2000.

Lorayne, Harry. *Super Memory—Super Student: How to Raise Your Grades in 30 Days*. Boston: Little, Brown & Company, 1990.

Lorayne, Harry. *The Memory Book: The Classic Guide to Improving Your Memory at Work, at School, and at Play*. New York: Ballantine Books, 1996.

Robbins, Harvey A. *How to Speak and Listen Effectively*. New York: AMACOM, 1992.

Roberts, Billy. *Working Memory: Improving Your Memory for the Workplace*. London: Bridge Trade, 1999.

Roberts, Billy. *Educate Your Memory: Improvement Techniques for Students of All Ages*. London: Allison & Busby, 2000.

INTERNET RESOURCES

ForgetKnot: A Source for Mnemonic Devices:
http://members.tripod.com/~ForgetKnot/

Prentice Hall Student Success Supersite—Study Skills:
www.prenhall.com/success/StudySkl/index.html

Helpful advice on listening from the Kishwaukee College Learning Skills Center:
kish.cc.il.us/lsc/ssh/listening.shtml

1. Ralph G. Nichols, "Do We Know How to Listen? Practical Helps in a Modern Age," *Speech Teacher* (March 1961): 118–124.

2. Walter Pauk, *How to Study in College*, 7th ed. Boston: Houghton Mifflin, 2001, pp. 236–241.

3. Herman Ebbinghaus, *Memory: A Contribution to Experimental Psychology*, trans. H. A. Ruger and C. E. Bussenius. New York: New York Teacher's College, Columbia University, 1885.

4. James Zull, *The Art of Changing the Brain: Enriching Teaching by Exploring the Biology of Learning.* Sterling, VA: Stylus Publishing, 2002.

5. Vyacheslav Kandyba, "Professor Uses Music to Bring Biology to Life," *The Chronicle of Higher Education.* March 30, 2003 [on-line]. Available: http://chronicle.com/weekly/v49/i38/38a01002.htm (March 2004).

IN THIS CHAPTER . . .

you will explore answers to the following questions:

Test Taking

SHOWING WHAT YOU KNOW

For a runner, a race is equivalent to a test because it measures ability at a given moment. Doing well in a race requires training similar to the studying you do for exams. The best runners—and test takers—understand that they train not just for the race or test, but to achieve a level of competence that they will use elsewhere.

When you successfully show what you know on tests, you achieve educational goals and develop confidence that you can perform well again and again. Exams also help you gauge your progress and, if necessary, improve your efforts. Most important, smart test preparation results in real learning that you take with you from course to course and into your career and life.

As you will see in this chapter, test taking is about preparation, persistence, and strategy—all of which tap into your analytical, creative, and practical abilities. It is also about conquering fears, paying attention to details, and learning from mistakes.

On the following page, read about student Peter Changsak's experience with test anxiety and his desire to overcome it.

- How can preparation improve test performance?
- How can you work through test anxiety?
- What general strategies can help you succeed on tests?
- How can you master different types of test questions?
- How can you learn from test mistakes?

How can I combat test anxiety?

I am a Yu'pik Eskimo from a village on the Yukon River. Before attending college, I worked for six years as a clerk at the Native Corporation, a gas station and general store. When the manager passed away, the business offered to make me a manager. Even though I knew how to do much of the work, I didn't feel I was ready, so I decided to go to school for more training.

College life is different from what I am accustomed to. The hardest part has been taking tests. I study hard, but then when I get in class and the test begins, my mind goes blank. When I read, I understand what I'm reading, but as soon as I close the book, I can't remember what I just read. My favorite class is Biology Lab—probably because we can walk around. I love mechanics and construction. When I worked at the Native Corporation, we built a new building. I felt like I was a success at work, but I don't feel successful as a student. Sometimes I feel like quitting, but I also think it can help me have more choices if I stick with it. I'm learning how to be a serious student, but it isn't easy. Can you give suggestions about how I can get over my test anxiety?

Peter Changsak

Sheldon-Jackson College,
Sitka, Alaska

Focus on preparation and work to change your attitude toward tests.

Many students experience test anxiety, especially students who are new to the educational setting. Often, anxiety is a result of feeling uncomfortable or distressed when charting unfamiliar waters. The first test administered in a class can bring about a great deal of anxiety.

First, it is important to adequately prepare for class exams:

- Attend class regularly.
- Pay attention in class and take *good notes*.
- Join a *study group* with fellow classmates.
- Spend three hours outside of the classroom studying for every hour you spend in class. Start studying early (don't wait until the week of the exam to study).
- Communicate with your instructor to make sure you understand course expectations, lecture information, and special projects that are due.
- Before the exam, get plenty of rest and eat a light breakfast or snack.

Second, when taking an exam:

- Close your eyes, take a deep breath, then review the test.
- Begin by responding to the questions you are most comfortable/familiar with.
- Continue reviewing the test to look for clues to answer those questions that you are not sure about.

Third, after taking the exam:

- After each test/exam, review your test/exam to learn about the areas you need to improve.
- Continue studying the information from the last exam along with new course information.

Finally, remember not all anxiety is bad—test anxiety, believe it or not, can encourage us to rise to an occasion. The stress of an upcoming test can help you work very hard and be prepared for the exam. Once the preparation is done, it is important for you to remind yourself that an exam is your opportunity to show off your knowledge. Changing your attitude toward the exam and looking forward to the opportunity to share your knowledge will help you think more positively about tests.

Tonjua Williams, M.Ed.

Associate Provost, Health Programs, St. Petersburg College

How can preparation improve *test performance?*

You prepare for exams every day of the semester. By attending class, staying on top of assignments, completing readings and projects, and participating in class discussions, you are actively learning and retaining what you need to know in order to do well on exams. This knowledge is the most important test-preparation tool you have.

The following additional measures will help you to be as prepared as possible for exam day because they will help you put your analytical, creative, and practical thinking skills into action.

Ninety percent of life is just showing up.

WOODY ALLEN

Identify test type and material covered

Before you begin studying, find out as much as you can about the test, including:

- Topics that will be covered. Will it cover everything since the semester began or will it be limited to a narrow topic?
- Types of questions. Objective (multiple choice, true/false, sentence completion), subjective (essay), or a combination?
- Material you will be tested on. Will the test cover only what you learned in class and in the text, or will it also cover outside readings?

Your instructors may answer many of these questions. They may tell you the question format and the topics that will be on the test. Some instructors may even drop hints about possible questions, either directly ("I might ask a question on this subject on your next exam") or more subtly ("One of my favorite theories is . . . ").

Here are other practical strategies for predicting what may be on a test.

Use SQ3R to identify what's important. Often, the questions you write and ask yourself when you read assigned materials may be part of the test. Textbook study questions are also good candidates.

Talk to people who already took the course. Try to get a sense of test difficulty, whether tests focus primarily on assigned readings or class notes, what materials are usually covered, and what types of questions are asked. Also ask about instructors' preferences. If you learn that the instructor pays close attention to specific facts, for example, use flash cards to drill yourself on details. If the instructor emphasizes a global overview, focus on concepts.

Examine old tests, if the instructor makes them available. You may find old tests in class, on-line, or on reserve in the library. Make sure you have the instructor's permission to consult them. Old tests will help you answer questions like:

- Do tests focus on examples and details, general ideas and themes, or a combination?
- Are the questions straightforward or confusing and sometimes tricky?

WRITE YOUR OWN TEST

Prepare for an upcoming exam using a pretest you create yourself.

Use the tips in this chapter to predict the material that will be covered, the types of questions that will be asked (multiple choice, essay, etc.), and the nature of the questions (a broad overview of the material or specific details).

Then be creative. Your goal is to write questions that your instructor is likely to ask—interesting questions that tap what you have learned and make you think about the material in different ways. Go through the following steps:

1. Write the questions you come up with on a separate sheet of paper.
2. Use what you created as a pretest. Set up test-like conditions—a quiet, timed environment—and see how well you do. Avoid looking at your text or notes unless the test is open book.
3. Evaluate your pretest answers against your notes and the text. How did you do?

_____

_____

4. Finally, after you take your instructor's exam, evaluate whether you think this exercise improved your performance on the actual exam. Would you use this technique again when you study for another exam? Why or why not?

_____

_____

- Will you be asked to integrate facts from different areas in order to draw conclusions?

After taking the first exam in the course, you will have a better idea of what to expect.

Create a study plan and schedule

Start your test preparation by deciding what you will study. Go through your notes, texts, related primary sources, and handouts, and set aside materials you don't need. Then prioritize the remaining materials. Your goal is to focus on information that is most likely to be on the exam. Next, use the time-management and goal-setting skills from Chapter 2 to prepare a schedule. Consider all of the relevant factors—your study materials, the number of days until the test, and the time you can study each day.

A checklist like the one in Key 7.1 will help you organize and stay on track as you prepare. Use a checklist to assign specific tasks to particular study times and sessions. Make extra copies of the checklist so that you can fill out a new one each time you have an exam.

Studying for final exams, which usually take place the last week of the semester, is a big commitment that requires careful time management. Your college may schedule study days, sometimes known as "reading period" or "dead days," between the end of classes and the beginning of

Course: _____ Instructor: _____

Date, time, and place of test: _____

Type of test (is it a midterm or a minor quiz?): _____

What the instructor said about the test, including the types of test questions, test length, and how much the test counts toward your final grade:

_____

_____

Topics to be covered on the test, in order of importance (information should also come from your instructor):

1. _____

2. _____

3. _____

4. _____

5. _____

Study schedule, including materials you plan to study (texts, class notes, homework problems, and so forth) and dates you plan to complete each:

MATERIAL   DATE OF COMPLETION

1. _____   _____

2. _____   _____

3. _____   _____

4. _____   _____

5. _____   _____

Materials you are expected to bring to the test (textbook, sourcebook, calculator, etc.):

_____

_____

_____

Special study arrangements (for example, plan study group meetings, ask the instructor for special help, get outside tutoring):

_____

_____

_____

Life-management issues (such as rearranging work hours):

_____

_____

_____

Source: Adapted from Ron Fry, "*Ace" Any Test,* 3rd ed. Franklin Lakes. NJ: Career Press, 1996, pp. 123–24.

finals. Lasting from a day or two to several weeks, these days give you uninterrupted hours to prepare for exams and finish papers.

End-of-year studying often requires flexibility. For example, instead of working at the library during this period, students at the University of Texas at Austin are often seen at Baron Springs, a spring-fed pool near campus. Anna Leeker and Jillian Adams chose this site to study Biology because of the beautiful surroundings—and because they had little choice. "We heard that the libraries are packed, and that students are waiting in line for tables," said Jillian. Both realize that they have to be vigilant about maintaining their focus, no matter where they study.[1]

Prepare through careful review

A thorough review, using analytical and practical strategies like the following, will give you the best shot at remembering the material you study:

Use SQ3R. The reading method you studied in Chapter 5 provides an excellent structure for reviewing your reading materials.

- *Surveying* gives you an overview of topics.
- *Questioning* helps you focus on important ideas and determine the meaning.
- *Reading* (or, in this case, rereading) reminds you of concepts and supporting information.
- *Reciting* helps to anchor the concepts in your head.
- *Reviewing,* such as quizzing yourself on the Q-stage questions, summarizing highlighted sections, making key-concept flash cards, and outlining chapters, helps solidify learning.

Review your notes. Use the following techniques to review your notes before an exam:

- Time your reviews carefully. Review notes for the first time within a day of the lecture, if you can, and then review again closer to the test day.
  - Mark up. Reread your notes, filling in missing information, clarifying points, writing out abbreviations, and highlighting key ideas

> Learning is what most adults will do for a living in the 21st century.
>
> **BOB PERELMAN**

- Organize. Consider adding headings and subheadings to your notes to clarify the structure of the information. Rewrite your notes using a different organizing structure—for example, an outline if you originally used a think link.
  - Summarize. Evaluate which ideas and examples are most important, then rewrite your notes in shortened form. Summarize your notes in writing or with a summary think link. Try summarizing from memory as a self-test.

Take a pretest

Use end-of-chapter text questions to create your own pretest. If your course doesn't have an assigned text, develop questions from your notes and assigned outside readings. Old homework problems will also help target areas you need to work on. Choose questions that are likely to be covered, then answer them under test-like conditions—in a quiet place, with no books or notes to help you (unless the exam is open book), and with a clock to tell you when to quit.

The same test-preparation skills you learn in college will help you do well on standardized tests for graduate school. Sharon Smith describes how students in her preparatory program used practice tests and other techniques to help boost their scores on the Medical College Admission Test (MCAT). They "started with un-timed practices in order to work on accuracy, and timed practices were incorporated as the semester progressed. Everyone tried to finish the tests/passages in the allotted time, and, at the end of each practice session, go over answer choices to understand why they are correct or incorrect." During spring semester they were "given mock exams, and it was important to treat the mock MCAT as if it were the real exam. This gave the best assessment of performance on test day."[2]

Prepare physically

Most tests ask you to work at your best under pressure. A good night's sleep will leave you rested and alert and improve your ability to remember the material you studied the night before. Eating a light, well-balanced meal is also important. When time is short, grab a quick-energy snack such as a banana, orange juice, or a granola bar. For more ideas on getting adequate sleep and eating a balanced diet, look ahead to the material on Personal Wellness (Chapter 9).

Make the most of last-minute studying

Cramming—studying intensively and around the clock right before an exam—often results in information going into your head and popping right back out shortly after the exam is over. If learning is your goal, cramming is not a good idea. The reality, however, is that nearly every student crams during college, especially during midterms and finals. Use these hints to make the most of this intensive study time:

- Review your flash cards. If you use flash cards, review them one last time.
- Focus on crucial concepts. Resist reviewing notes or texts page by page.
- Create a last-minute study sheet. On a single sheet of paper, write down key facts, definitions, formulas, and so on. If you prefer visual notes, use think links to map out ideas and supporting examples.
- Arrive early. Study the sheet or your flash cards until you are asked to clear your desk.

After your exam, evaluate how cramming affected your recall. Within a few days, you will probably remember very little—a reality that will work against you in advanced courses that build on this knowledge and in careers that require it. Think ahead about how you can start studying earlier to prepare for your next exam.

Whether you cram or not, you may experience anxiety on test day. Many students do. Following are some ideas for how to handle test anxiety when it strikes.

How can you work through *test anxiety?*

TEST ANXIETY

A bad case of nerves that can make it hard to think or to remember.

A certain amount of stress can be a good thing. Your body is alert, and your energy motivates you to do your best. Some students, however, experience incapacitating stress before and during exams, especially midterms and finals.

Test anxiety can cause sweating, nausea, dizziness, headaches, and fatigue. It can reduce your ability to concentrate, make you feel overwhelmed, and cause you to "blank out." As a result, test anxiety often results in lower grades that may not reflect what you really know. Take two steps to minimize your anxiety: Prepare thoroughly and build a positive attitude.

Preparation

The more confident you feel about the material, the better you will perform on test day. In this sense, consider all the preparation and study information in *Keys to Success* as test-anxiety assistance. Also, finding out what to expect on the exam will help you feel more in control. Seek out information about the material that will be covered, the question format, the length of the exam, and the points assigned to each question.

Creating a detailed study plan builds your knowledge as it combats anxiety. Divide the plan into small tasks. As you finish each, you gain an increased sense of accomplishment, confidence, and control.

Attitude

Here are ways to maintain an attitude that will help you succeed.

- **See the test as an opportunity to learn.** Instead of thinking of tests as contests that you either "win" or "lose," think of them as signposts along the way to mastering the material. Learning is far more important than "winning."

- **Understand that tests measure performance, not personal value.** Your grade does not reflect your ability to succeed. Whether you get an A or an F, you are the same person.

- **Appreciate your instructor's purpose.** Your instructors want to help you succeed. Don't hesitate to visit them during office hours and send e-mail questions to clarify material.

- **Seek study partners who challenge you.** Find study partners who can inspire you to do your best. Try to avoid people who are also anxious, because you both may pick up on each other's fears and negativity. (For more on study groups, see Chapter 5.)

- **Set yourself up for success.** Expect progress and success—not failure. Take responsibility for creating success through your work and attitude.
- **Practice relaxation.** When you feel test anxiety mounting, breathe deeply, close your eyes, and visualize positive mental images such as getting a good grade and finishing with time to spare. Try to ease muscle tension—stretch your neck, tighten and then release your muscles.
- **Practice positive self-talk.** Tell yourself that you can do well and that it is normal to feel anxious, particularly before an important exam. As you walk into the testing room, give yourself a pep talk that builds confidence—something like, "I know this stuff, and I'm going to show everyone what I know." Also, slay your perfection monster by telling yourself, "I don't have to get a perfect score."

Students from other cultures may not experience test anxiety in the same way as Americans. Because of cultural differences, U. S. students may experience more anxiety than students from countries, such as England, where group achievement tends to be emphasized more than individual achievement.

When you study in a group, you can compare your information, gain from what others know, and solidify your learning through teaching others.

Test anxiety and the returning student

If you're returning to school after years away, you may wonder how well you will handle exams. To deal with these feelings, focus on what you have learned through life experience, including the ability to handle work and family pressures. Without even knowing it, you have developed the time-management, planning, and communication skills necessary for college success.

In addition, your life experiences will give real meaning to abstract classroom ideas. For example, workplace relationships may help you understand Social Psychology concepts, and refinancing your home mortgage may help you grasp the importance of interest-rate swings—a key concept in economics.

Parents who have to juggle child care with study time can find the challenge especially difficult before a test. Here are some suggestions that might help:

- **Find help.** This is especially important with younger children.
- **Plan activities.** If you have younger children, have a supply of games, books, and videos on hand to use while you study.
- **Explain the time frame.** Tell school-aged children your study schedule and the test date. Plan a reward after your test.

Preparing for an exam sets the stage for taking the exam. You are now ready to focus on methods to help you succeed when the test begins.

Test Preparation

If the topic or format of a test challenges your stronger or weaker intelligences, these tips will help you make the most of your time and ability.

INTELLIGENCE	SUGGESTED STRATEGIES	WHAT WORKS FOR YOU? WRITE NEW IDEAS HERE
Verbal–Linguistic	• Think of and write out questions your instructor may ask on a test. Answer the questions and then try rewriting them in a different format (essay, true/false, and so on). • Underline important words in review questions or practice questions.	
Logical–Mathematical	• Make diagrams of review or practice questions. • Outline the key steps involved in topics on which you may be tested.	
Bodily–Kinesthetic	• Use your voice to review out loud. Recite concepts, terms and definitions, important lists, dates, and so on. • Create a sculpture, model, or skit to depict a tough concept that will be on your test.	
Visual–Spatial	• Create a think link to map out an important topic and its connections to other topics in the material. Study it and redraw it from memory a day before the test. • Make drawings related to possible test topics.	
Interpersonal	• Develop a study group and encourage each other. • In your group, come up with as many possible test questions as you can. Ask each other these questions in an oral exam–type format.	
Intrapersonal	• Brainstorm test questions. Then, come back to them after a break or even a day's time. On your own, take the sample "test" you developed. • Make time to review in a solitary setting.	
Musical	• Play music while you read if it does not distract you. • Study concepts by reciting them to rhythms you create or to music.	
Naturalistic	• Bring your text, lecture notes, and other pertinent information to an outdoor spot that inspires you and helps you to feel confident, and review your material there.	

What *general strategies* can help you succeed on tests?

Even though every test is different, there are general strategies that will help you handle almost all tests, including short-answer and essay exams.

Write down key facts

Before you even look at the test, write down key information—including formulas, rules, and definitions—that you studied recently and that you don't want to forget. Use the back of the question sheet or some scrap paper for your notes. (Be sure your instructor knows that you made these notes after the test began.)

Begin with an overview

Although exam time is precious, spend a few minutes at the start of the test gathering information about the questions—how many there are in each section, what types, and their point values. Then, analyze the situation and think practically to schedule your time. For example, if a two-hour test is divided into two sections of equal point value—an essay section with four questions and a short-answer section with 60 questions—you might spend an hour on the essays (15 minutes per question) and an hour on the short answers (one minute per question).

You may need to take level of difficulty into account as you come up with options for how to parcel out your time. For example, if you think you can get through the short-answer questions in 45 minutes and sense that you'll have a tougher time with the writing section, you can budget an hour and a quarter for the essays.

Read test directions

Reading test directions carefully can save you trouble. For example, although a History test of 100 true/false questions and one essay may look straightforward, the directions may tell you to answer 80 of the 100 questions or that the essay is optional. If the directions indicate that you are penalized for incorrect answers—meaning that you lose points instead of simply not gaining points—avoid guessing unless you're fairly certain.

When you read the directions, you may learn that some questions or sections are weighted more heavily than others. For example, the short-answer questions may be worth 30 points, whereas the essays are worth 70. In this case, it's smart to spend more time on the essays than the short answers. To stay aware of the specifics of the directions, use the practical strategy of circling or underlining key information.

Mark up the questions

Highlight instructions and keywords to avoid careless errors. As you read each question, circle qualifiers such as *always, never, all, none,* and *every,* verbs that communicate specific test instructions, and concepts that are tricky or need special attention.

Take special care on machine-scored tests

Use the correct pencil (usually a number 2) on machine-scored tests, and mark your answer in the proper space, filling the space completely. Periodically, use your practical thinking skills to check the answer number against the question number to make sure they match. If you mark the answer to question 4 in the space for question 5, not only will your response to question 4 be wrong, but your responses to all subsequent questions will be off by a line. To avoid this problem, put a small dot next to any number you skip and plan to return to later.

Neatness counts on these tests because the computer can misread stray pencil marks or partially erased answers. If you mark two answers to a question and partially erase one, the computer will read both responses and charge you with a wrong answer.

While it's tempting to rush through a test to get it over with, taking time to think when you need to will help you be more sure of your answers and may even help you stay calm.

Work from easy to hard

Begin with the easiest questions, and answer them as quickly as you can without sacrificing accuracy. This will boost your confidence and leave more time for questions that require more focus and effort. Mark tough questions as you reach them, and return to them after answering the questions you know.

Watch the clock

Keep track of how much time is left and how you are progressing. Some students are so concerned about time that they rush through the test and have time left over. If this happens to you, spend the remaining time refining and checking your work instead of leaving early. You may be able to correct mistakes, change answers, or add more information to an essay.

Master the art of intelligent guessing

When you are unsure of an answer on a short-answer test, you can leave it blank or guess. As long as you are not penalized for incorrect answers, guessing helps you. "Intelligent guessing," writes Steven Frank, an authority on student studying and test taking, "means taking advantage of what you do know in order to try to figure out what you don't. If you guess intelligently, you have a decent shot at getting the answer right."[3]

When you check your work at the end of the test, use your analytical ability to decide whether you would make the same guesses again. Chances are that you will leave your answers alone, but you may notice something that changes your mind—a qualifier that affects meaning, a miscalculation in a math problem. Or you may recall information that you drew a blank on the first time around.

Maintain academic integrity

Cheating as a strategy to pass a test or get a better grade robs you of the opportunity to learn the material, which, ultimately, is your loss. Cheating also jeopardizes your future if you are caught. You may be seriously reprimanded—or even expelled—if you violate your school's code of academic integrity.

Now that you have explored these general strategies, you can use what you've learned to address specific types of test questions.

How can you master *different types* of test questions?

Every type of test question has a different way of finding out how much you know about a subject. For objective questions, you choose or write a short answer, often making a selection from a limited number of choices. Multiple-choice, fill-in-the-blank, matching, and true/false questions fall into this category. Subjective questions require you to plan, organize, draft, and refine a response. All essay questions are subjective. In general, subjective questions tap your creative abilities more than short-answer questions do.

Key 7.2 shows samples of real test questions from Western Civilization, Macroeconomics, Spanish, and Biology college texts published by Pearson Education. Included are multiple-choice, true/false, fill-in-the-blank, matching, and essay questions, including a short-answer essay. Seeing these questions firsthand will help you feel more comfortable with testing formats and question types when you take your first exams.

Multiple-choice questions

Multiple-choice questions are the most popular type of question on standardized tests. The following analytical and practical strategies can help you answer them:

Carefully read the directions. Directions can be tricky. For example, whereas most test items ask for a single correct answer, some give you the option of marking several choices that are correct. For some tests, you might be required to answer only a certain number of questions.

Read each question thoroughly. Then look at the choices, and try to choose an answer. This strategy makes it less likely that you'll get confused.

OBJECTIVE QUESTIONS

Short-answer questions that test your ability to recall, compare, and contrast information and to choose the right answer from a limited number of choices.

SUBJECTIVE QUESTIONS

Essay questions that require you to express your answer in terms of your own personal knowledge and perspective.

From Chapter 29, "The End of Imperialism," in *Western Civilization: A Social and Cultural History*, 2nd edition.[4]

■ **MULTIPLE-CHOICE QUESTION**

India's first leader after independence was:

A. Gandhi   B. Bose   C. Nehru   D. Sukharno   *(answer: C)*

■ **FILL-IN-THE-BLANK QUESTION**

East Pakistan became the country of _____ in 1971.

A. Burma   B. East India   C. Sukharno   D. Bangladesh   *(answer: D)*

■ **TRUE/FALSE QUESTION**

The United States initially supported Vietnamese independence.   T   F   *(answer: false)*

■ **ESSAY QUESTION**

Answer one of the following:

1. What led to Irish independence? What conflicts continued to exist after independence?
2. How did Gandhi work to rid India of British control? What methods did he use?

From Chapter 6, "Unemployment and Inflation," in *Macroeconomics: Principles and Tools*, 3rd edition.[5]

■ **MULTIPLE-CHOICE QUESTION**

If the labor force is 250,000 and the total population 16 years of age or older is 300,000, the labor-force participation rate is

A. 79.5%   B. 83.3%   C. 75.6%   D. 80.9%   *(answer: B)*

■ **FILL-IN-THE-BLANK QUESTION**

Mike has just graduated from college and is now looking for a job, but has not yet found one. This causes the employment rate to _____ and the labor-force participation rate to _____.

A. increase; decrease   C. stay the same; stay the same

B. increase; increase   D. increase; stay the same   *(answer: C)*

■ **TRUE/FALSE QUESTION**

The Consumer Price Index somewhat overstates changes in the cost of living because it does not allow for substitutions that consumers might make in response to price changes.   T   F   *(answer: true)*

■ **SHORT-ANSWER ESSAY QUESTION**

During a press conference, the Secretary of Employment notes that the unemployment rate is 7.0%. As a political opponent, how might you criticize this figure as an underestimate? In rebuttal, how might the Secretary argue that the reported rate is an overestimate of unemployment?

(Possible answer: The unemployment rate given by the secretary might be considered an underestimate because discouraged workers, who have given up the job search in frustration, are not counted as unemployed. In addition, full-time workers may have been forced to work part-time. In rebuttal, the secretary might note that a portion of the unemployed have voluntarily left their jobs. Most workers are unemployed only briefly and leave the ranks of the unemployed by gaining better jobs than they had previously held.)

Continued.

From *Mosaicos: Spanish as a World Language*, 3rd edition.[6]

■ **MATCHING QUESTION**

You are learning new words and your teacher asks you to think of an object similar to or related to the words he says. His words are listed below. Next to each word, write a related word from the list below.

el reloj	el cuaderno	el pupitre	una computadora
el televisor	la tiza	el lápiz	la mochila

1. el escritorio _____

2. el bolígrafo _____

3. la videocasetera _____

4. la pizarra _____

5. el libro _____

(answers: 1. el pupitre; 2. el lápis; 3. el televisor; 4. la tiza; 5. el cuaderno)

■ **ESSAY QUESTION**

Your mother always worries about you and wants to know what you are doing with your time in Granada. Write a short letter to her describing your experience in Spain. In your letter, you should address the following points:

1. What classes you take

2. When and where you study

3. How long you study every day

4. What you do with your time (mention three activities)

5. Where you go during your free time (mention two places)

From Chapter 13, "DNA Structure and Replication," in *Biology: A Guide to the Natural World*, 2nd edition.[7]

■ **MULTIPLE-CHOICE QUESTION**

What units are bonded together to make a strand of DNA?

A. chromatids   B. cells   C. enzymes   D. nucleotides   E. proteins   *(answer: D)*

■ **TRUE/FALSE QUESTION**

Errors never occur in DNA replication, because the DNA polymerases edit out mistakes.   T   F

(answer: false)

■ **FILL-IN-THE-BLANK QUESTION**

In a normal DNA molecule, adenine always pairs with _____ and cytosine always pairs with _____.

(answers: thymine; guanine)

■ **MATCHING QUESTION**

Match the scientist and the approximate time frames (decades of their work) with their achievements.

Column 1

____ 1. Modeled the molecular structure of DNA

____ 2. Generated X-ray crystallography images of DNA

____ 3. Correlated the production of one enzyme with one gene

Column 2

A. George Beadle and Edward Tatum, 1930s and 1940s

B. James Watson and Francis Crick, 1950s

C. Rosalind Franklin and Maurice Wilkins, 1950s

(answers: 1–B; 2–C; 3–A)

Underline keywords and phrases. If the question is complicated, try to break it down into small sections that are easy to understand.

Pay attention to words that could throw you off. For example, it is easy to overlook negatives in a question ("Which of the following is not . . . ").

If you don't know the answer, eliminate answers that you know or suspect are wrong. If you can leave yourself with two possible answers, you will have a 50–50 chance of making the right choice. To narrow down, ask questions about each of the choices:

- Is the choice accurate on its own terms? If there's an error in the choice—for example, a term that is incorrectly defined—the answer is wrong.

- Is the choice relevant? An answer may be accurate, but unrelated to the question.

- Are there any qualifiers? Absolute qualifiers, like *always, never, all, none,* or *every,* often signal an exception that makes a choice incorrect. For example, the statement "Normal children always begin talking before the age of two" is untrue (most normal children begin talking before age two, but some start later). Analysis has shown that choices containing conservative qualifiers like *often, most, rarely,* or *may sometimes be* are often correct.

- Do the choices give clues? Does a puzzling word remind you of a word you know? Does any part of an unfamiliar word—its prefix, suffix, or root—ring a bell?

Make an educated guess by looking for patterns. Certain patterns tend to appear in multiple-choice questions and may help you make smart guesses. Although these patterns may not apply to the specific test questions you encounter, they're important to keep in mind. Experts advise you to:

- consider the possibility that a choice that is *more general* than the others is the right answer.

  - consider the possibility that a choice that is *longer* than the others is the right answer.

  - look for a choice that has a *middle value in a range* (the range can be from small to large or from old to recent). It is likely to be the right answer.

  - look for two choices that have *similar meanings.* One of these answers is probably correct.

  - look for answers that *agree grammatically* with the question. For example, a fill-in-the-blank question that has an *a* or *an* before the blank gives you a clue to the correct answer.

Make sure you read every word of every answer. Instructors have been known to include answers that are almost right, except for a single word. Focus especially on qualifying words such as *always, never, tend to, most, often,* and *frequently.*

When questions are linked to a reading passage, read the questions first. This will help you focus on the information you need to answer the questions.

Here are some examples of the kinds of multiple-choice questions you might encounter in an Introduction to Psychology course[8] (the correct answer follows each question):

1. Arnold is at the company party and has had too much to drink. He releases all of his pent-up aggression by yelling at his boss, who promptly fires him. Arnold normally would not have yelled at his boss, but after drinking heavily he yelled because_____.

    A. parties are places where employees are supposed to be able to "loosen up"

    B. alcohol is a stimulant

    C. alcohol makes people less concerned with the negative consequences of their behavior

    D. alcohol inhibits brain centers that control the perception of loudness

(The correct answer is C)

2. Which of the following has not been shown to be a probable cause of or influence in the development of alcoholism in our society?

    A. intelligence   C. personality

    B. culture   D. genetic vulnerability

(The correct answer is A)

3. Geraldine is a heavy coffee drinker who has become addicted to caffeine. If she completely ceases her intake of caffeine over the next few days, she is likely to experience each of the following EXCEPT_____.

    A. depression   C. insomnia

    B. lethargy   D. headaches

(The correct answer is C)

True/false questions

Read true/false questions carefully to evaluate what they are asking. If you're stumped, guess (unless you're penalized for wrong answers).

Look for qualifiers in true/false questions—such as *all, only,* and *always* (the absolutes that often make a statement false) and *generally, often, usually,* and *sometimes* (the conservatives that often make a statement true)—that can turn a statement that would otherwise be true into one that is false or vice versa. For example, "The grammar rule 'I before E except after C' is *always* true" is false, whereas "The grammar rule 'I before E except after C' is *usually* true" is true. The qualifier makes the difference.

Matching questions

Matching questions ask you to match the terms in one list with the terms in another list, according to the directions. For example, the directions may tell you to match a communicable disease with the germ that usually causes it. The following practical strategies will help you handle these questions.

Make sure you understand the directions. The directions tell you whether each answer can be used only once or more than once.

Work from the column with the longest entries. The left-hand column usually contains terms to be defined or questions to be answered, whereas the right-hand column contains definitions or answers. As a result, entries in the right-hand column are usually longer than those on the left. Reading the items on the right only once each will save time as you work to match them with the shorter phrases on the left.

Start with the matches you know. On your first run-through, mark these matches with a penciled line, waiting to finalize your choices after you've completed all the items. Keep in mind that if you can use an answer only once, you may have to change answers if you reconsider any of your original choices.

Finally, tackle the matches you're not sure of. On your next run-through, focus on the more difficult matches. Look for clues and relationships you might not have considered.

If one or more phrases seem to have no correct answer, look back at your easy matches to be sure that you did not jump too quickly. Consider the possibility that one of your sure-thing answers is wrong.

Fill-in-the-blank questions

Fill-in-the-blank questions, also known as sentence completion questions, ask you to supply one or more words or phrases with missing information that completes the sentence. These strategies will help you make successful choices.

Be logical. Insert your answer, then reread the sentence from beginning to end to be sure it is factually and grammatically correct and makes sense.

Note the length and number of the blanks. These are important clues but not absolute guideposts. If two blanks appear right after one another, the instructor is probably looking for a two-word answer. If a blank is longer than usual, the correct response may require additional space. However, if you are certain of an answer that doesn't seem to fit the blanks, trust your knowledge and instincts.

Pay attention to how blanks are separated. If there is more than one blank in a sentence and the blanks are widely separated, treat each one separately. Answering each as if it were a separate sentence-completion question increases the likelihood that you will get at least one answer correct. Here is an example:

> When Toni Morrison was awarded the _____ Prize for Literature, she was a professor at _____ University.
> *(Answer: Morrison received the Nobel Prize and is a professor at Princeton University.)*

Think out of the box. If you can think of more than one correct answer, put them both down. Your instructor may be impressed by your assertiveness and creativity.

If you are uncertain of an answer, make an educated guess. Have faith that after hours of studying, the correct answer is somewhere in your subconscious mind and that your guess is not completely random.

Here are examples of fill-in-the-blank questions you might encounter in an Introduction to Astronomy course[10] (correct answers follow questions):

1. A _____ is a collection of hundreds of billions of stars. *(galaxy)*

2. Rotation is the term used to describe the motion of a body around some _____. *(axis)*

3. The solar day is measured relative to the Sun; the sidereal day is measured relative to the _____. *(stars)*

4. On December 21, known as the _____ _____, the Sun is at its _____ _____. *(winter solstice; southernmost point)*

Essay questions

An essay question allows you to express your knowledge and views more extensively than a short-answer question. With this freedom comes the challenge to organize and express that knowledge clearly.

The following steps will help improve your responses to essay questions. The process is basically a less extensive version of the writing process—you plan, draft, revise, and edit your response. The primary differences here are that you are writing under time pressure and that you are working from memory.

1. **Start by reading the questions.** Decide which to tackle (if there's a choice). Use your analytical ability to focus on what each question is asking. Then engage practical strategies as you read the directions carefully and do everything asked.

Some essay questions may contain more than one part, so it is important to budget your time. For example, if you have one hour to answer three question sections, you might budget 20 minutes for each section, and break that down into writing stages (3 minutes for planning, 15 minutes for drafting, 2 minutes for revising and editing).

2. **Watch for action verbs.** Certain verbs can help you figure out how to think. Key 7.3 explains some words commonly used in essay questions. Underline these words as you read and use them to guide your writing.

3. **Plan.** Use your creative thinking skills to brainstorm ideas and examples. Create an informal outline or a think link to map your ideas and list supporting examples.

Focus on action verbs on essay tests.

key
7.3

Analyze—Break into parts and discuss each part separately.	**Explain**—Make the meaning of something clear, often by making analogies or giving examples.
Compare—Explain similarities and differences.	**Illustrate**—Supply examples.
Contrast—Distinguish between items being compared by focusing on differences.	**Interpret**—Explain your personal view of facts and ideas and how they relate to one another.
Criticize—Evaluate the positive and negative effects of what is being discussed.	**Outline**—Organize and present the main examples of an idea or sub-ideas.
Define—State the essential quality or meaning. Give the common idea.	**Prove**—Use evidence and argument to show that something is true, usually by showing cause and effect or giving examples that fit the idea to be proven.
Describe—Visualize and give information that paints a complete picture.	**Review**—Provide an overview of ideas and establish their merits and features.
Discuss—Examine in a complete and detailed way, usually by connecting ideas to examples.	**State**—Explain clearly, simply, and concisely, being sure that each word gives the image you want.
Enumerate/List/Identify—Recall and specify items in the form of a list.	**Summarize**—Give the important ideas in brief.
Evaluate—Give your opinion about the value or worth of something, usually by weighing positive and negative effects, and justify your conclusion.	**Trace**—Present a history of the way something developed, often by showing cause and effect.

4. **Draft.** Start with a thesis statement that states clearly what your essay will say. Then, devote one or more paragraphs to the main points in your outline. Back up the general statement that starts each paragraph with evidence in the form of examples, statistics, and so on. Use simple, clear language, and look back at your outline to make sure you cover everything. Wrap it up with a short, pointed conclusion. Since you probably won't have time for redrafting, try to be as complete and organized as possible.

5. **Revise.** Make sure you answer the question completely and include all of your points. Look for ideas you left out, general statements that need more support, paragraphs that don't hold together well, unnecessary material, and confusing sentences. Fix problems by adding new material in the margins and crossing out what you don't need. When adding material, you can indicate with an arrow where it fits or note that inserts can

WRITE TO THE VERB

Hone your ability to read and follow essay instructions accurately.

Focusing on the action verbs in essay test instructions can mean the difference between giving instructors what they want and answering off the mark.

get analytical!

- Start by choosing a topic you learned about in this text—for example, the concept of successful intelligence or internal and external barriers to listening. Write your topic here:

  _____

  _____

- Put yourself in the role of instructor. Write an essay question on this topic, using one of the action verbs in Key 7.3 to frame the question. For example, "List the three aspects of successful intelligence," or "Analyze the classroom-based challenges associated with internal barriers to listening."

  _____

  _____

- Now choose three other action verbs from Key 7.3. Use each one to rewrite your original question.

  1. _____

  2. _____

  3. _____

- Finally, analyze how each new verb changes the focus of the essay.

  1. _____

     _____

  2. _____

     _____

  3. _____

be found on separate pages. If you have more than one insert, label each to avoid confusion (e.g., Insert #1, Insert #2, etc.).

6. **Edit.** Check for mistakes in grammar, spelling, punctuation, and usage. No matter your topic, being technically correct in your writing makes your work more impressive.

Neatness is a crucial factor in essay writing. No matter how good your ideas are, if your instructor can't read them, your grade will suffer. If your handwriting is a problem, try printing your answers, skipping every other line, and writing on only one side of the paper. Students with illegible handwriting might ask to take the test on a laptop computer.

To answer the third essay question from the box below, one student created the planning outline shown in Key 7.4. Notice how abbreviations and shorthand help the student write quickly. It is much faster to write "Role of BL in IC" than "Role of Body Language in Interpersonal Communication" (see Chapter 6 for shorthand strategies). Key 7.5 shows the student's essay, including the word changes and inserts she made while revising the draft.

Here are some examples of essay questions you might encounter in an Interpersonal Communication course. In each case, notice the action verbs from Key 7.3.

1. Summarize the role of the self-concept as a key to interpersonal relationships and communication.

2. Explain how internal and external noise affects the ability to listen effectively.

3. Describe three ways that body language affects interpersonal communication.

Create an informal outline during essay tests.

7.4

Roles of BL in IC

1. To contradict or reinforce words

   —e.g., friend says "I'm fine"

2. To add shades of meaning

   —saying the same sentence in 3 diff. ways

3. To make lasting 1st impression

   —impact of nv cues and voice tone greater than words

   —we assume things abt person based on posture, eye contact, etc.

Response to an essay question with revision marks.

7.5

QUESTION: Describe three ways that body language affects interpersonal communication.

Body language plays an important role in interpersonal communication and helps

, especially when
you meet someone
for the first time
shape the impression you make. Two of the most important functions of body

language are to contradict and reinforce verbal statements. When body

delivered
language contradicts verbal language, the message ~~conveyed~~ by the body is

dominant. For example, if a friend tells you that she is feeling "fine," but her

her eye contact
minimal,
posture is slumped, and her facial expression troubled, you have every reason to

wonder whether she is telling the truth. If the same friend tells you that

she is feeling fine and is smiling, walking with a bounce in her step, and has

accurately reflecting
and reinforcing her
words.
direct eye contact, her body language is ~~telling the truth.~~

The nonverbal cues that make up body language also have the power to add

shades of meaning. Consider this statement: "This is the best idea I've heard

all day." If you were to say this three different ways—in a loud voice while

standing up; quietly while sitting with arms and legs crossed and

maintaining
looking away; and while ~~maintening~~ eye contact and taking the receiver's

hand—you might send three different messages.

Although first
impressions emerge
from a combination
of nonverbal cues,
tone of voice, and
choice of words,
nonverbal elements
(cues and tone)
usually come across
first and strongest.
Finally, the impact of nonverbal cues can be greatest when you meet

someone for the first time. When you meet someone, you tend to make

assumptions based on nonverbal behavior such as posture, eye contact, gestures,

and speed and style of movement.

crucial
In summary, nonverbal communication plays a ~~crucial~~ role in interpersonal

relationships. It has the power to send an accurate message that may

belie
~~destroy~~ the speaker's words, offer shades of meaning, and set the tone

of a first meeting.

How can you learn from *test mistakes?*

The purpose of a test is to see how much you know, not merely to get a grade. Use the following strategies to analyze and learn from your mistakes so that you avoid repeating them.

Try to identify patterns in your mistakes. Look for the following:

- **Careless errors.** In your rush to finish, did you misread the question or directions, blacken the wrong box on the answer sheet, skip a question, write illegibly?
- **Conceptual or factual errors.** Did you misunderstand a concept? Did you fail to master facts or concepts? Did you skip part of the text or miss classes in which ideas were covered?

Rework the questions you got wrong. Based on instructor feedback, try to rewrite an essay, recalculate a math problem from the original question, or redo questions following a reading selection. If you discover a pattern of careless errors, redouble your efforts to be more careful and save time to double-check your work.

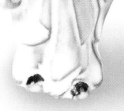

> Our greatest glory is not in never falling, but in rising every time we fall.
>
> **CONFUCIUS**

After reviewing your mistakes, fill in your knowledge gaps. If you made mistakes because of a lack of understanding, develop a plan to learn the material. Solidifying your knowledge can help you on future exams and in life situations that involve the subject you're studying.

Talk to your instructors. Talk with your instructor about your specific mistakes on short-answer questions or about a weak essay. If you are not sure why you were marked down on an essay, ask what you could have done to improve your grade. Take advantage of this opportunity to determine how to do better on the next exam.

If you fail a test, don't throw it away. Use it as a way to review material that you had trouble with or didn't know as well as you should have. You might also want to keep it as a reminder that you can improve if you have the will to succeed. When you compare a failure to later successes, you'll see how far you've come.

The willingness to learn from test mistakes is critical for all students, including those with reading-related learning disabilities. When CAST researcher Roxanne Ruzic examined how students who are learning disabled prepare for tests, she found that successful students took advantage of instructor feedback; they applied what they learned from their mistakes on one test to their preparation for others. Students who dismissed this feedback did not excel.

Jack is a case in point, as Ruzic explains: "When Jack received his graded midterm exam [in Introduction to International Business], he discounted some of what the instructor wrote in his blue book, claiming she was wrong, rather than trying to figure out how to ensure that he knew

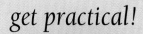

LEARN FROM YOUR MISTAKES

Examine what went wrong on a recent exam to build knowledge for next time.

Look at an exam on which your performance fell short of expectations. If possible, choose one that contains different types of objective and subjective questions. With the test and answer sheet in hand, use your analytical and practical thinking skills to answer the following questions:

- Identify the types of questions on which you got the most correct answers (for example, matching, essay, multiple choice).

  _____

- Identify the types of questions on which you made the greatest number of errors.

  _____

- Analyze your errors to identify patterns—for example, did you misread test instructions, or did you ignore qualifiers that changed the questions' meanings? What did you find?

  _____

  _____

- Finally, what are two practical actions you are committed to take during your next exam to avoid the same problems?

  Action 1: _____

  Action 2: _____

the material and she knew that he knew it. While Jack did not do as well on the midterm as he would have liked, he used the same study techniques to prepare for the final exam as he had used for the midterm. Had Jack talked more to other people (including instructors) regularly to assess his understanding of content and expectations and worked in study-groups, he would have been much more successful in his courses." Jack's final course grade was a C+—not where he could have been had he made the effort to learn from earlier setbacks.[11]

Sine qua non

Although Latin is no longer spoken and is considered a "dead" language, it plays an important role in modern English, since many English words and phrases have Latin roots. The Latin phrase *sine qua non* (pronounced sihn-ay kwa nahn) means, literally, "without which not." In other words, a sine qua non is "an absolutely indispensable or essential thing."

Think of learning as the sine qua non of test taking. When you have worked hard to learn, review, and retain information, you will be well prepared for tests, no matter what form they take. Focus on knowledge to transform test taking from an intimidating challenge into an opportunity to demonstrate what you know.

FOR COLLEGE, CAREER, AND LIFE SUCCESS

Developing Successful Intelligence

PUTTING IT ALL TOGETHER

Prepare effectively for tests. Take a detailed look at your performance on and preparation for a recent test.

Step 1. Think it through: *Analyze how you did.* Were you pleased or disappointed with your performance and grade? Why?

_____

_____

Thinking about your performance, look at the potential problems listed below. Circle any that you feel were a factor in this exam. Fill in the empty spaces with any key problems not listed.

- Incomplete preparation
- Fatigue
- Feeling rushed during the test
- Shaky understanding of concepts
- Poor guessing techniques

- Feeling confused about directions
- Test anxiety
- _____
- _____
- _____

If you circled any problems, think about why you made mistakes (if it was an objective exam) or why you didn't score well (if it was an essay exam).

Step 2. Think out of the box: *Be creative about test-preparation strategies.* If you had absolutely no restrictions on time or on access to materials, how would you have prepared for this test?

create your future

Describe briefly what your plan would be and how it would minimize any problems you encountered.

_____

_____

_____

Now think back to your actual preparation for this test. Describe techniques you used and note time
spent.

_____

_____

_____

How does what you would like to do differ from what you actually did?

_____

_____

Step 3. Make it happen: *Improve preparation for the future.* Think about
the practical actions you will take the next time you face a similar test.

Actions I took this time, but do not intend to take next time:

_____

_____

Actions I did not take this time, but intend to take next time:

_____

_____

Team Building

COLLABORATIVE SOLUTIONS

Test study group. Form a study group with two or three other students.
When your instructor announces the next exam, ask each study group
member to record everything he or she does to prepare for the exam,
including:

- learning what to expect on the test (topics and material that will be
  covered, types of questions that will be asked)
- examining old tests
- creating and following a study schedule and checklist
- using SQ3R to review material
- taking a pretest
- getting a good night's sleep before the exam
- doing last-minute cramming
- mastering general test-taking strategies
- mastering test-taking strategies for specific types of test questions
  (multiple choice, true/false, matching, fill in the blank, essay)

After the exam, come together to compare preparation strategies. What important differences can you identify in the routines followed by group members? How did learning styles play a role in those differences? How do you suspect that different routines affected test performance and outcome? On a separate piece of paper, for your own reference, write down what you learned from the test-preparation habits of your study mates that may help you as you prepare for upcoming exams.

Writing

DISCOVERY THROUGH JOURNALING

Record your thoughts on a separate piece of paper or in a journal.

Test anxiety. Do you experience test anxiety? Describe how tests generally make you feel (you might include an example of a specific test situation and what happened). Identify your specific test-taking fears, and brainstorm ideas for how to overcome fears and self-defeating behaviors.

Career Portfolio

PLAN FOR SUCCESS

Complete the following in your electronic portfolio or on separate sheets of paper.

On-the-job testing. Depending on what careers you are considering, you may encounter one or more tests throughout your career. Some are for entry into the field (e.g., medical boards); some test your proficiency on particular equipment (e.g., a proficiency test on Microsoft Word); some move you to the next level of employment (e.g., a technical certification test to become a certified actuary). Choose one career you are thinking about and investigate what tests are involved as you advance through different stages of the field. Be sure to look for tests in any of the areas described above. Write down everything you find out about each test involved. For example:

- what it tests you on
- when, in the course of pursuing this career, you would need to take the test
- what preparation is necessary for the test (including course work)
- whether the test needs to be retaken at any time (e.g., airline pilots usually need to be recertified every few years)

Finally, see if you can review any of the tests you will face if you pursue this career. For example, if your career choice requires proficiency on a specific computer program, your college's career or computer center may have the test available.

SUGGESTED READINGS

Browning, William G., Ph.D. *Cliffs Memory Power for Exams*. Lincoln, NE: CliffsNotes Inc., 1990.

Frank, Steven. *Test Taking Secrets: Study Better, Test Smarter, and Get Great Grades*. Holbrook, MA: Adams Media Corporation, 1998.

Fry, Ron. *"Ace" Any Test*, 5th ed. Florence, KY: Thomson Delmar Learning, 2004.

Hamilton, Dawn. *Passing Exams: A Guide for Maximum Success and Minimum Stress*. New York: Continuum International, 2003.

Kesselman-Turkel, Judy and Franklynn Peterson. *Test Taking Strategies*. Madison, WI: University of Wisconsin Press, 2004.

Luckie, William R. and Wood Smethurst. *Study Power: Study Skills to Improve Your Learning and Your Grades*. Cambridge, MA: Brookline Books, 1997.

Meyers, Judith N. *Secrets of Taking Any Test: Learn the Techniques Successful Test-Takers Know*. New York: Learning Express, July 2000.

INTERNET RESOURCES

Prentice Hall Student Success SuperSite (testing tips in study skills section): www.prenhall.com/success

Florida State University (list of sites offering information on test-taking skills): http://osi.fsu.edu/hot/testtaking/skills.htm

Test Taking Tips.com (test taking and study skills): www.testtakingtips.com

University of North Dakota (study strategies home page): www.d.umn.edu/student/loon/acad/strat/

ENDNOTES

1. Ben Gose, "Notes from Academe: Living It Up on the Dead Days," *The Chronicle of Higher Education*, June 7, 2002 [on-line]. Available: http://chronicle.com/weekly/v48/i39/39a04801.htm (April 2004).

2. "Students Speak," MEDPREP: Medical/Dental Education Preparatory Program, Southern Illinois University School of Medicine [on-line]. Available: www.som.siu.edu/medprep/students_speak.html (March 2004).

3. Steven Frank, *The Everything Study Book*. Holbrook, MA: Adams Media Corporation, 1996, p. 208.

4. King, Margaret L., *Instructor's Manual with Tests for Western Civilization: A Social & Cultural History*, 2nd Edition, ©2003. Reprinted by permission of Pearson Education, Inc., Upper Saddle River, NJ.

5. O'Sullivan, Arthur, *Test Item File #2 for Macroeconomics: Principles & Tools*, 3rd Edition, ©2003. Reprinted by permission of Pearson Education, Inc., Upper Saddle River, NJ.

6. Castells, Matilde Olivella, *Testing Program for Mosaicos: Spanish as a World Language*, 3rd Edition, ©2002. Reprinted by permission of Pearson Education, Inc., Upper Saddle River, NJ.

7. Krogh, David, *Test Item File for Biology: A Guide to the Natural World*, 2nd Edition, ©2002. Reprinted by permission of Pearson Education, Inc., Upper Saddle River, NJ.

8. Piggrem, Gary W.; Morris, Charles G., *Test Item File for Understanding Psychology*, 3rd Edition, ©1996. Reprinted by permission of Pearson Education, Inc., Upper Saddle River, NJ.

9. Ibid.

10. Chaisson, Eric; McMillan, Steve, *Astronomy Today*, 3rd Edition, ©1999. Reprinted by permission of Pearson Education, Inc., Upper Saddle River, NJ.

11. Roxanne Ruzic, "Lessons for Everyone: How Students with Reading-Related Learning Disabilities Survive and Excel in College Courses with Heavy Reading Requirements," Paper presented at the Annual Meeting of the American Educational Research Association, April 13, 2001 [on-line]. Available: www.cast.org/ud1/index.cfm?i=1540 (March 2004).

IN THIS CHAPTER . . .

*you will explore answers
to the following questions:*

Relating to Others
COMMUNICATING IN A DIVERSE WORLD

Among your most meaningful, life-changing experiences at college will be those that take you out of your "comfort zone" and force you to question your thinking and even your basic beliefs. Encountering the diversity of the people around you can inspire this kind of questioning. As you read this chapter, you will explore how accepting differences and rejecting prejudice can lead to respect for others and strong teamwork skills, both of which are key ingredients for success in school and beyond.

In this chapter, you will investigate how analytical, creative, and practical abilities can help you build the cultural competence that will allow you to relate successfully to others. You will explore how to communicate effectively, investigating different communication styles and methods for handling conflict. Finally, you will look at how your personal relationships can inspire you and enhance your college and life experience.

On the following page, read how student Nisar Nikzad is seeking to connect to a new community while staying in touch with his own culture.

- **How do you experience diversity?**
- **How can you develop cultural competence?**
- **How can minority students make the most of college?**
- **How can you communicate effectively?**
- **How do you make the most of personal relationships?**

How can I adjust to a new society and connect to my college fellows and people of my community?

I came to the United States a little over two and a half years ago from Afghanistan. I am a Biology student aiming to go to medical school. My goal is to join the team of doctors called "Doctors Without Borders" and travel to underdeveloped countries where I can help people in need of medical services.

I am sociable and like hanging out with friends from a variety of different backgrounds. However, I often feel that in order to connect with American students on my campus, I need to do what they do—even when it comes to partying. I learn better when I am connecting to people, but I want to be myself and not to have to change to meet others' expectations. I like learning new cultures but still want to keep mine and this makes it tougher for me to adjust well.

How can I connect to my community without losing myself and my culture?

Nisar Nikzad
Community College of Denver
Denver, Colorado

Find a way to incorporate both your home country culture and U. S. culture into who you are.

The challenge you are facing—to adapt and to integrate—is called *acculturation* and it is common, not only for students, but for all those who come to a new country. I faced a similar situation when I came to the United States from Iran to go to college. You already possess three characteristics essential to successful acculturation. First, you are aware of cultural differences and you are able to approach them without negative judgment. Second, you are also aware of your own culture and have a desire to preserve it. Third, you have recognized that adaptation does not happen overnight, and you are willing to put in the work and resolve conflicts.

Given that your home country culture and your new U. S. culture are both important to you, your goal is to bring the two together and create a new culture of sorts for yourself. The first step is to continue learning about the United States. Although it may appear that there is a uniform culture among American college students, there actually are considerable differences and diversity in beliefs, values, and behaviors. Because Americans are used to seeing different people around us, we tend to be more open to other cultures. Additionally, although we each may have a dominant culture, we are all part of many different cultures that make up who we are. You are Afghani, American, male, part of the medical profession (or planning to be), and so forth.

The other thing you can do to help your acculturation is to be an ambassador about your values and your way of life. Talk to your friends here about your country, religion, language, school, family, and so forth. You are likely to find them eager to learn, although sometimes their early stereotypes and assumptions may be simplistic. Learning about your culture will increase the richness of everyone's cultural context.

Don't give up your identity. You will change as a result of your experiences; you are likely to feel more "American," but you will also change those around you and they will become a little more "Afghani." This give-and-take will enrich both you and those around you and allow you to be successful.

Afsaneh Nahavandi Professor of Management and Director of Freshman Programs Arizona State University West

How do you experience *diversity*?

A century ago it was possible to live an entire lifetime knowing no one from a culture different from your own. Not so today. With waves of new immigrants continually arriving, just as they have done throughout U.S. history, American society consists of people from a multitude of countries and cultural backgrounds.

The speed of cultural change is dramatic: In the 2000 census, American citizens described themselves in terms of 63 different racial categories, compared with only 5 in 1990.[1] Technology and economic interdependence add to our growing cultural awareness. Cable television, the Internet, and the global marketplace link people from all over the world in ways that were unimaginable less than a decade ago. You have unprecedented access to information about what people do and how they live in nearly every corner of the globe.

Diversity affects everyone

As you read in Chapter 1, diversity exists both within each person and among all people:

- **The diversity within each person.** Your physical being, personality, learning style, talents and skills, and analytical, creative, and practical abilities set you apart from everyone else. *No one else has been or will ever be exactly like you.*

- **The diversity among people.** Differences in skin color, gender, ethnicity and national origin, age, physical characteristics and abilities, and sexual orientation are among the major differences that exist among people. Differences in cultural and religious beliefs and practices, education and socioeconomic status, family background, and marital and parental status add to our country's cultural mosaic.

You may work with people from different backgrounds. You may encounter all kinds of people as you attend religious services, buy groceries and stamps, swim at a pool, or socialize. You may experience diversity within your family—often the kind of diversity that is not visible. Even if friends or family members have the same racial and ethnic background as you do, they might be completely different in how they learn, the way they communicate, what they value, and what they do well.

Workplaces and college campuses are filled with people of every age and stage of life. On track to receive her bachelor's degree, this 85-year-old student is determined to achieve her goal.

Diversity on campus

In college you are likely to meet classmates or instructors who reflect America's growing diversity, including

- bi- or multiracial individuals or those who come from families with more than one religious tradition.

- non-native English speakers who may have immigrated from countries outside the United States.
- people older than "traditional" 18- to 22-year-old students.
- persons living with various kinds of disabilities.
- persons practicing different lifestyles—often expressed in the way they dress, their interests, their sexual orientation, and their leisure activities.

Being able to appreciate and adjust to differences among people is crucial to your success at school, at work, and in your personal relationships. You can accomplish this goal by using your analytical, creative, and practical abilities to develop cultural competence.

How can you develop *cultural competence?*

As you learned in Chapter 2, *cultural competence* refers to the ability to understand and appreciate differences among people and change your behavior in a way that enhances, rather than detracts from, relationships and communication. According to the National Center for Cultural Competence, to develop cultural competence you must act upon the following five steps:[2]

1. Value diversity.
2. Identify and evaluate personal perceptions and attitudes.
3. Be aware of what happens when different cultures interact.
4. Build knowledge about other cultures.
5. Use what you learn to adapt to diverse cultures as you encounter them.

As you develop cultural competence, you heighten your ability to analyze how people relate to one another. Most important, you develop practical skills that enable you to connect to others by bridging the gap between who you are and who they are.[3]

Value diversity

Valuing diversity means having a basic respect for, and acceptance of, the differences among people. Every time you meet someone new, you have a choice about how to relate. If you value diversity, you will choose to treat people with tolerance and respect, granting them the right to think, feel, and believe without being judged.

Being open-minded in this way will help your relationships thrive, as shown in Key 8.1. Even though you won't like every person you meet, you can make an effort to show respect while focusing on the person as an individual.

YOUR ROLE	SITUATION	CLOSED-MINDED ACTIONS	OPEN-MINDED ACTIONS
Fellow student	For an assignment, you are paired with a student old enough to be your mother.	You assume the student will be clueless about the modern world. You think she might preach to you about how to do the assignment.	You get to know the student as an individual. You stay open to what you can learn from her experiences and knowledge.
Friend	You are invited to dinner at a friend's house. When he introduces you to his partner, you realize that he is gay.	You are turned off by the idea of two men in a relationship. You make an excuse to leave early. You avoid your friend after that.	You have dinner with the two men and make an effort to get to know more about them, individually and as a couple.
Employee	Your new boss is of a different racial and cultural background than yours.	You assume that you and your new boss don't have much in common. You think he will be distant and uninterested in you.	You rein in your stereotypes. You pay close attention to how your new boss communicates and leads. You adapt to his style and make an effort to get to know him better.

Identify and evaluate personal perceptions and attitudes

Whereas people may value the *concept* of diversity, attitudes and emotional responses may influence how they act when they confront the *reality* of diversity in their own lives. As a result, many people have prejudices that lead to damaging stereotypes.

Prejudice

Almost everyone has some level of (prejudice,) meaning that they prejudge others, usually on the basis of characteristics such as gender, race, sexual orientation, and religion. People judge others without knowing anything about them because of . . .

PREJUDICE

A preconceived judgment or opinion, formed without just grounds or sufficient knowledge.

- influence of family and culture. Children learn attitudes, including intolerance, superiority, and hate, from their parents, peers, and community.
- fear of differences. It is human to fear, and to make assumptions about, the unfamiliar.
- experience. One bad experience with a person of a particular race or religion may lead someone to condemn all people with the same background.

Stereotypes

Prejudice is usually based on (stereotypes)—assumptions made, without proof or critical thinking, about the characteristics of a person or group of people. Stereotyping emerges from . . .

STEREOTYPE

A standardized mental picture that represents an oversimplified opinion or uncritical judgment.

- a desire for patterns and logic. People often try to make sense of the world by using the labels, categories, and generalizations that stereotypes provide.

- **media influences.** The more people see stereotypical images—the airhead beautiful blonde, the jolly fat man—the easier it is to believe that stereotypes are universal.
- **laziness.** Labeling group members according to a characteristic they seem to have in common takes less energy than exploring the qualities of individuals.

Stereotypes stall the growth of relationships, because pasting a label on a person makes it hard for you to see the real person underneath. Even stereotypes that seem "positive" may not be true and may get in the way of perceiving people as individuals. Key 8.2 shows some "positive" and "negative" stereotypes.

Use your analytical abilities to question your own ideas and beliefs and to weed out the narrowing influence of prejudice and stereotyping. Giving honest answers to questions like the following is an essential step in the development of cultural competence:

- How do I react to differences?
- What prejudices or stereotypes come to mind when I see people, in real life or the media, who are a different color than I am? From a different culture? Making different choices?
- Where did my prejudices and stereotypes come from?
- Are these prejudices fair? Are these stereotypes accurate?
- What harm can having these prejudices and believing these stereotypes cause?

With the knowledge you build as you answer these questions, move on to the next stage: Looking carefully at what happens when people from different cultures interact.

Stereotypes involve generalizations that may not be accurate.

key 8.2

POSITIVE STEREOTYPE	NEGATIVE STEREOTYPE
Women are nurturing.	Women are too emotional for business.
African Americans are great athletes.	African Americans struggle in school.
Hispanic Americans are family oriented.	Hispanic Americans have too many kids.
White people are successful in business.	White people are cold and power hungry.
Gay men have a great sense of style.	Gay men are sissies.
People with disabilities have strength of will.	People with disabilities are bitter.
Older people are wise.	Older people are set in their ways.
Asian Americans are good at math and science.	Asian Americans are poor leaders.

get creative!

Heighten your awareness of diversity by examining your own uniqueness.

Being able to respond to people as individuals requires that you become more aware of the diversity that is not always on the surface. Brainstorm 10 words or phrases that describe you. The challenge: Keep references to your ethnicity or appearance (brunette, Cuban American, wheelchair dependent, and so on) to a minimum, and fill the rest of the list with characteristics others can't see at a glance (laid-back, only child, 24 years old, drummer, marathoner, interpersonal learner, and so on).

1. _____   6. _____
2. _____   7. _____
3. _____   8. _____
4. _____   9. _____
5. _____   10. _____

Use a separate piece of paper to make a similar list for someone you know well—a friend or family member. Again, stay away from the most obvious visible characteristics. See if anything surprises you about the different image you create of this familiar person.

Be aware of what happens when cultures interact

As history has shown, when people from different cultures interact, they often experience problems caused by lack of understanding, prejudice, and stereotypic thinking. At their mildest, these problems create roadblocks that obstruct relationships and communication. At their worst, they set the stage for acts of discrimination and hate crimes.

Discrimination

Discrimination refers to actions that deny people equal employment, educational, and housing opportunities, or treat people as second-class citizens. Federal law says that you cannot be

Minds are like parachutes. They only function when they are open.

SIR JAMES DEWAR

denied basic opportunities and rights because of your race, creed, color, age, gender, national or ethnic origin, religion, marital status, potential or actual pregnancy, or potential or actual illness or disability (unless the illness or disability prevents you from performing required tasks and unless accommodations are not possible).

Despite these legal protections, discrimination is common and often appears on college campuses. Students may not want to work with students of other races. Members of campus clubs may reject prospective members because of religious differences. Outsiders may harass students attending gay and lesbian alliance meetings. Instructors may judge students according to their weight, accent, or body piercings.

Hate crimes

HATE CRIME

A crime motivated by a hatred of a specific characteristic thought to be possessed by the victim.

When prejudice turns violent, it often manifests itself in hate crimes directed at racial, ethnic, and religious minorities and homosexuals:

- In Wyoming in 1998, Matthew Shepard, a gay college student, was kidnapped and tied to a fence where his captors beat and abandoned him. He died of his injuries.
- In California in 1999, Buford O. Furrow Jr. entered a community center and shot five people because they were Jewish. He then shot and killed a Filipino-American letter carrier.

The increase in hate crimes in recent years is alarming. According to FBI statistics, reported hate crimes more than doubled from 1991 to 2001.[4] Incidents categorized as hate crimes include simple assault (the most common hate crime), aggravated assault, forcible sex offenses, arson, manslaughter, and murder. Because the statistics include only reported incidents, they tell only a part of the story—many more crimes likely go unreported by victims fearful of what might happen if they contact authorities.

Build cultural knowledge

The successfully intelligent response to discrimination and hate, and the next step in your path toward cultural competence, is to gather knowledge. You have a personal responsibility to learn about people who are different from you, including those you are likely to meet on campus.

What are some practical ways to begin?

- *Read* newspapers, books, magazines, and Web sites.
- *Ask questions* of all kinds of people, about themselves and their traditions.
- *Observe* how people behave, what they eat and wear, how they interact with others.
- *Travel internationally* to unfamiliar places where you can experience different ways of living firsthand.
- *Travel locally* to equally unfamiliar, but close-by, places where you will encounter a variety of people.
- *Build friendships* with fellow students or coworkers you would not ordinarily approach.

Some colleges have international exchange students who can help you appreciate the world's cultural diversity. When Yiting Liu left China to study mathematics and economics at a U.S. college, she knew little about the United States. Dorothy Smith, her African American roommate, helped her adjust. "Yiting didn't know much about race relations when she first got to America," explained Dorothy, "but from hanging around us, she's been able to get an interpretive experience." Also, said Dorothy, when Yiting "first came here, she was an outsider. She didn't know what the taboos were. Now she's able to cross into different groups."[5]

Building knowledge also means exploring yourself. Talk with family, read, seek experiences that educate you about your own cultural heritage. Then share what you know with others.

Adapt to diverse cultures

Here's where you take everything you have gathered—your value of diversity, your self-knowledge, your understanding of how cultures interact, your information about different cultures—and put it to work with practical actions. With these actions you can improve how you relate to others, and perhaps even change how people relate to one another on a larger scale. Think carefully, and creatively, about what kinds of actions feel right to you. Make choices that you feel comfortable with, that cause no harm, and that may make a difference, however small.

Dr. Martin Luther King Jr. believed that careful thinking could change attitudes. He said:

> The tough-minded person always examines the facts before he reaches conclusions: in short, he postjudges. The tender-minded person reaches conclusions before he has examined the first fact; in short, he prejudges and is prejudiced. . . . There is little hope for us until we become tough minded enough to break loose from the shackles of prejudice, half-truths, and down-right ignorance.[6]

Try the following suggestions. In addition, let them inspire your own creative ideas about what else you can do in your daily life to improve how you relate to others.

When you meet different people, you discover many ways of being and learning. After having a stroke, this student learned how to write with her feet using a special device.

Look past external characteristics. If you meet a woman with a disability, get to know her. She may be an accounting major, a daughter, and a mother. She may love baseball, politics, and science fiction novels. These characteristics— not just her physical person—describe who she is.

Put yourself in other people's shoes. Shift your perspective and try to understand what other people feel, especially if there's a conflict. If you make a comment that someone interprets as offensive, for example, think about why what you said was hurtful. If you can talk about it with the person, you may learn even more about how he or she heard what you said and why.

Adjust to cultural differences. When you understand someone's way of being and put it into practice, you show respect and encourage communication. If a friend's family is formal at home, dress appropriately and behave formally when you visit. If an instructor maintains a lot of personal space, keep a respectful distance when you visit during office hours. If a study group member takes offense at a particular kind of language, avoid it when you meet.

Help others in need. Newspaper columnist Sheryl McCarthy wrote about an African American who, in the midst of the 1992 Los Angeles riots, saw an Asian American man being beaten and helped him to safety: "When asked why he risked grievous harm to save an Asian man he didn't even know, the African-American man said, 'Because if I'm not there to help someone else, when the mob comes for me, will there be someone there to save me?'"[7]

Stand up against prejudice, discrimination, and hate. When you hear a prejudiced remark or notice discrimination taking place, think about what you can do to encourage a move in the right direction. You may choose to make a comment, or to get help by approaching an authority such as an instructor or dean. Sound the alarm on hate crimes—let authorities know if you suspect that a crime is about to occur, join campus protests, support organizations that encourage tolerance.

Recognize that people everywhere have the same basic needs. Everyone loves, thinks, hurts, hopes, fears, and plans. When you are trying to find common ground with diverse people, remember that you are united first through your essential humanity.

When people use successful intelligence to work through problems, changes can happen. After a gay tutor left a job at a university rather than face harassment, his friends organized an intercollegiate meeting on intolerance. Chandra J. Johnson, assistant to the president at the University of Notre Dame, asked participants to start by examining themselves: "This is an opportunity to see how our own biases have been formed," she said. "We are not born with notions of racism. These kinds of social ills have been projected onto us. . . . These things are very, very real and people's spirits are destroyed every day as a result of a bias or a misconception."

Ada Maxwell, a student attendee, believes that talking about intolerance is the key to eliminating it. "It doesn't have to be taboo," she said. "Half of the education . . . is the classes and the professors, but the other half—and it's a really important half—is what you can learn from other people. Your thinking can change and other people's thinking can change."[8]

Many minority students experience a dimension to college life unknown to majority students. Examining their experiences and choices will help all students understand the complexity of what it means to be a minority in America.

How can *minority students* make the most of college?

Who fits into the category of "minority student" at your school? The term *minority* includes students of color; students who are not part of the majority Christian sects; and gay, lesbian, and bisexual students. However, even for members of these groups, there is no universal "minority" experience. Each person's experiences are unique.

If you are a minority student, two actions will help you make the most of college: Defining your perspective and defining your experience.

Define your perspective

You have a choice about what perspective to bring to your new relationships. Do you expect others to stereotype you right away, or do you expect that they will be open to getting to know you as an individual? What might be the consequences of each perspective? For your part, do you plan to try to approach each person as an individual rather than to type them according to their ethnic or cultural status, age or gender, values or choices?

Part of getting off to a positive and productive start at college means being open-minded and avoiding assumptions as you get to know people. Yes, everyone will have their own ideas, values, and ways of living. It is possible, however—as well as productive—to get to know these ideas and values in the people you encounter without immediately making assumptions or placing judgments. Working toward understanding is the key. As Paul Barrett Jr., political science major at Earlham College, says,

> As a black male, I am faced with situations very different from that of a white male, a white female, a black female, an Asian-American male, and so on. We must have the ability to approach situations with a panoramic perspective rather than the narrow scope of our own worlds. Is that not the very essence of diversity? Is it not the ability to at least try to understand differences in culture and understand what makes a person act or think the way that he or she does?[9]

University of Michigan student Fiona Rose describes the benefits of a positive approach to diversity this way:

> My years at U-M have been enhanced by relationships with men and women from all cultures, classes, races, and ethnicities. Such interactions are essential to an education. While courses teach us the history and academic value of diversity, friendships prepare us to survive and thrive in our global community. Good institutions consider not only what a potential student will gain from classes and course work, but what he or she will bring to the campus community.[10]

Consider the mind-set you want to take as you begin college. Adopt the perspective that will open you to new friendships and horizon-broadening experiences.

Define your experience

When you start school, it's natural to want to live with, sit next to, or socialize with people similar to you. However, if you define your entire college experience by these ties, you may limit your understanding of others and your opportunities for growth.

Along with activities that appeal to the general student population, most colleges have organizations and services that support minority groups. Among these are specialized student associations, cultural centers, arts groups with a minority focus, minority fraternities and sororities, and political-action groups. Many minority students look for a balance, involving themselves in activities with members of their group as well as with the college mainstream. For example, a student may join the African-American Students Association as well as clubs for all students such as the campus newspaper or an athletic team.

To make choices as a minority student on campus, ask yourself these questions:

- How much time do I want to spend pursuing minority-related activities? Do I want to focus my studies on a minority-related field, such as African American studies?
- Do I want to minimize my ties with my minority group? Will I care if other minority students criticize my choices?
- Do I want to spend part of my time among people who share my background and part with students from other groups?

The attitudes and habits you develop now may have implications for the rest of your life—in your choice of friends, where you decide to live, your work, and even your family. Think carefully about the path you take, and follow your head and heart.

I have a dream that one day on the red hills of Georgia the sons of former slaves and the sons of former slave owners will be able to sit down together at the table of brotherhood.

MARTIN LUTHER KING JR.

So far, the chapter has focused on the need to accept and adapt to diversity in its many forms. Just as there is diversity in skin color and ethnicity, there is also diversity in the way people communicate. Effective communication helps people of all cultures understand one another and make connections.

get practical! **MAKE A DIFFERENCE**

Find personal ways to connect with other cultures.

Rewrite three strategies in the "Adapt to Diverse Cultures" section on pages 225–226 as specific actions to which you commit. For example, "Help others in need" might become "Sign up to tutor in the Writing Center." Circle or check the number when you have completed each task or, if it is ongoing, when you have begun the change.

1. _____

   _____

   _____

2. _____

   _____

   _____

3. _____

   _____

   _____

How can you *communicate effectively?*

Clear-spoken communication promotes success at school, at work, and in personal relationships. Successfully intelligent communicators analyze and adjust to communication styles, learn to give and receive criticism, analyze and make practical use of body language, and work through communication problems.

Adjust to communication styles

When you speak, your goal is for listeners to receive the message as you intended. Problems arise when one person has trouble "translating" a message coming from someone using a different communication style. Your knowledge of the Personality Spectrum (see Chapter 3) will help you understand and analyze the ways diverse people communicate.

Identifying your styles

Following are some communication styles that tend to be associated with the four dimensions in the Personality Spectrum. No one style is better than another. Successful communication depends on understanding your personal style and becoming attuned to the styles of others.

Thinker-dominant communicators focus on facts and logic. As speakers, they tend to rely on logical analysis to communicate ideas and prefer quantitative concepts to those that are conceptual or emotional. As listeners, they often do best with logical messages. Thinkers may also need time to process what they have heard before responding. Written messages—on paper or via e-mail—are often useful for these individuals because writing can allow for time to put ideas together logically.

Organizer-dominant communicators focus on structure and completeness. As speakers, they tend to deliver well-thought-out, structured messages that fit into an organized plan. As listeners, they often appreciate a well-organized message that defines practical tasks in concrete terms. As with Thinkers, a written format is often an effective form of communication to or from an Organizer.

Giver-dominant communicators focus on concern for others. As speakers, they tend to cultivate harmony, analyzing what will promote closeness in relationships. As listeners, they often appreciate messages that emphasize personal connection and address the emotional side of an issue. Whether speaking or listening, Givers often favor in-person talks over written messages.

Adventurer-dominant communicators focus on the present. As speakers, they focus on creative ideas, tending to convey a message as soon as the idea arises and move on to the next activity. As listeners, they appreciate up-front, short, direct messages that don't get sidetracked. Like Givers, Adventurers tend to communicate and listen more effectively in person.

Use this information as a jumping-off point for your self-exploration. Just as people tend to demonstrate characteristics from more than one Personality Spectrum dimension, communicators may demonstrate different styles. Analyze your style by thinking about the communication styles associated with your dominant Personality Spectrum dimensions. Compare them to how you tend to communicate and how others seem to respond to you. Then, use creative and practical thinking skills to decide what works best for you as a communicator.

Speakers adjust to listeners

Listeners may interpret messages in ways you never intended. Think about practical solutions to this kind of problem as you read the following example involving a Giver-dominant instructor and a Thinker-dominant student (the listener):

Instructor: "Your essay didn't communicate any sense of your personal voice."

Student: "What do you mean? I spent hours writing it. I thought it was on the mark."

- **Without adjustment:** The instructor ignores the student's need for detail and continues to generalize. Comments like, "You need to elaborate. Try writing from the heart. You're not considering your audience," might confuse or discourage the student.
- **With adjustment:** Greater logic and detail will help. For example, the instructor might say: "You've supported your central idea clearly, but you didn't move beyond the facts into your interpretation of what they mean. Your essay reads like a research paper. The language doesn't sound like it is coming directly from you."

Listeners adjust to speakers

As a listener, improve understanding by being aware of stylistic differences and translating the message into one that makes sense to you. The following example of an Adventurer-dominant employee speaking to an Organizer-dominant supervisor shows how adjusting can pay off.

Employee: "I'm upset about the e-mail you sent me. You never talked to me directly and you let the problem build into a crisis. I haven't had a chance to defend myself."

- **Without adjustment:** If the supervisor is annoyed by the employee's insistence on direct personal contact, he or she may become defensive: "I told you clearly what needs to be done. I don't know what else there is to discuss."
- **With adjustment:** In an effort to improve communication, the supervisor responds by encouraging the in-person exchange that is best for the employee. "Let's meet after lunch so you can explain to me how you believe we can improve the situation."

Although adjusting to communication styles helps you speak and listen more effectively, you also need to understand, and learn how to effectively give and receive, criticism.

Communication

Using techniques corresponding to your stronger intelligences boosts your communication skills both as a speaker and as a listener.

INTELLIGENCE	SUGGESTED STRATEGIES	WHAT WORKS FOR YOU? WRITE NEW IDEAS HERE
Verbal–Linguistic	• Find opportunities to express your thoughts and feelings to others—either in writing or in person. • Remind yourself that you have two ears and only one mouth. Listening is more important than talking.	
Logical–Mathematical	• Allow yourself time to think through solutions before discussing them—try writing out a logical argument on paper and then rehearsing it orally. • Accept the fact that others may have communication styles that vary from yours and that may not seem logical.	
Bodily–Kinesthetic	• Have an important talk while walking or performing a task that does not involve concentration. • Work out physically to burn off excess energy before having an important discussion.	
Visual–Spatial	• Make a drawing or diagram of points you want to communicate during an important discussion. • If your communication is in a formal classroom or work setting, use visual aids to explain your main points.	
Interpersonal	• Observe how you communicate with friends. If you tend to dominate the conversation, brainstorm ideas about how to communicate more effectively. • Remember to balance speaking with listening.	
Intrapersonal	• When you have a difficult encounter, take time alone to evaluate what happened and to decide how you can communicate more effectively next time. • Remember that, in order for others to understand clearly, you may need to communicate more than you expect to.	
Musical	• Play soft music during an important discussion if it helps you, making sure it isn't distracting to the others involved.	
Naturalistic	• Communicate outdoors if that is agreeable to all parties. • If you have a difficult exchange, imagine how you might have responded differently had it taken place outdoors.	

Know how to give and receive criticism

CONSTRUCTIVE

Promoting improvement or development.

Criticism can be either (constructive) or nonconstructive. Constructive criticism is a practical problem-solving strategy, involving goodwill suggestions for improving a situation. In contrast, nonconstructive criticism focuses on what went wrong, doesn't offer alternatives or help that might help solve the problem, and is often delivered negatively, creating bad feelings.

When offered constructively and carefully, criticism can help bring about important changes. Consider a case in which someone has continually been late to study group sessions. The group leader can comment in one of two ways. Which comment would encourage you to change your behavior?

- Constructive. The group leader talks privately with the student: "I've noticed that you've been late a lot. We count on you, because our success depends on what each of us contributes. Is there a problem that is keeping you from being on time? Can we help?"
- Nonconstructive. The leader watches the student arrive late and says, in front of everyone, "If you can't start getting here on time, there's really no point in your coming."

While at school, your instructors will criticize your class work, papers, and exams. On the job, criticism may come from supervisors, coworkers, or customers. No matter the source, constructive comments can help you grow as a person. Be open to what you hear, and always remember that most people want to help you succeed.

Offering constructive criticism

When offering constructive criticism, use the following strategies to be effective:

- Criticize the behavior rather than the person. Avoid personal attacks. "You've been late to five group meetings" is much preferable to "You're lazy."
- Define the problematic behavior specifically. Try to focus on the facts, substantiating with specific examples and minimizing emotions. Avoid additional complaints—people can hear criticisms better if they are discussed one at a time.
- Suggest new approaches and offer help. Talk about practical ways of handling the situation. Work with the person to develop creative options. Help the person feel supported.
- Use a positive approach and hopeful language. Express the conviction that changes will occur and that the person can turn the situation around.

Receiving criticism

When you find yourself on criticism's receiving end, use the following techniques:

- Analyze the comments. Listen carefully, then evaluate what you heard. What does it mean? What is the intent? Try to let nonconstructive comments go without responding.

GIVE CONSTRUCTIVE CRITICISM

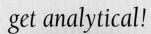

get analytical!

Imagine how you would offer constructive criticism.

Briefly describe a situation in your life that could be improved if you were able to offer constructive criticism to a friend or family member. Describe the improvement you want:

_____

_____

Imagine that you have a chance to speak to this person. First describe the setting—time, place, atmosphere—where you think you would be most successful:

_____

_____

Now develop your "script." Keeping in mind what you know about constructive criticism, analyze the situation and decide on what you think would be the best approach. Freewrite what you would say. Keep in mind the goal you want your communication to achieve.

_____

_____

_____

_____

_____

_____

Finally, if you can, make your plan a reality. Will you do it?   Yes   No

If you do have the conversation, note here: Was it worth it?   Yes   No

- Request suggestions on how to change your behavior. Ask, "How would you like me to handle this in the future?"
- Summarize the criticism and your response to it. Make sure everyone understands the situation.
- Use a specific strategy. Use problem-solving skills to analyze the problem, brainstorm ways to change, choose a strategy, and take practical action to make it happen.

Criticism, as well as other thoughts and feelings, may be communicated nonverbally. You will become a more effective communicator if you understand body language.

Understand body language

Body language has an extraordinary capacity to express people's real feelings through gestures, eye movements, facial expressions, body positioning and posture, touching behaviors, vocal tone, and use of personal space. Why is it important to know how to analyze body language?

233

Nonverbal cues shade meaning. What you say can mean different things depending on body positioning or vocal tone. The statement "That's a great idea" sounds positive. However, said while sitting with your arms and legs crossed and looking away, it may communicate that you dislike the idea. Said sarcastically, the tone may reveal that you consider the idea a joke.

Culture influences how body language is interpreted. For example, in the United States, looking away from someone may be a sign of anger or distress; in Japan, the same behavior is usually a sign of respect.

Nonverbal communication strongly influences first impressions. First impressions emerge from a combination of verbal and nonverbal cues. Nonverbal elements, including tone of voice, posture, eye contact, and speed and style of movement, usually come across first and strongest.

Although reading body language is not an exact science, the following practical strategies will help you use it to improve communication.

- Pay attention to what is said through nonverbal cues. Focus on your tone, your body position, whether your cues reinforce or contradict your words. Then do the same for those with whom you are speaking. Look for the level of meaning in the physical.
- Note cultural differences. Cultural factors influence how an individual interprets nonverbal cues. In cross-cultural conversation, discover what seems appropriate by paying attention to what the other person does on a consistent basis, and by noting how others react to what you do.
- Adjust body language to the person or situation. What body language might you use when making a presentation in class? Meeting with your advisor? Confronting an angry coworker? Think through how to use your physicality to communicate successfully.

Communicate across cultures

As you meet people from other countries and try to form relationships with them, you may encounter communication issues that are linked to cultural differences.[11] As you recall from Chapter 2, these problems often stem from the different communication styles that are found in high-context and low-context cultures.

You cannot shake hands with a clenched fist.

INDIRA GANDHI

In the United States and other low-context cultures, communication is linked primarily to words and to the explicit messages sent through these words. In contrast, in high-context cultures, such as those in the Middle and Far East, words are often considered less important than such factors as context, situation, time, formality, personal relationships, and nonverbal behavior.

Key 8.3 will help you see how 12 world cultures fit on the continuum of high- to low-context communication styles. Key 8.4 summarizes some major communication differences you should be aware of when talking with someone from a different culture. Being attuned to culture-

The continuum of high- and low-context cultures.

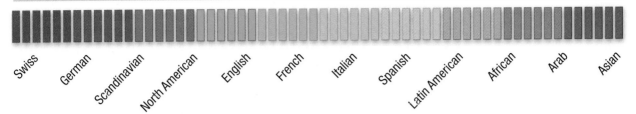

LOW-CONTEXT CULTURES   HIGH-CONTEXT CULTURES

Swiss   German   Scandinavian   North American   English   French   Italian   Spanish   Latin American   African   Arab   Asian

based communication differences will help you interact comfortably with people who come from different parts of the world.

Language barriers may also arise when communicating cross-culturally. When speaking with someone who is struggling with your language, make the conversation easier by choosing words the person is likely to know, avoiding slang expressions, being patient, and using body language to fill in what words can't say. Also, invite questions—and ask them yourself—so that you both can be as clear as possible.

Some ways communication differs in high- and low-context cultures.

FACTORS AFFECTING COMMUNICATION	LOW-CONTEXT CULTURES	HIGH-CONTEXT CULTURES
Personal Relationships	The specific details of the conversation are more important than what people know about each other.	Personal trust is the basis for communication, so sharing personal information forms a basis for strong, long-lasting relationships.
Time	People expect others to be punctual and to meet schedules.	Time is seen as a force beyond the person's control. Therefore lateness is common, and not considered rude.
Formality	A certain degree of civility is expected when people meet, including hand-shakes and introductions.	People often require formal introductions that emphasize status differences. As a result, a student will speak with great respect to an instructor.
Eye Contact	Expect little direct eye contact.	• Arab natives may use prolonged, direct eye contact. • Students from Japan and other Far Eastern countries are likely to turn their eyes away from instructors as a sign of respect.
Personal Space	In the United States, people converse while remaining between 4 and 12 feet apart.	People from Latin America and the Middle East may sit or stand between 18 inches and 4 feet away from you.

Source: Adapted from Louis E. Boone, David L. Kurtz, and Judy R. Block. *Contemporary Business Communication,* 2nd ed. Upper Saddle River, NJ: Prentice Hall, 1997, p. 72.

One of the biggest barriers to successful communication is conflict, which can result in anger and even violence. With effort, you can successfully manage conflict and stay away from those who cannot.

Manage conflict

Conflicts, both large and small, arise when there is a clash of ideas or interests. You may have small conflicts with a housemate over a door left unlocked. You may have major conflicts with your partner about finances or with an instructor about a failing grade. Conflict, as unpleasant as it can be, is a natural element in the dynamic of getting along with others. Prevent it when you can—and when you can't, use problem-solving strategies to resolve it.

Conflict prevention strategies

These two strategies can help you to prevent conflict from starting in the first place.

ASSERTIVE

Able to declare and affirm one's own opinions while respecting the rights of others to do the same.

Being assertive. No matter what your dominant learning styles, you tend to express yourself in one of three ways—aggressively, assertively, or passively. Aggressive communicators focus primarily on their own needs and can become impatient when needs are not satisfied. Assertive communicators are likely both to get their message across and to give listeners the opportunity to speak, without attacking others or sacrificing their own needs. Passive communicators focus primarily on the needs of others and often deny themselves power, causing frustration.

Key 8.5 contrasts the characteristics of these three. Assertive behavior strikes a balance between aggression and passivity and promotes the most productive communication. Aggressive and passive communicators can use practical strategies to move toward a more assertive style of communication.

- Aggressive communicators might take time before speaking, use "I" statements, listen to others, and avoid giving orders.
- Passive communicators might acknowledge anger, express opinions, exercise the right to make requests, and know that their ideas and feelings are important.

Send "I" messages. "I" messages help you communicate your needs rather than attacking someone else. Creating these messages involves some simple rephrasing: "You didn't lock the door!" becomes "I felt uneasy when I came to work and the door was unlocked." Similarly, "You never called last night" becomes "I was worried when I didn't hear from you last night."

"I" statements soften the conflict by highlighting the effects that the other person's actions have on you, rather than focusing on the person or the actions themselves. These statements help the receiver feel freer to respond, perhaps offering help and even acknowledging mistakes.

Conflict resolution

All too often, people deal with conflict through avoidance (a passive tactic that shuts down communication) or escalation (an aggressive tactic that often leads to fighting). Conflict resolution demands calm communication,

Assertiveness fosters successful communication.

AGGRESSIVE	ASSERTIVE	PASSIVE
Loud, heated arguing	Expressing feelings without being nasty or overbearing	Concealing one's own feelings
Blaming, name-calling, and verbal insults	Expressing oneself and giving others the chance to express themselves	Feeling that one has no right to express anger
Walking out of arguments before they are resolved	Using "I" statements to defuse arguments	Avoiding arguments
Being demanding: "Do this"	Asking and giving reasons: "I would appreciate it if you would do this, and here's why . . ."	Being noncommittal: "You don't have to do this unless you really want to . . ."

motivation, and careful thinking. Use your analytical, creative, and practical thinking skills to apply the problem-solving plan (Chapter 4):

- Define and analyze the problem.
- Brainstorm possible solutions.
- Analyze potential solutions.
- Choose a solution and make it happen with practical action.

Trying to calm anger is an important part of resolving conflict. All people get angry at times—at people, events, and themselves. However, excessive anger can contaminate relationships, stifle communication, and turn friends and family away.

Manage anger

Strong emotions can get in the way of happiness and success. It is hard to concentrate on American History when you are raging over being cut off in traffic or can't let go of your anger with a friend. Psychologists report that angry outbursts may actually make things worse. When you feel yourself losing control, try some of these practical anger-management techniques.

- **Relax.** Breathe deeply. Slowly repeat a calming phrase or word like "Take it easy" or "Relax."
- **Change your environment.** Take a break from what's upsetting you. Go for a walk, go to the gym, see a movie. Come up with some creative ideas about what might calm you down.
- **Think before you speak.** When angry, most people tend to say the first thing that comes to mind, even if it's hurtful. Inevitably, this escalates the hard feelings and the intensity of the argument. Instead, wait to say something until you are in control.
- **Do your best to solve a problem, but remember that not all problems can be solved.** Instead of blowing up, think about how you can handle

what's happening. Analyze a challenging situation, make a plan, resolve to do your best, and begin. If you fall short, you will know you made an effort and be less likely to turn your frustration into anger.

- **Get help if you can't keep your anger in check.** If you consistently lash out, you may need the help of a counselor. Many schools have mental health professionals available to students.

Your ability to communicate and manage conflict has a major impact on your relationships with friends and family. Successful relationships are built on self-knowledge, good communication, and hard work.

How do you make the most of *personal relationships?*

Personal relationships with friends, classmates, spouses and partners, and parents can be sources of great satisfaction and inner peace. Good relationships can motivate you to do your best in school, on the job, and in life. When relationships fall apart, however, nothing may seem right. You may be unable to eat, sleep, or concentrate. Relationships have enormous power.

Use positive relationship strategies

Here are some strategies for improving personal relationships.

Make personal relationships a high priority. Life is meant to be shared. In some marriage ceremonies, the bride and groom share a cup of wine, symbolizing that the sweetness of life is doubled by tasting it together and the bitterness is cut in half when shared by two.

Invest time. You devote time to education, work, and sports. Relationships benefit from the same investment. In addition, spending time with people you like can relieve stress.

Spend time with people you respect and admire. Life is too short to hang out with people who bring you down or encourage you to ignore your values. "Try to nurture at least one friendship in each class," advises a Palo Alto College student. "If you know negative people who will try to discourage you and crush your spirit, avoid them. . . . You need nurturing and positivity."[12]

If you want a friend, be a friend. If you treat others with the kind of loyalty and support that you appreciate yourself, you are likely to receive the same in return.

Work through tensions. Negative feelings can fester when left unspoken. Get to the root of a problem by discussing it, compromising, forgiving, and moving on.

Take risks. It can be frightening to reveal your deepest dreams and frustrations, to devote yourself to a friend, or to fall in love. However, if you open yourself up, you stand to gain the incredible benefits of companionship, which for most people outweigh the risks.

Find a pattern that suits you. Some students date exclusively and commit early. Some students prefer to socialize in groups. Some students date casually. Be honest with yourself—and others—about what you want in a relationship.

If a relationship fails, find ways to cope. When an important relationship becomes strained or breaks up, analyze the situation and choose practical strategies to help you move on. Some people need time alone; others need to be with friends and family. Some seek counseling. Some throw their energy into school or exercise. Some cry. Whatever you do, believe that in time you will emerge from the experience stronger.

Avoid destructive relationships

On the far end of the spectrum are relationships that turn destructive. College campuses see their share of violent incidents. The more informed you are, the less likely you are to add to the sobering statistics.

Sexual harassment

Both men and women can be victims, although the most common targets are women. Sexual harassment basically consists of these two types:

- *Quid pro quo harassment* refers to a request for a sexual favor or activity in exchange for something else. "If you don't do X for me, I will fail you/fire you/make your life miserable."
- *Hostile environment harassment* indicates any situation where sexually charged remarks, behavior, or items cause discomfort. Examples include lewd jokes and pornography.

How to cope. If you feel degraded by anything that goes on at school or work, address the person whom you believe is harassing you, or speak to a dean or supervisor.

Violence in relationships

Statistics indicate that violent relationships among students are increasing.[13]

- One in five college students has experienced and reported at least one violent incident while dating, from being slapped to more serious violence.
- In three of four violent relationships, problems surface after the couple has dated for a while.
- In six of ten cases, drinking and drugs are associated with the violence.

Women in their teens and twenties are more likely to be victims of domestic violence than older women. Here's why: First, when trouble

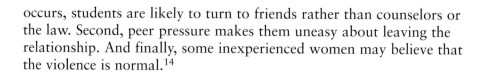

occurs, students are likely to turn to friends rather than counselors or the law. Second, peer pressure makes them uneasy about leaving the relationship. And finally, some inexperienced women may believe that the violence is normal.[14]

How to cope. Analyze your situation and use problem-solving skills to come up with options. If you see warning signs such as controlling behavior, unpredictable mood swings, personality changes associated with alcohol and drugs, and outbursts of anger, consider ending the relationship. If you are being abused, call a shelter or abuse hotline or seek counseling at school or at a community center. If you need medical attention, go to a clinic or hospital emergency room. If you believe that your life is in danger, get out and obtain a restraining order that requires your abuser to stay away from you.

Rape and date rape

Any intercourse or anal or oral penetration by a person against another person's will is defined as rape. Rape is primarily an act of rage and control, not a sexual act. Acquaintance rape, or date rape, refers to sexual activity during a date that is against one partner's will, including situations where one partner is too drunk or drugged to give consent. A drug called Rohypnol, known as roofies, is sometimes used by date rapists to sedate victims and is difficult to detect in a drink.

Campus Advocates for Rape Education (C.A.R.E.), an organization at Wheaton College, MA, describes date rape's particular damage. "One's trust in a friend, date, or acquaintance is violated . . . fear, self-blame, guilt, and shame are magnified because the assailant is known."[15]

How to cope. Communicate—clearly and early—what you want and don't want to do. When on a date with someone who seems unstable or angry, stick to safe, public places. Keep a cell phone handy. Avoid alcohol or drugs that might make it difficult for you to stay in control.

If you are raped, whether by an acquaintance or a stranger, seek medical attention immediately. Next, talk to a close friend or counselor. Consider reporting the incident to the police or to campus officials. Whether or not you take legal action, continue to get help through counseling, a rape survivor group, or a hotline.

Choose communities that enhance your life

Personal relationships often take place within communities, or groups, that include people who share your interests—for example, sororities and fraternities, athletic clubs, and political groups. So much of what you accomplish in life is linked to your network of personal contacts.

If you affiliate with communities that are involved in positive activities, you are more likely to surround yourself with responsible and character-rich people who may become your friends and colleagues. You may find among them your future spouse or partner, your best friend, a person who helps you land a job, your doctor, accountant, real estate agent, and so on.

DATE RAPE

Sexual assault perpetrated by the victim's escort during an arranged social encounter.

PERSONAL TRIUMPH

GUSTAVO MINAYA Student at Essex Community College, Baltimore, Maryland

Connecting with others can be difficult, especially if you start out feeling exceptionally different. Gustavo Minaya spoke no English when he came to the United States as a child. Through learning and getting involved in activities, he has found his niche. Read the account, then use a separate piece of paper to answer the questions on page 243.

I am a native of Peru. When I was six years old, my mother told me that we were going to America for a better life. My father was already living in the United States so my mother went to the embassy to apply for a visa, but our visa was denied. In desperation, she decided to hire "coyotes." These are people who know secret routes to the United States. Their job was to help us cross the border.

Our journey began at night with cold train rides. At different points, we stopped to eat or to get on a different train. Along the way other families joined us. At the Mexico–Texas border, the coyotes instructed us to walk under a highway. Once we were out again in the open, everyone began running for the U. S. border. Helicopters were circling overhead with their search lights on, and people were shouting. It was pandemonium.

Exhausted, we made it across the border and into a van, where people were stacked on top of each other. At another border check, my mother and I were arrested and taken into custody by immigration officers who took our fingerprints. They arranged to have us transported to an emergency shelter run by the American Red Cross. Meanwhile, my dad completed the paperwork for legal immigration, and we joined him a few months later.

Of course, I didn't know English. When I started school in the second grade I looked different from the other kids, and I sounded different because of my accent. Some of the kids picked on me. I cried a lot back then. The next year I took English as a Second Language (ESL) classes. Gradually, I learned English and began to feel like I fit in.

When I look back over my experiences, I believe the one thing that has helped me adjust to the changes is friendliness. I like to make people laugh, and I go into things with a positive attitude. Being friendly with other students, and people in general, has helped me gain a sense of belonging.

My main advice to international students who want to make the most of their education is to participate in campus activities. You can join a club or work on campus, maybe at the school store or library. This way you meet new people, and you'll learn English faster. You can't fit in if you isolate yourself.

Participation is also important for developing leadership skills. I look at clubs and other campus activities as opportunities to enhance my education. For example, I joined the International Student Association (ISA) and am now the president. During the meetings, I give my ideas and show my support by volunteering for projects. I've discovered that one of my strengths is bringing people together for a good cause.

I'm very proud of my parents for how hard they worked to make a better life for me and my brothers and sisters. In my native country of Peru, you can work as hard as you want, but it gets you nowhere. Some of the smartest people there are taxicab drivers because they can't find jobs doing anything else. Here, if you are willing to work, you can have a profession and achieve what you want. I plan to achieve as much as I can.

Finding and working with a community of people with similar interests can have positive effects in personal relationships and in workplace readiness, as Eastern Kentucky University student Kasey Doyle explains:

> During my sophomore year, a friend persuaded me to join a service sorority on campus. I was hesitant at first, but once I began to get involved, I realized that I had missed out on many opportunities. Not only have I made many friends, I have also become more outgoing and personable. . . . I found a place where I fit in.
>
> Joining this organization also prepared me for my major and my job at [the campus newspaper] The Progress.
>
> As a reporter, you are expected to be outgoing and personable, and before joining an organization, I was extremely shy. I'm definitely not timid anymore, and I have matured and become more self-confident.[16]

If you find yourself drawn toward communities that encourage negative and even harmful behavior, such as gangs or groups that haze pledges, stop and think. Analyze why you are drawn to these groups. Resist the temptation to join. If you are already involved and want out, stand up for yourself and be determined.

Kente

The African word *kente* means "that which will not tear under any condition." Kente cloth is worn by men and women in African countries such as Ghana, Ivory Coast, and Togo. There are many brightly colored patterns of kente, each beautiful, unique, and special.

Think of how this concept applies to people. Like the cloth, all people are unique, with brilliant and subdued aspects. Despite mistreatment or misunderstanding by others, you need to remain strong so that you don't tear, allowing the weaker fibers of your character to show through. The kente of your character can help you endure, stand up against injustice, and fight peacefully, but relentlessly, for the rights of all people.

BUILDING SKILLS

FOR COLLEGE, CAREER, AND LIFE SUCCESS

Developing Successful Intelligence

PUTTING IT ALL TOGETHER

Learn from the experiences of others. Look back to Gustavo Minaya's Personal Triumph on page 241. After you've read his story, relate his experience to your own life by completing the following:

Step 1. Think it through: *Analyze your experience and compare it to Gustavo's.* When in your life have you felt like an outsider, and how does this relate to Gustavo's experience? What was his key to finding his place in his new world? What was yours?

Step 2. Think out of the box: *Create a challenge.* Think about the activities and organizations at your school with which you would most feel "at home." Then imagine that none of those are available—and that you are required to get involved with three organizations or activities that you would never naturally choose. How would you challenge yourself? Name the three choices and describe what you think you could gain from your experiences. Consider trying one—for real!

Step 3. Make it happen: *Use practical strategies to connect with others.* Choose one of those organizations or activities that feel natural to you. Then choose one from your list of those that would be your challenges. Now try them both. Contact a person involved with each organization or activity and ask them for details—when the group meets, what they do, what the time commitment would likely be, what the benefit would be. Then join both in the coming semester, making an effort to get to know others who are involved.

create your future

Writing

DISCOVERY THROUGH JOURNALING

Record your thoughts on a separate piece of paper or in a journal.

Opening your mind. On what topic is it most difficult for you to be accepting? Describe your difficulty with race, culture, ethnic origin, weight, gender, sexual orientation, or any other human characteristic. What do you think is the source of your uneasiness—parents, peers, experience, any other source? Describe what you can do now to think more openly, and think about why it may help you to combat your prejudices.

Team Building

COLLABORATIVE SOLUTIONS

Problem solving close to home. Divide into groups of two to five students. Assign one group member to take notes. Discuss the following questions, one at a time:

1. What are the three largest problems the world faces with regard to how people get along with and accept others?

2. What could we do to deal with these three problems?

3. What can each individual student do to make improvements? (Talk about what you specifically feel that you can do.)

When all groups have finished, gather as a class and hear each group's responses. Observe the variety of problems and solutions. Notice whether more than one group came up with one or more of the same problems. If there is time, one person in the class, together with your instructor, could gather the responses to question 3 into an organized document that you can send to your school or local paper.

Career Portfolio

PLAN FOR SUCCESS

Complete the following in your electronic portfolio or on separate sheets of paper.

Compiling a résumé. What you have accomplished in various work and school situations will be important for you to emphasize as you strive to land a job that is right for you. Your roles—on the job, in school, at home, or in the community—help you gain knowledge and experience.

On one electronic page or sheet of paper, list your education and skills information. On the other, list job experience. For each job, record job title, the dates of employment, and the tasks that this job entailed (if the job had no particular title, come up with one yourself). Be as detailed as possible—it's best to write down everything you remember. When you

Désirée Williams

237 Custer Street, San Francisco, CA 94101 • 650/555-5252 (w) or 415/555-7865 (h) • fax: 707/555-2735 • e-mail: desiree@zzz.com

---

EDUCATION

2001 to present	San Francisco State University, San Francisco, CA
	Pursuing a B.A. in the Spanish BCLAD (Bilingual, Cross-Cultural Language Acquisition Development) Education and Multiple Subject Credential Program. Expected graduation: June, 2005

PROFESSIONAL EMPLOYMENT

10/02 to present	**Research Assistant, Knowledge Media Lab**
	Developing ways for teachers to exhibit their inquiry into their practice of teaching in an on-line, collaborative, multimedia environment.
5/01 to present	**Webmaster/Web Designer**
	Work in various capacities at QuakeNet, an Internet Service Provider and Web Commerce Specialist in San Mateo, CA. Designed several sites for the University of California, Berkeley, Graduate School of Education, as well as private clients such as A Body of Work and Yoga Forever.
9/01 to 6/02	**Literacy Coordinator**
	Coordinated, advised, and created literacy curriculum for an America Reads literacy project at Prescott School in West Oakland. Worked with non-reader 4th graders on writing and publishing, incorporating digital photography, Internet resources, and graphic design.
8/01	**Bilingual Educational Consultant**
	Consulted for Children's Television Workshop, field-testing bilingual materials. With a research team, designed bilingual educational materials for an ecotourism project run by an indigenous rain forest community in Ecuador.
1/01 to 6/01	**Technology Consultant**
	Worked with 24 Hours in Cyberspace, an on-line worldwide photojournalism event. Coordinated participation of schools, translated documents, and facilitated public relations.

SKILLS

Languages:	Fluent in Spanish.
	Proficient in Italian and Shona (majority language of Zimbabwe).
Computer:	Programming ability in HTML, Javascript, Pascal, and Lisp. Multimedia design expertise in Adobe Photoshop, Netobjects Fusion, Adobe Premiere, Macromedia Flash, and many other visual design programs.
Personal:	Perform professionally in Mary Schmary, a women's a cappella quartet. Have climbed Mt. Kilimanjaro.

compile your résumé, you can make this material more concise. Keep this list current by adding experiences and accomplishments as you go along.

Using the information you have gathered and Key 8.6 as your guide, draft a résumé for yourself. Remember that there are many ways to construct a résumé; consult other resources, such as those listed in the bibliography, for different styles. You may want to reformat your résumé according to a style that your career counselor or instructor recommends, that best suits the career area you plan to enter, or that you like best.

Keep your résumé draft on hand—and on a computer disk. When you need to submit a résumé with a job application, update the draft and print it out on high-quality paper.

Here are some general tips for writing a résumé:

- Always put your name and contact information at the top. Make it stand out.
- State an objective if it is appropriate—if your focus is specific or you are designing this résumé for a particular interview or career area.
- List your post-secondary education, starting from the latest and working backward. This may include summer school, night school, seminars, and accreditations.
- List jobs in reverse chronological order (most recent job first). Include all types of work experience (full-time, part-time, volunteer, internship, and so on).
- When you describe your work experience, use action verbs and focus on what you have accomplished, rather than on the description of assigned tasks.
- Include keywords that are linked to the description of the jobs for which you will be applying.
- List references on a separate sheet. You may want to put "References upon request" at the bottom of your résumé.
- Use formatting (larger font sizes, different fonts, italics, bold, and so on) and indents selectively to help the important information stand out.
- Get several people to look at your résumé before you send it out. Other readers will have ideas that you haven't thought of and may find errors that you have missed.

SUGGESTED READINGS

Dublin, Thomas, ed. *Becoming American, Becoming Ethnic: College Students Explore Their Roots.* Philadelphia: Temple University Press, 1996.

Feagin, Joe R., Hernan Vera, and Nikitah O. Imani. *The Agony of Education: Black Students at White Colleges and Universities.* New York: Routledge, 1996.

Gonzales, Juan L., Jr. *The Lives of Ethnic Americans*, 2nd ed. Dubuque, IA: Kendall/Hunt, 1994.

Hockenberry, John. *Moving Violations.* New York: Hyperion, 1996.

Levey, Marc, Michael Blanco, and W. Terrell Jones. *How to Succeed on a Majority Campus: A Guide for Minority Students.* Belmont, CA: Wadsworth Publishing Co., 1997.

Qubein, Nido R. *How to Be a Great Communicator: In Person, on Paper, and at the Podium.* New York: John Wiley & Sons, 1996.

Schuman, David. *Diversity on Campus.* Dubuque, IA: Kendall/Hunt, 2001.

Suskind, Ron. *A Hope in the Unseen: An American Odyssey from the Inner City to the Ivy League.* New York: Broadway Books, 1999.

Takaki, Ronald. *A Different Mirror: A History of Multi-cultural America.* Boston: Little, Brown & Company, 1994.

Tannen, Deborah. *You Just Don't Understand: Women and Men in Conversation.* New York: Perennial Currents, 2001.

Tatum, Beverly Daniel. *"Why Are All the Black Kids Sitting Together in the Cafeteria?" and Other*

Conversations About Race: A Psychologist Explains the Development of Racial Identity. Philadelphia: Basic Books, 2003.

Terkel, Studs. *Race: How Blacks and Whites Think and Feel About the American Obsession.* New York: Free Press, 1995.

Trotter, Tamera and Joycelyn Allen. *Talking Justice: 602 Ways to Build and Promote Racial Harmony.* Saratoga, FL: R & E Publishers, 1993.

INTERNET RESOURCES

Prentice Hall Student Success Supersite (success stories from students from a diversity of backgrounds): www.prenhall.com/success

Asian-American Resources: www.ar.mit.edu/people/irie/aar/

Britannica Guide to Black History: http://blackhistory.eb.com

Latino USA: www.latinousa.org

The Sociology of Race and Ethnicity (with multiple links to other resources): www.trinity.edu/~mkear/race.html

ENDNOTES

1. "For 7 Million, One Census Race Category Wasn't Enough," *New York Times*, March 13, 2001, pp. A1 and A14.

2. "Conceptual Frameworks/Models, Guiding Values and Principles," National Center for Cultural Competence, 2002 [on-line]. Available: http://gucchd.georgetown.edu/nccc/framework.html (May 2004).

3. Information in the sections on the five stages of building competency is based on Mark A. King, Anthony Sims, and David Osher, "How Is Cultural Competence Integrated in Education?" Cultural Competence [on-line]. Available: www.air.org/cecp/cultural/Q_integrated.htm#def (May 2004).

4. FBI Hate Crime statistics, from a grid created by the Anti-Defamation League, 2001 [on-line]. Available: www.adl.org/combating_hate/ (May 2004).

5. Jen Lin-Liu, "China's 'Harvard Girl': A College Student Has Become an Example for a New Style of Raising Children," *The Chronicle of Higher Education*, May 30, 2003 [on-line]. Available: http://chronicle.com/weekly/v49/i38/38a04001.htm (March 2004).

6. Martin Luther King Jr., from his sermon "A Tough Mind and a Tender Heart," *Strength in Love*. Philadelphia: Fortress Press, 1986, p. 14.

7. Sheryl McCarthy, *Why Are the Heroes Always White?* Kansas City, MO: Andrews and McMeel, 1995, p. 137.

8. Doug Gavel, "Students Speak Out at Hate Crime Forum," *Harvard University Gazette*, www.news.harvard.edu/gazette/2001/02.15/01-hatecrime.html.

9. Paul Barrett Jr., "Solutions Offered to Address Racism On Campus," *Earlham Word Online*, Volume XIII, Issue 11, November 20, 1998. Available: http://word.cs.earlham.edu/issues/XIII/112098/opin91.html (November 2004).

10. Media Watch, *Diversity Web*, Fall 1997. Available: www.diversityweb.org/Digest/F97/mediawatch.html#top (November 2004).

11. Information for this section from Philip R. Harris and Robert T. Moran. *Managing Cultural Differences*, 3rd ed. Houston, TX: Gulf Publishing Company, 1991 and Lennie Copeland and Lewis Griggs, *Going International: How to Make Friends and Deal Effectively in the Global Marketplace*. New York: Random House, 1985.

12. Student essay submitted by the First Year Experience students of Patty Parma, Palo Alto College, San Antonio, Texas, January 2004.

13. Tina Kelley, "On Campuses, Warnings About Violence in Relationships," *New York Times*, February 13, 2000, p. 40.

14. Ibid.

15. U.S. Department of Justice, Bureau of Justice Statistics, "Sex Offenses and Offenders," 1997, and "Criminal Victimization," 1994.

16. Kasey Doyle, "Getting Involved on Campus Important," *The Eastern Progress,* November 4, 2004 [on-line]. Available: www.easternprogress. com/news/2004/11/04/Perspective/Getting.Involved.On. Campus.Important-792180.shtml.

IN THIS CHAPTER . . .

You will explore answers to the
following questions:

Creating Your Life
BUILDING A SUCCESSFUL FUTURE

As you come to the end of your work in this course, you have built up a wealth of knowledge. You will soon be analyzing how you fared in your first college semester. You are facing important decisions about what direction you want to go in school—and starting to think about where the choices you make now will ultimately lead you.

This chapter will help you build life skills that can fuel your future success—maintaining wellness, preparing for a career, and budgeting your money, including information on financial aid and credit cards. You will gather 20 important tools that will help you transfer the power of successful intelligence into your post-college life. Finally, you will create your personal mission, exploring how to use it to guide your dreams.

On the following page, read how student Rachel Faison is looking for ways in which she can translate her college experience into life success.

- How can you maintain a healthy body and mind?
- How can you make smart decisions about substances and sex?
- How can you prepare for a successful career?
- How can you create a budget that works?
- How can you continue to activate your successful intelligence?
- How can you create and live your personal mission?

What knowledge will help me succeed in a changing world?

At my school, we are required to focus on an area of interest starting in the second semester of sophomore year. At this point I'm planning on studying acting, with an intent to pursue an acting career after I graduate. Since I'm a sophomore now, I will soon have to load my schedule with classes in the theater department. I know that acting is an unreliable profession, but it's what I want to do; plus, these days it seems that you can't find job security anywhere, even in areas that traditionally were pretty solid.

I do want to take time in college to explore other areas of interest. Art history and religion both interest me although I don't know how I would translate those interests into a career. I believe that as long as you have basic areas of knowledge and study a variety of things, you'll have options—you will find something to do and will be able to do it well. I'm just not sure of the specifics of how that works. How will what I'm doing in college serve me, outside of the specific training I'll receive in acting? What will help me keep my footing in a career once I graduate?

Rachel Faison
Bard College, Annandale-on-Hudson, New York

Internship experience and exploring your passions will help you achieve success.

You are absolutely right that if you learn to use your mind to the fullest, you will prepare yourself well for any profession you decide to pursue. The key right now is to develop several skill sets to complement your academic learning so that you will be versatile. Here are some ideas about how to build your general skills and explore your specific passions and interests.

First, work at least two internships before you graduate. You will learn volumes from experiencing the culture and politics in different workplaces and by proving your instincts and skills in the real-world environment. This experience will also help you discover whether you like or dislike the areas in which you intern. Knowing what you don't like can be just as important as knowing what you like. Many students select fields that sound good or pay a lot without discovering what succeeding in that field really entails. Do your homework on what interests you.

Second, look for areas where you can build your leadership skills. What organization can you join? What leadership role can you play? How will that organization be different and better because you have been a part of it? Stretch yourself. Sometimes when we move into areas that scare us, we grow the most. Develop a healthy outlook toward success and failure as you participate and lead within organizations in college.

Finally, think carefully about what you love (and don't love) doing. Ask yourself probing questions regarding your values. Listen to your heart as well as your head. What makes you feel purposeful, creative, joyful, and valued? What makes you want to wake up every morning? You may not come up with answers right away, but committing yourself to the process of asking the questions and "holding" the questions will allow you to dig genuinely and deeply for the way that you can make your mark in the world of work. Good luck and congratulations for being brave enough to ask meaningful questions!

Carol Carter
President and Founder, LifeBound, Denver, Colorado

How can you maintain a healthy *body and mind?*

The healthier you are, the more you'll be able to reach your potential. Make your physical health a priority by eating right, exercising, and getting enough sleep. Make your mental health a priority by recognizing mental health problems, related to stress or other causes, and understanding ways to get help.

Eat right

College life can make it tough to eat well. Students spend hours sitting in class or studying and tend to eat on the run, build social events around food, and eat as a reaction to stress. Many new students find that the "freshman 15"—referring to 15 pounds that people say freshmen tend to gain in the first year of school—is much more than a myth.

Making healthier choices about what you eat can lead to more energy, better general health, and an improved quality of life. These practical tips will help you pay attention to how you eat, and make changes when you need to, so that you can stay healthy or lose weight if necessary.

- Eat a diet consisting of a variety of foods, including plenty of vegetables, fruits, and grain products.
- Reduce portion size and consume sugar and salt in moderation.
- Choose a diet low in fat and cholesterol.
- Plan your meals and avoid skipping meals.
- Eat because you're hungry; avoid using food for stress relief.
- If you need to lose weight, find a support group, such as Weight Watchers or an on-campus organization, that can help you stay on target.

Exercise

Being physically fit enhances your general health, increases your energy, and helps you cope with stress. During physical activity, the brain releases endorphins, chemical compounds that have a positive and calming effect on the body.

College athletes use daily exercise as a stress reliever. Larisa Kindell, a senior and co-captain of Wesleyan University's swimming team, credits her athletic routine with helping her balance her life. "If I didn't have swimming, a place to release my academic stress, I don't think I'd be as effective in the classroom or studying at night," she said. Swimming has taught her "discipline, time management, and motivation" and has contributed to her academic success.[1] Always check with a physician before beginning an exercise program.

Types of exercise

There are three general categories of exercises. The type you choose depends on your exercise goals, available equipment, your time and fitness level, and other factors.

- *Cardiovascular training* strengthens your heart and lung capacity. Examples include running, swimming, in-line skating, aerobic dancing, and biking.

- *Strength training* strengthens different muscle groups. Examples include using weight machines and free weights and doing push-ups and abdominal crunches.
- *Flexibility training* increases muscle flexibility. Examples include stretching and yoga.

Busy students often have trouble getting to the gym, even when there is a fully equipped athletic center on campus. Even in the busiest weeks, you can stay on the move by walking to classes and meetings, using the stairs in your buildings, or using home exercise equipment such as weights, a treadmill, or an elliptical trainer.

Get enough sleep

College students are infamous for being sleep deprived. While research indicates that students need eight to nine hours of sleep a night to function well, recent studies show that students average six to seven hours—and often get much less.[2]

Students, overwhelmed with responsibilities, often feel that they have no choice but to prioritize schoolwork over sleep. Michelle Feldman, a sophomore at Syracuse University, stays up regularly until 4:00 A.M. getting her reading and studying done. Fellow Syracuse student Brian Nelson, a junior aiming to complete a triple major, only manages two hours a night as he works to keep up with the 24 credits he's taking in one semester.[3]

The groundwork of all happiness is health.

LEIGH HUNT

For the sake of both your health and your GPA, find a way to get the sleep you need. Sleep expert Gregg D. Jacobs, Ph.D., recommends the following practical suggestions for improving sleep habits:[4]

- Reduce consumption of alcohol and caffeine.
- Exercise regularly, especially in the afternoon or early evening.
- Take naps.
- Be consistent with wake times and bed times.
- Complete tasks an hour or so before sleep.
- Establish a comfortable sleeping environment.

Recognize mental health problems

No one is happy all the time. However, some people experience emotional disorders that make it more difficult than usual to cope with life's ups and downs. If you recognize yourself in any of the following descriptions, take practical steps to improve your health. Most student health centers and campus counseling centers can provide both medical and psychological help for students with emotional disorders. Treatment may involve psychotherapy, drug therapy, and even hospitalization or residence in a treatment center.

IMPROVE YOUR PHYSICAL HEALTH

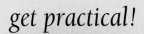

get practical!

Make a change in how you eat, exercise, or sleep.

First, decide what you most need to change. What's most important to your health right now—
to eat better, exercise more, or get more sleep? Name it: _____

Now, considering your individual situation and looking at the strategies in this chapter, list
five practical actions you can take right away to improve in this area. Word them as action
statements. *Examples:* "I will leave earlier so that I can walk to my first class." "I will stop
keeping candy bars in my room." "I will take a nap whenever I'm dragging in the afternoon."

1. _____
2. _____
3. _____
4. _____
5. _____

The final step: Just do it!

Depression. A depressive disorder is an illness that requires a medical evaluation and is treatable. Symptoms include constant sadness or anxiety, loss
of interest in activities that you normally like, eating too much or too little,
and low self-esteem. Depression can have a genetic, a psychological, a
physiological, or an environmental cause, or a combination of causes. In
extreme cases, severe depression can lead to suicide.

Anorexia nervosa. This condition, occurring mainly in young women, creates an intense desire to be thin. People with anorexia become dangerously
thin through restricting food intake, constant exercise, and use of laxatives,
all the time believing they are overweight. An estimated 5 to 7 percent of
college undergraduates in the United States suffer from anorexia.[5] Effects
of anorexia-induced starvation include loss of menstrual periods in women,
impotence in men, organ damage, heart failure, and death.

Bulimia. People who binge on excessive amounts of food, usually sweets
and fattening foods, and then purge through self-induced vomiting, have
bulimia. They may also use laxatives or exercise obsessively. Effects of
bulimia include damage to the digestive tract and even heart failure due to
the loss of important minerals.

Binge eating. Like bulimics, people with binge eating disorder eat large
amounts of food and have a hard time stopping. However, they do not
purge afterwards. Binge eaters are often overweight and feel unable to control their eating. Binge eaters may suffer from health problems associated
with obesity.

Situations involving substances or sex are sources of stress for many
college students. Use the following information and your successful intelligence to make decisions that are right for you.

How can you make successfully *intelligent decisions* about substances and sex?

You are responsible for the choices you make regarding alcohol, tobacco, drugs, and sexual practices. As you read, think about the effects of your actions on yourself and others, and consider how to make positive, life-affirming choices.

Alcohol

Alcohol is a depressant that slows vital body functions and is the most frequently abused drug on campus. Even a few drinks affect thinking and muscle coordination. Heavy drinking can damage the liver, the digestive system, and brain cells and can impair the central nervous system. Prolonged use also leads to addiction, making it seem impossible to quit. In addition, alcohol contributes to the deaths of 100,000 people every year through both alcohol-related illnesses and accidents involving drunk drivers.[6]

Of all alcohol consumption, binge drinking is associated with the greatest problems. Here are statistics from a recent survey:[7]

- Forty-three percent of the students surveyed labeled themselves as binge drinkers, and 21 percent said that they binge drink frequently.
- Eight out of ten of the students who do not binge drink reported experiencing such "secondhand effects" as vandalism, sexual assault or unwanted sexual advances, or interrupted sleep or study.[8]
- Students who binge drink are more likely to miss classes, be less able to work, have hangovers, become depressed, and engage in unplanned or unsafe sexual activity.[9]

From what Darra Clark, a freshman at a large university in the Southwest, has seen, it is not possible to be a successful student if you drink too much. You can't do well in school and have friends if you "get drunk and stoned out of your gourd every night," she explains. "I think that the whole drinking scene is probably the thing I've found most appalling about college (our student handbook specifically outlaws beer funnels, for example). The problem, of course, is that drinking becomes a really hard behavior to regulate. . . . Drinking and drugs have done some awful things to some of the kids I've seen around here."[10]

Tobacco

The National Institute on Drug Abuse (NIDA) found that nearly 40 percent of college students reported smoking at least once in the year before they were surveyed, and 25 percent had smoked once within the previous month.[11]

When people smoke they inhale nicotine, a highly addictive drug found in all tobacco products. Nicotine's immediate effects may include an increase in blood pressure and heart rate, sweating, and throat irritation. Long-term effects may include high blood pressure, bronchitis, emphysema, stomach ulcers, and heart disease. Pregnant women who smoke increase their risk of having infants with low birth weight, premature births, or stillbirths. Furthermore, inhaling tobacco smoke damages the cells that line the air sacs of the lungs and can cause lung cancer. Lung cancer causes more deaths in the United States than any other type of cancer.[12]

Quitting smoking is difficult and should be attempted gradually, ideally with the support of friends and family. The positive effects of quitting—increased life expectancy, greater lung capacity, and more energy—may inspire any smoker to consider making a lifestyle change. Weigh your options and make a responsible choice.

There are many ways to have a good time in college. Many students take entertaining short courses such as ballroom dancing, which is a social event as well as an educational experience.

Drugs

The NIDA reports that nearly 32 percent of college students have used illicit drugs at least once in the year prior to being surveyed, and 16 percent in the month before.[13] College students may use drugs to relieve stress, be accepted by peers, or just to try something new.

In most cases, the negative consequences of drug use outweigh any temporary high. Drug use violates federal, state, and local laws, and you may be arrested, tried, and imprisoned for possessing even a small amount of drugs. You can jeopardize your reputation, your student status, and your ability to get a job if you are caught using drugs or if drug use impairs your performance. Finally, long-term drug use can damage your body and mind. Key 9.1 shows commonly used drugs and their potential effects.

One drug that doesn't fit cleanly into a particular category is methylenedioxymethamphetamine (MDMA), better known as Ecstasy. The use of this drug, a combination stimulant and hallucinogen, is on the rise at college parties, raves, and concerts. Its immediate effects include diminished anxiety and relaxation. When the drug wears off, nausea, hallucinations, shaking, vision problems, anxiety, and depression replace these highs. Long-term users risk permanent brain damage in the form of memory loss, chronic depression, and other disorders.[14]

You are responsible for analyzing the potential consequences of what you introduce into your body. Ask questions like the following: Why do I want to do this? What positive and negative effects might my behavior have? Why do others want me to take drugs? What do I really think of these people? How would my drug use affect the people in my life? The more carefully you analyze your situation, the more likely you will be to make choices that are in your own best interest.

The ways in which drugs affect body and mind.

DRUG CATEGORY	DRUG TYPES	HOW THEY MAKE YOU FEEL	PHYSICAL EFFECTS	DANGER OF PHYSICAL DEPENDENCE	DANGER OF PSYCHOLOGICAL DEPENDENCE
Stimulants	Cocaine, amphetamines	Alert, stimulated, excited	Nervousness, mood swings, stroke or convulsions, psychoses, paranoia, coma at large doses	Relatively strong	Strong
Depressants	Alcohol, Valium, Xanax, Rohypnol	Sedated, tired, high	Cirrhosis; impaired blood production; greater risk of cancer, heart attack, and stroke; impaired brain function	Strong	Strong
Opiates	Heroin, codeine, other pain pills	Drowsy, floating, without pain	Infection of organs, inflammation of the heart, hepatitis	Yes, with high dosage	Yes, with high dosage
Cannabinols	Marijuana, hashish	Euphoria, mellowness, little sensation of time	Impairment of judgment and coordination, bronchitis and asthma, lung and throat cancers, anxiety, lack of energy and motivation, reduced ability to produce hormones	Moderate	Relatively strong
Hallucinogens	LSD (acid), mushrooms	Heightened sensual perception, hallucinations, confusion	Impairment of brain function, circulatory problems, agitation and confusion, flashbacks	Insubstantial	Insubstantial
Inhalants	Glue, aerosols	Giddiness, lightheadedness	Damage to brain, heart, liver, and kidneys	Insubstantial	Insubstantial

Source: Adapted from *Educating Yourself about Alcohol and Drugs: A People's Primer* by Marc Alan Schuckit, M.D. New York: HarperCollins, 1998.

Facing addiction

People with addictions have lost control. If you think you may be addicted, take the initiative to seek help. Because substances often cause physical and chemical changes and psychological dependence, habits are tough to break and quitting may involve a painful withdrawal. Asking for help isn't an admission of failure but a courageous move to reclaim your life. The following resources can help you generate options and generate practical plans for recovery.

Counseling and medical care. You can find help from school-based, private, government-sponsored, or workplace-sponsored resources. Ask your school's counseling or health center, your personal physician, or a local hospital for a referral.

Detoxification ("detox") centers. If you have a severe addiction, you may need a controlled environment where you can separate yourself completely from drugs or alcohol.

Support groups. Alcoholics Anonymous (AA) is the premier support group for alcoholics. AA has led to other support groups for addicts such as Overeaters Anonymous (OA) and Narcotics Anonymous (NA). Many schools have AA, NA, or other group sessions on campus.

Another important aspect of both physical and mental health involves being comfortable with your sexuality and making wise sexual decisions. Choosing birth control and knowing how to avoid sexually transmitted diseases have short- and long-term consequences for the rest of your life.

Sexual decision making

What sexuality means to you and the role it plays in your life are your own business. However, the physical act of sex goes beyond the private realm. Individual sexual conduct can result in an unexpected pregnancy and in contracting or passing a sexually transmitted infection (STI). These consequences affect everyone involved in the sexual act and, often, their families.

Your self-respect depends on making choices that maintain health and safety—yours as well as those of the person with whom you are involved. Analyze sexual issues carefully, weighing the positive and negative effects of your choices.

Birth control

Using birth control is a choice, and it is not for everyone. If you do choose to use it, evaluate the pros and cons of each option for yourself as well as for your partner. Consider cost, ease of use, reliability, comfort, and protection against STIs. Communicate with your partner and together make a choice that is comfortable for both of you.

For more information, check your library, the Internet, or a bookstore; talk to your doctor; or ask a counselor at the student health center. Key 9.2 describes established methods, with effectiveness percentages and STI prevention based on proper and regular use.

Sexually transmitted infections

STIs spread through sexual contact (intercourse or other sexual activity that involves contact with the genitals). All are highly contagious. The only birth control methods that offer protection are the male and female condoms (latex or polyurethane only), which prevent skin-to-skin contact. Most STIs can also spread to infants of infected mothers during birth.

Make an educated decision about birth control.

METHOD	APPROXIMATE EFFECTIVENESS	PREVENTS STIs?	DESCRIPTION
Abstinence	100%	Only if no sexual activity occurs	Just saying no. No intercourse means no risk of pregnancy. However, alternative modes of sexual activity can still spread STIs.
Condom (male)	94%	Yes, if made of latex	A sheath that fits over the penis and prevents sperm from entering the vagina.
Condom (female)	90%	Yes	A sheath that fits inside the vagina, held in place by two rings, one of which hangs outside. Made of polyurethane.
Diaphragm or cervical cap	85%	No	A bendable rubber cap that fits over the cervix and pelvic bone inside the vagina (the cervical cap is smaller and fits over the cervix only). Both must be fitted initially by a gynecologist and used with a spermicide.
Oral contraceptives (the pill)	97%	No	A dosage of hormones taken daily by a woman, preventing the ovaries from releasing eggs. Side effects can include headaches, weight gain, and increased chances of blood clotting. Various brands and dosages; must be prescribed by a gynecologist.
Spermicidal foams, jellies, inserts	84% if used alone	No	Usually used with diaphragms or condoms to enhance effectiveness, they have an ingredient that kills sperm cells (but not STIs). They stay effective for a limited period of time after insertion.
Intrauterine device (IUD)	94%	No	A small coil of wire inserted into the uterus by a gynecologist (who must also remove it). Prevents fertilized eggs from implanting in the uterine wall. Possible side effects include bleeding.
Depo-Provera (the shot)	Nearly 100%	No	An injection that a woman must receive from a doctor every few months. Possible side effects may resemble those of oral contraceptives.
Tubal ligation	Nearly 100%	No	Surgery for women that cuts and ties the fallopian tubes, preventing eggs from traveling to the uterus. Difficult and expensive to reverse. Recommended for those who do not want any, or any more, children.
Vasectomy	Nearly 100%	No	Surgery for men that blocks the tube that delivers sperm to the penis. Like tubal ligation, difficult to reverse and recommended only for those who don't want any, or any more, children.
Rhythm method	Variable	No	Abstaining from intercourse during the ovulation segment of the woman's menstrual cycle. Can be difficult to time and may not account for cycle irregularities.
Withdrawal	Variable	No	Pulling the penis out of the vagina before ejaculation. Unreliable, because some sperm can escape in the fluid released prior to ejaculation. Dependent on a controlled partner.

To stay safe, know these facts about sexually transmitted diseases.

DISEASE	SYMPTOMS	HEALTH PROBLEMS IF UNTREATED	TREATMENTS
Chlamydia	Discharge, painful urination, swollen or painful joints, change in menstrual periods for women	Can cause pelvic inflammatory disease (PID) in women, which can lead to sterility or ectopic pregnancies; infection; miscarriage or premature birth.	Curable with full course of antibiotics; avoid sex until treatment is complete.
Gonorrhea	Discharge, burning while urinating	Can cause PID, swelling of testicles and penis, arthritis, skin problems, infections.	Usually curable with antibiotics; however, certain strains are becoming resistant to medication.
Genital herpes	Blisterlike itchy sores in the genital area, headache, fever, chills	Symptoms may subside and then reoccur, often in response to high stress levels; carriers can transmit the virus even when it is dormant.	No cure; some medications, such as Acyclovir, reduce and help heal the sores and may shorten recurring outbreaks.
Syphilis	A genital sore lasting one to five weeks, followed by a rash, fatigue, fever, sore throat, headaches, swollen glands	If it lasts over four years, it can cause blindness, destruction of bone, insanity, or heart failure; can cause death or deformity of a child born to an infected woman.	Curable with full course of antibiotics.
Human Papilloma Virus (HPV, or genital warts)	Genital itching and irritation, small clusters of warts	Can increase risk of cervical cancer in women; virus may remain in body and cause recurrences even when warts are removed.	Treatable with drugs applied to warts or various kinds of wart removal surgery.
Hepatitis B	Fatigue, poor appetite, vomiting, jaundice, hives	Some carriers will have few symptoms; others may develop chronic liver disease that may lead to other diseases of the liver.	No cure; some will recover, some will not. Bed rest may help ease symptoms. Vaccine is available.

Have a doctor examine any irregularity or discomfort as soon as you detect it. Key 9.3 describes common STIs.

The most serious of the STIs is AIDS (acquired immune deficiency syndrome), which is caused by the human immunodeficiency virus (HIV). Not everyone who tests positive for HIV will develop AIDS, but AIDS has no cure and results in eventual death. Medical science continues to develop drugs to combat AIDS and its related illnesses. The drugs can cause severe side effects, however, and none are cures.

HIV is transmitted through two types of bodily fluids: fluids associated with sex (semen and vaginal fluids) and blood. People have acquired HIV through sexual relations, by sharing hypodermic needles for drug

use, and by receiving infected blood transfusions. You cannot become infected unless one of those fluids is involved. Therefore, it is unlikely you can contract HIV from toilet seats, hugging, kissing, or sharing a glass. Other than not having sex at all, a latex condom is the best defense against AIDS. Although some people dislike using condoms, it's a small price to pay for preserving your life.

To be safe, have an HIV test done at your doctor's office or at a government-sponsored clinic. Your school's health department may also administer HIV tests, and home HIV tests are available over the counter. If you are infected, first inform all sexual partners and seek medical assistance. Then, contact support organizations in your area or call the National AIDS Hotline at 1-800-342-AIDS.

Health, both mental and physical, is one asset that will serve you well as you move along the path toward success in the workplace. The education you are receiving in college is another. Following are more ideas about preparing for career success.

How can you prepare for *workplace success*?

Whether you have no idea of your career path or have worked for years and are looking for a career change, now is the time to take steps toward a fulfilling career. You are already preparing for career success with your work in this course, because every skill in this book—thinking, teamwork, writing skills, and goal setting, among others—prepares you to thrive in the workplace. Use the following strategies to get more specific in your preparation.

Investigate career paths

The working world changes all the time. You can get an idea of what's out there—and what you think of it all—by exploring potential careers and building knowledge and experience.

Explore potential careers. Career possibilities extend far beyond what you can imagine. Ask instructors, relatives, mentors, and fellow students about careers they are familiar with. Explore your school's career center. Check your library for books on careers or biographies of people who worked in fields that interest you. Use your analytical thinking skills to broaden your investigation. Look at Key 9.4 for the kinds of questions that will aid your search. You may discover that a wide array of job possibilities exists for most career fields, and that within each job there lies a variety of tasks and skills.

What can I do in this area that I like and do well?	Do I respect the company or the industry? The product or service?
What are the educational requirements (certificates or degrees, courses)?	Does this company or industry accommodate special needs (child care, sick days, flex time)?
What skills are necessary?	Do I need to belong to a union? What does union membership involve?
What wage or salary and benefits can I expect?	Are there opportunities near where I live (or want to live)?
What personality types are best suited to this kind of work?	What other expectations exist (travel, overtime, etc.)?
What are the prospects for moving up to higher-level positions?	Do I prefer the service or production end of this industry?

Build knowledge and experience. Having knowledge and experience specific to the career you wish to pursue is valuable on the job hunt. Courses, internships, jobs, and volunteering are four great ways to build both.

- Courses. Take a course or two in your areas of interest to determine if you like the material. Find out what courses are required for a major in those areas.
- Internships. An internship is a great way to gain real-world experience that you can't get in the classroom. Your career center may be able to help you explore summer or year-round internship opportunities.
- Jobs. You may discover career opportunities while earning money during a part-time job. Someone who answers phones for a newspaper company, for example, might be drawn into journalism.
- Volunteering. Helping others in need can introduce you to careers and increase your experience. Many employers look favorably on volunteering.

Know what employers want

In the jobs you seek after you graduate, employers will look for specific technical skills, work experience, and academic credentials. They will also look for other skills and qualities that indicate that you are a promising candidate.

Key 9.5 describes the particular skills and qualities that tell an employer that you are likely to be an efficient and effective employee. These skills, which you have built throughout this book, are as much a part of your school success as they are of your work success. The more you develop them now, the more employable and promotable you will be.

INTERNSHIP

A temporary work program in which a student can gain supervised practical experience in a particular professional field.

Employers look for candidates with these important skills.

SKILLS	WHY IS IT USEFUL?
Communication	Good listening, speaking, and writing skills are keys to working with others, as is being able to adjust to different communication styles.
Analytical thinking	An employee who can analyze choices and challenges, as well as assess the value of new ideas, stands out.
Creativity	The ability to come up with new concepts, plans, and products helps companies improve and innovate.
Practical thinking	No job gets done without employees who can think through a plan for achieving a goal, put it into action, and complete it successfully.
Teamwork	All workers interact with others on the job. Working well with others is essential for achieving workplace goals.
Goal setting	Teams fail if goals are unclear or unreasonable. Employees and company benefit from setting realistic, specific goals and achieving them reliably.
Cultural competence	The workplace is increasingly diverse. An employee who can work with, adjust to, and respect people from different backgrounds and cultures is valuable.
Leadership	The ability to influence and motivate others in a positive way earns respect and career advancement.
Positive attitude	Other employees will gladly work with, and often advance, someone who completes tasks with positive, upbeat energy.
Integrity	Acting with integrity at work—communicating promptly, being truthful and honest, following rules, giving proper notice—enhances value.
Flexibility	The most valuable employees understand the constancy of change and have developed the skills to adapt to its challenge.
Continual learning	The most valuable employees take personal responsibility to stay current in their fields.

Expect change

The working world is always in flux, responding to technological developments, global competition, and other factors. Reading newspapers and magazines, scanning business sites on the Internet, and watching television news all help you keep abreast of what you face as you make career decisions. Think about the following as you prepare to adjust to change.

Growing and declining career areas. Rapid workplace change means that a growth area today may be declining tomorrow—witness the

CONNECT VALUES TO CAREER

Use your values as a career exploration guide.

First, look at the following list of "value words." Put a checkmark by those qualities that are most important to you as a working person. Circle your top five.

- Accepting
- Adventurous
- Ambitious
- Calm
- Caring
- Conscientious
- Cooperative
- Creative

- Decisive
- Demonstrating leadership
- Efficient
- Enthusiastic
- Focused on learning
- Honest/fair
- Independent
- Kind

- Loyal
- Organized
- Powerful
- Prompt
- Serious
- Trustworthy
- Wealthy

Keeping your top values in mind, answer the following questions:

The kind of work I enjoy most is _____

I can't see myself working as a _____

Self-fulfillment at work consists of _____

Being in charge of others makes me feel _____

Being responsible makes me feel _____

Working independently makes me feel _____

Working in a team makes me feel _____

Imagining that I'm being promoted after two years on a job, I think my employer would say it is because of these exemplary characteristics:

_____

_____

Source: Adapted from Gary Izumo et al., *Keys to Career Success.* Upper Saddle River, NJ: Prentice Hall, 2002, pp. 67–69.

---

sudden drop in Internet company jobs and fortunes in 2001. The U.S. Bureau of Labor keeps updated statistics on the status of various career areas. For example, for the period 1998–2008, of the 10 fastest growing occupations identified by the Bureau, five are computer-related occupations.

Workplace trends. What's happening now? Companies, to save money, are hiring more temporary employees (temps) and fewer full-time employees. Temporary jobs offer flexibility, few obligations, and often more take-home pay, but have limited benefits. Also, in response to the changing needs of the modern workforce, companies are offering more "quality of life" benefits such as telecommuting, job sharing, and on-site child care.

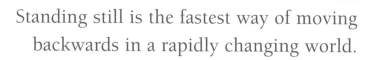

> Standing still is the fastest way of moving backwards in a rapidly changing world.

LAUREN BACALL

Personal change. Even difficult personal changes can open doors that you never imagined were there. For example, Susan Davenny Wyner, a successful classical singer, was hit by a car while biking. The accident damaged her vocal cords beyond repair. She later discovered that conducting held an opportunity for her to express herself musically in a way she didn't think she could ever do again.[15]

Consider learning style

What you know about your learning style from Chapter 3 will give you important clues in the search for the right career. The Multiple Intelligences assessment points to information about your innate learning strengths and challenges, which, in turn, can lead you to careers that involve these strengths. Your Personality Spectrum assessment results are perhaps even more significant to career success, because they provide insight on how you work best with others. Career success depends, in large part, on your ability to function in a team.

Key 9.6 focuses the four dimensions of the Personality Spectrum on career ideas and strategies. Look for your strengths and decide what you may want to keep in mind as you search. Look also at the skills that challenge you because even the most ideal job involves some tasks that may not be in your area of comfort. Identifying ways to boost your abilities in those areas will help you succeed.

Now that you've done your homework, it's time to get to the search. What you know, along with the strategies that follow, will help you along the path to a career that works for you.

Searching for a job—and a career

Maximize your career opportunities by using the resources available to you, making a strategic search plan, and knowing some basics about résumés and interviews. The information in this section will help you right away if you are one of the many who want or need to work while in school. Key 9.7 shows more about who works while enrolled in college.

NETWORKING

The exchange of information or services among individuals, groups, or institutions.

Use available resources

Use your school's career planning and placement office, your (networking) skills, classified ads, and on-line services to help you explore possibilities for jobs you need right away and for postgraduation career opportunities.

Personality Spectrum dimensions indicate strengths and challenges.

DIMENSION	STRENGTHS ON THE JOB	CHALLENGES ON THE JOB	LOOK FOR JOBS/CAREERS THAT FEATURE . . .
Thinker	• Problem solving • Development of ideas • Keen analysis of situations • Fairness to others • Efficiency in working through tasks • Innovation of plans and systems • Ability to look strategically at the future	• A need for private time to think and work • A need, at times, to move away from established rules • A dislike of sameness—systems that don't change, repetitive tasks • Not always being open to expressing thoughts and feelings to others	• Some level of solo work/think time • Problem solving • Opportunity for innovation • Freedom to think creatively and to bend the rules • Technical work • Big-picture strategic planning
Organizer	• High level of responsibility • Enthusiastic support of social structures • Order and reliability • Loyalty • Ability to follow through on tasks according to requirements • Detailed planning skills with competent follow-through • Neatness and efficiency	• A need for tasks to be clearly, concretely defined • A need for structure and stability • A preference for less rapid change • A need for frequent feedback • A need for tangible appreciation • Low tolerance for people who don't conform to rules and regulations	• Clear, well-laid-out tasks and plans • Stable environment with consistent, repeated tasks • Organized supervisors • Clear structure of how employees interact and report to one another • Value of, and reward for, loyalty
Giver	• Honesty and integrity • Commitment to putting energy toward close relationships with others • Finding ways to bring out the best in self and others • Peacemaker and mediator • Ability to listen well, respect opinions, and prioritize the needs of coworkers	• Difficulty in handling conflict, either personal or between others in the work environment • Strong need for appreciation and praise • Low tolerance for perceived dishonesty or deception • Avoidance of people perceived as hostile, cold, or indifferent	• Emphasis on teamwork and relationship building • Indications of strong and open lines of communication among workers • Encouragement of personal expression in the workplace (arrangement of personal space, tolerance of personal celebrations, and so on)
Adventurer	• Skillfulness in many different areas • Willingness to try new things • Ability to take action • Hands-on problem-solving skills • Initiative and energy • Ability to negotiate • Spontaneity and creativity	• Intolerance of being kept waiting • Lack of detail focus • Impulsiveness • Dislike of sameness and authority • Need for freedom, constant change, and constant action • Tendency not to consider consequences of actions	• A spontaneous atmosphere • Less structure, more freedom • Adventuresome tasks • Situations involving change • Encouragement of hands-on problem solving • Travel and physical activity • Support of creative ideas and endeavors

Many students are working while in school.

Community college students

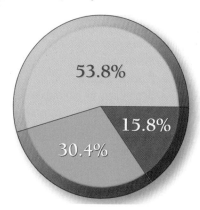

53.8%

15.8%

30.4%

Four-year college students

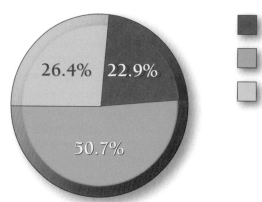

26.4% 22.9%

50.7%

■ Not employed

■ Worked part-time

□ Worked full-time

Source: U.S. Department of Education, National Center for Educational Statistics. *Profile of Undergraduates in U.S. Postsecondary Education Institutions:* 1999–2000. (NCES 98-084), July 2002, Table 5.1.

CONTACT

A person who serves as a carrier or source of information.

Your school's career planning and placement office. Generally, the career planning and placement office deals with postgraduation job opportunities, whereas the student employment office, along with the financial aid office, has information about working during school. At either location you might find general workplace information, listings of job opportunities, interview sign-up sheets, and company contact information. The career office may hold frequent informational sessions on different topics. Your school may also sponsor job or career fairs that give you a chance to explore job opportunities. Start exploring your school's career office early in your college life.

Networking. The most basic type of networking—talking to people about fields and jobs that interest you—is one of the most important job-hunting strategies. Networking contacts can answer questions regarding job hunting, job responsibilities and challenges, and salary expectations. You can network with friends and family members, instructors, administrators, counselors, alumni, employers, coworkers, and others.

Classified ads. Some of the best job listings are in newspapers. Individual ads describe the position available, including background requirements, and provide contact information. Some ads also include job requirements and salary or wages offered.

On-line services. The Internet has exploded into one of the most fruitful sources of job listings. There are many different ways to hunt for a job on the Web:

Professors are often valuable resources for information about majors and careers. Don't hesitate to ask questions.

• Look up career-focused and job listing Web sites such as CareerBuilder.com, Monster.com, Yahoo Hotjobs, or futurestep.com.

- Access job search databases such as the Career Placement Registry and U.S. Employment Opportunities.
- Check the Web pages of individual associations and companies, which may post job listings and descriptions.

If nothing happens right away, keep at it. New job postings appear, new people sign on to look at your résumé. Plus, sites change all the time. Do a general search using the keywords "hot job sites" or "job search sites" to stay current on what sites are up and running.

Make a strategic job search plan

After gathering information, make a practical plan to achieve your career goals by mapping out your long-term time line and keeping track of specific actions.

Make a big-picture time line. Make a career time line that illustrates the steps toward your goal, as shown in Key 9.8. Write in the steps when you

A career time line helps you plan ahead.

key 9.8

1 month	Enter community college on a part-time schedule
6 months	Meet with advisor to discuss desired major and required courses
1 year	Declare major in secondary education
2 years	Switch to full-time class schedule
3 years	Graduate with associate's degree / Transfer to 4-year college
4 years	Work part-time as a classroom aide
5 years	Student teaching / Graduate with bachelor's degree and teaching certificate
6 years	Have a job teaching high school

Use a file card like this to keep records of your job search.

Job/company:	Child-care worker at Morningside Day Care
Contact:	Sally Wheeler, Morningside Day Care,
	17 Parkside Rd, Silver Spring, MD 20910
Phone/fax/e-mail:	(301) 555-3353 phone, (301) 555-3354 fax,
	no e-mail
Communication:	Saw ad in paper, sent résumé & cover letter on Oct. 7
Response:	Call from Sally to set up interview
	—Interview on Oct. 15 at 2 p.m., seemed to get a positive
	response, said she would contact me again by end of the week
Follow-up:	Sent thank-you note on Oct. 16

think they should happen. If your plan is five years long, indicate what you plan to do by the fourth, third, and second years, and then the first year, including a six-month goal and a one-month goal for that first year. Your path may change, of course; use your time line as a guide rather than as an inflexible plan.

Keep track of details. After you establish your time frame, make an organized plan for pursuing the jobs or careers that have piqued your interest. Set goals that establish whom you will talk to, what courses you will take, what skills you will work on, what jobs or internships you will investigate, and any other research you need to do. Do you plan to make three phone calls per day? Will you fill out one job application each week? Keep a record—on 3 by 5 cards, in a computer file, or in a notebook—of people you contact, companies to which you apply, and any response to your communications. Key 9.9 illustrates a sample file card.

Compile an effective résumé and cover letter. Your résumé should always be typed or printed on high-quality paper. Design your résumé neatly, using an acceptable format (books or your career office can show you some standard formats). Proofread it for errors and have someone else proofread it as well. Type or print it on a heavier bond paper than is used for ordinary copies. Include a cover letter along with your résumé that tells the employer what job you are interested in and why he or she should hire you.

Interview. Be clean, neat, on time, and appropriately dressed. Choose a nice pair of shoes—people notice. Bring an extra copy of your résumé and any other materials that you want to show the interviewer. Avoid chewing gum or smoking. Offer a confident handshake. Make eye contact. Show your integrity by speaking honestly about yourself. After the interview, no matter what the outcome, follow up right away with a formal but pleasant thank-you note.

No matter where your money comes from—job paychecks or financial aid—budgeting skills will help you stretch it as far as it can go.

How can you *create a budget* that works?

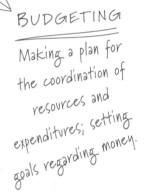

For the vast majority of college students, money is tight. You may have to rely on loans or money from a job in order to cover tuition, textbooks, and the products and services you need every day. Even if your family pays for your education, you will almost certainly need to monitor your monthly personal expenses. Effective budgeting relieves money-related stress and helps you feel more in control.

Your biggest expense right now is probably the cost of your education, including tuition and room and board. However, that expense may not hit you fully until after you graduate and begin to pay back your student loans. For now, include in your budget only the part of the cost of your education you are paying while you are in school.

Budgeting demands analytical, creative, and practical thinking. You gather information about your resources (money flowing in) and expenditures (money flowing out) and analyze the difference. Next, you come up with ideas about how you can make changes. Finally, you take practical action to adjust spending or earning so that you come out even or ahead. Most people budget on a month-by-month basis.

BUDGETING

Making a plan for the coordination of resources and expenditures; setting goals regarding money.

Figure out what you earn

Add up all of the money you receive during the year—the actual after-tax money you have to pay your bills. Common sources of income include:

- take-home pay from a regular full-time or part-time job during the school year
- take-home pay from summer and holiday employment
- money you earn as part of a work-study program
- money you receive from your parents or other relatives for your college expenses
- scholarships or grants that provide spending money

If you have savings specifically earmarked for your education, decide how much you will withdraw every month for your school-related expenses.

Figure out what you spend

Start by recording every check you write for fixed expenses like rent and telephone. Then, over the next month, record personal expenditures in a small notebook. Indicate any expenditure over five dollars, making sure to count smaller expenditures if they are frequent (for example, a bus pass for a month, soda or newspaper purchases per week).

Some expenses, like automobile and health insurance, may be billed only a few times a year. In these cases, convert the expense to monthly by dividing the yearly cost by 12. Be sure to count only current expenses, not expenses that you will pay after you graduate. Among these are the following:

- rent or mortgage
- tuition that you are paying right now (the portion remaining after all forms of financial aid, including loans, scholarships and grants, are taken into account)
- books, lab fees, and other educational expenses
- regular bills (electric, gas, oil, phone, water)
- food, clothing, toiletries, and household supplies
- child care
- transportation and auto expenses (gas, maintenance)
- credit cards and other payments on credit (car payments)
- insurance (health, auto, homeowner's or renter's, life)
- entertainment and related items (cable TV, movies, eating out, books and magazines)
- computer-related expenses, including the cost of your on-line service
- miscellaneous unplanned expenses

Use the total of all your monthly expenses as a baseline for other months, realizing that your expenditures will vary depending on what is happening in your life.

Evaluate the difference

Focusing again on your current situation, subtract your monthly expenses from your monthly income. Ideally, you have money left over—to save or to spend. However, if you are spending more than you take in, your first job is to analyze the problem by looking carefully at your budget, your spending patterns, and priorities. Use your analytical thinking skills to ask some focused questions.

Question your budget. Did you forget to budget for recurring expenses, or was your budget derailed by an emergency expense that you did not foresee? Is your income sufficient for your needs?

Question your spending patterns and priorities. Did you spend money wisely or did you overspend on luxuries? Are you putting too many purchases on your credit card and being hit by high interest payments? When you are spending more than you are taking in during a "typical month," you may have to adjust your budget over the long term.

Adjust spending or earning

Look carefully at what may cause you to overspend and brainstorm possible solutions that address those causes. Solutions can involve either increasing resources or decreasing spending. To deal with spending, prioritize your expenditures and trim the ones you really don't need to make.

As for resources, investigate ways to take in more money, such as taking a part-time job or hunting down scholarships or grants.

Budgeting

Looking into the strategies associated with your strongest intelligences helps you identify effective ways to manage your money.

INTELLIGENCE	SUGGESTED STRATEGIES	WHAT WORKS FOR YOU? WRITE NEW IDEAS HERE
Verbal–Linguistic	• Talk over your budget with someone you trust. • Write out a detailed budget outline. If you can, keep it on a computer where you can change and update it regularly.	
Logical–Mathematical	• Focus on the numbers; using a calculator and amounts as exact as possible, determine your income and spending. • Calculate how much money you'll have in 10 years if you start now to put $2,000 in an IRA account each year.	
Bodily–Kinesthetic	• Consider putting money, or a slip with a dollar amount, each month in different envelopes for various budget items—rent, dining out, etc. When the envelope is empty or the number is reduced to zero, your spending stops.	
Visual–Spatial	• Set up a budgeting system that includes color-coded folders and colored charts. • Create color-coded folders for papers related to financial and retirement goals—investments, accounts, etc.	
Interpersonal	• Whenever budgeting problems come up, discuss them right away. • Brainstorm a solid five-year financial plan with one of your friends.	
Intrapersonal	• Schedule quiet time and think about how you want to develop, follow, and update your budget. Consider financial-management software, such as Quicken. • Think through the most balanced allocation of your assets—where you think your money should go.	
Musical	• Include a category of music-related purchases in your budget—going to concerts, buying CDs—but keep an eye on it to make sure you don't go overboard.	
Naturalistic	• Remember to include time and money in your budget to enjoy nature. • Sit in a spot you like. Brainstorm how you will achieve your short- and long-term financial goals.	

In addition, think analytically about the big picture of where your money goes. Every budgetary decision you make has particular effects, often involving a trade-off among options. When you spend $80 for that new pair of sneakers, for example, you may not have enough for movie tickets and dinner with friends that weekend. Often, making some short-term sacrifices in order to save money can help you tremendously in the long run. If you do what you can to spend less than you make and to "pay yourself"—put some money away in your savings, each month if possible—you'll have a better chance of providing for your future wants and needs.

Financial aid

Financing your education—alone or with the help of your family—involves gathering financial knowledge and making financial decisions. Visit your school's financial aid office in person or on the Internet, research the available options and decide what works best, and then apply early. Apply your successful intelligence; never assume you are not eligible for aid. The types of aid available are student loans, grants, and scholarships.

Student loans. As the recipient of a student loan, you are responsible for paying back the amount you borrow, plus interest, according to a predetermined payment schedule that may stretch over a number of years. The federal government administers or oversees most student loans. To receive aid from any federal program, you must be a citizen or eligible non-citizen and be enrolled in a program that meets government requirements. Federal loan programs include Perkins (for those with exceptional financial need), Stafford (available to students enrolled at least half-time, exceptional need not required), and PLUS (available to students enrolled at least half-time and who are claimed as dependents by their parents).

Grants. Unlike student loans, grants do not require repayment. Grants, funded by federal, state, or local governments as well as private organizations, are awarded to students who show financial need. Federal grant programs include Pell (need-based, available to undergraduates) and FSEOG (need-based; encourages community service work or work related to your course of study).

Scholarships. Scholarships are awarded to students who show talent or ability in specific areas (academic achievement, sports, the arts, citizenship, or leadership). They may be financed by government or private organizations, schools, or individuals.

It can take work to locate financial aid opportunities; many aren't widely advertised. Start digging at your financial aid office and visit your library, bookstore, and the Internet. Guides to funding sources catalog thousands of financial aid offers, and the Internet features on-line scholarhip search services. Additional information about federal grants and loans is available in the current version (updated yearly) of *The Student Guide to Financial Aid*. This publication can be found at your school's financial aid office, or you can request it by mail or phone (800-433-3243). The publication is also available on-line at www.ed.gov/prog_info/SFA/StudentGuide/.

When you are applying for aid, fill out applications as neatly as possible and submit them on time. You can find the Free Application for Federal Student Aid (FAFSA) form at your library, at the Federal Student Aid Information Center, through your college's financial aid office or Web site, or via the U.S. Department of Education's Web site at www.ed.gov/finaid.html.

Finally, if you are receiving aid from your college, follow all the rules and regulations, including meeting application deadlines and remaining in academic good standing. In most cases, you will have to reapply yearly for aid. Take a new look at what's available to you each year you are in school; you may be eligible for different grants or scholarships at various points in your college career.

Managing your credit cards

College students often receive dozens of credit card offers. These offers—and the cards that go along with them—are a double-edged sword: They have the power to help you manage your money, but they also can plunge you into a hole of debt that may take you years to dig out of. Some recent statistics from a Nellie May survey of undergraduates illustrate the challenging situation:[16]

- Average number of credit cards per student—3.2
- Average credit card debt per student—$1,843
- Average available credit card limit—$3,683
- Percentage of students with debt between $3,000 and $7,000— 9 percent
- Percentage of students with more than $7,000 in credit card debt— 5 percent

Every time you charge a textbook, a present, or a pair of pants, you are creating a debt that must be repaid. The credit card issuer earns money by charging interest on your unpaid balance. When used properly, credit cards are a handy alternative to cash. They give you the peace of mind of knowing that you always have money for emergencies and that you have a record of all your purchases. In addition, if you pay your bills on time, you will be building a strong credit history that will affect your ability to take out future loans. However, it takes self-control to avoid overspending, especially because it is so easy to hand over your credit card when you see something you like. To avoid unmanageable debt that can lead to a personal financial crisis, learn as much as you can about credit cards, starting with the important concepts in Key 9.10.

The majority of American citizens have some level of debt, and many people go through periods when they have a hard time paying bills. Falling behind on payments, however, could result in a poor credit rating that makes it difficult for you to make large purchases or take out loans. Particular resources can help you solve credit problems; two are the National Foundation for Credit Counseling (www.nfocc.org) and the Consumer Credit Counseling Service (1-800-338-2227; for Spanish, 1-800-682-9832).

Debbie Alford, a student at the University of Central Oklahoma, realized too late how poor financial decisions would affect her future. As a freshman, Debbie charged only "necessities," such as books and tuition,

Learn to be a smart credit consumer.

WHAT TO KNOW ABOUT . . .	. . . AND HOW TO USE WHAT YOU KNOW
Account balance—a dollar amount that includes any unpaid balance, new purchases and cash advances, finance charges, and fees. Updated monthly on your card statement.	Charge only what you can afford to pay at the end of the month. Keep track of your balance. Hold on to receipts and call customer service if you have questions about recent purchases.
Annual fee—the yearly cost some companies charge for owning a card.	Look for cards without an annual fee or, if you've paid your bills on time, ask your current company to waive the fee.
Annual percentage rate (APR)—the amount of interest charged on your unpaid balance, meaning the cost of credit if you carry a balance in any given month. The higher the APR, the more you pay in finance charges.	Credit card companies compete by charging different APRs. Shop around, especially on the Web. Two sites with competitive APR information are www.studentcredit.com and www.bankrate.com. Also, watch out for low, but temporary, introductory rates that skyrocket to over 20 percent after a few months. Look for *fixed* rates (guaranteed not to change).
Available credit—the unused portion of your credit line. Determine available credit by deducting your current card balance from your credit limit.	It is important to have credit available for emergencies, so avoid charging to the limit.
Cash advance—an immediate loan, in the form of cash, from the credit card company. You are charged interest immediately and may also pay a separate transaction fee.	Use a cash advance only in emergencies because the finance charges start as soon as you complete the transaction. It is a very expensive way to borrow money.
Credit limit—the debt ceiling the card company places on your account (e.g., $1,500). The total owed, including purchases, cash advances, finance charges, and fees, cannot exceed this limit.	Credit card companies generally set low credit limits for college students. Many students get around this limit by owning more than one card, which increases the credit available but most likely increases problems as well.
Delinquent account—an account that is not paid on time or for which the minimum payment has not been met.	Avoid having a delinquent account at all costs. Not only will you be charged substantial late fees, but you also risk losing your good credit rating, affecting your ability to borrow in the future.
Finance charges—the total cost of credit, including interest and service and transaction fees.	Your goal is to incur no finance charges. The only way to do that is to pay your balance in full by the due date on your monthly statement.
Minimum payment—the smallest amount you can pay by the statement due date. The amount is set by the credit card company.	Making only the minimum payment each month can result in disaster if you continue to charge more than you can realistically afford. When you make a purchase, think in terms of total cost, not monthly payments.
Outstanding balance—the total amount you owe on your card.	If you carry a balance over several months, additional purchases are immediately hit with finance charges. Pay cash instead.
Past due—your account is considered "past due" when you fail to pay the minimum required payment on schedule.	Three credit bureaus note past due accounts on your credit history: Experian, Trans Union, and Equifax. You can contact each bureau for a copy of your credit report to make sure there are no errors.

and paid her credit card debt in full when her financial aid check arrived every semester. Her debt began to escalate when she started using her cards to cover expenses, like car repairs, food, and clothes. At age 23, and only a junior in college, Debbie filed for bankruptcy. Looking back, she blames credit card companies for making it so easy to accumulate debt and herself for not understanding the financial hole she was digging until it was too late.[17]

The most basic way to stay in control is to pay bills regularly and on time. On credit card bills, pay at least the minimum amount due. If you get into trouble, address the problem immediately to minimize damages. Call the creditor and see if you can pay your debt gradually using a payment plan. Finally, examine what got you into trouble and avoid it in the future if you can. Cut up a credit card or two if you have too many. If you clean up your act, your credit history will gradually clean up as well.

CREDITOR

A person or company to whom a debt is owed, usually money.

Throughout this text you have connected analytical, creative, and practical thinking to academic and life skills. You have put them together in order to solve problems and make decisions. You have seen how these skills, used consistently and balanced, can help you succeed.

As you complete your work in the course, know that you are only just beginning your career as a successfully intelligent learner. You will continue to discover the best ways to use your analytical, creative, and practical thinking skills to achieve goals that are meaningful to you.

How can you continue to activate your *successful intelligence*?

Robert Sternberg has found that successfully intelligent people, despite differences in thinking and in personal goals, have several particular characteristics in common. He calls them "self-activators"—things that get you moving and keep you going. According to Sternberg, successfully intelligent people:[18]

1. **Motivate themselves.** They make things happen, spurred on by a desire to succeed and a love of what they are doing.

2. **Learn to control their impulses.** Instead of going with their first quick response, they sit with a question or problem. They allow time for thinking and let ideas surface before making a decision.

3. **Know when to persevere.** When it makes sense, they push past frustration and stay on course, confident that success is in their sights. They also are able to see when they've hit a dead end—and, in those cases, to stop pushing.

4. **Know how to make the most of their abilities.** They understand what they do well and capitalize on it in school and in work.

5. **Translate thought into action.** Not only do they have good ideas; they are able to turn those ideas into practical actions that bring ideas to fruition.

6. **Have a product orientation.** They want results; they focus on what they are aiming for rather than on how they are getting there.

7. **Complete tasks and follow through.** With determination, they finish what they start. They also follow through to make sure all the loose ends are tied and the goal has been achieved.

8. **Are initiators.** They commit to people, projects, and ideas. They make things happen rather than sitting back and waiting for things to happen to them.

9. **Are not afraid to risk failure.** Because they take risks and sometimes fail, they often enjoy greater success and build their intellectual capacity. Like everyone, they make mistakes—but tend not to make the same mistake twice.

10. **Don't procrastinate.** They are aware of the negative effects of putting things off, and they avoid them. They create schedules that allow them to accomplish what's important on time.

11. **Accept fair blame.** They strike a balance between never accepting blame and taking the blame for everything. If something is their fault, they accept the responsibility and don't make excuses.

12. **Reject self-pity.** When something goes wrong, they find a way to solve the problem. They don't get caught in the energy drain of feeling sorry for themselves.

13. **Are independent.** They can work on their own and think for themselves. They take responsibility for their own schedule and tasks.

14. **Seek to surmount personal difficulties.** They keep things in perspective, looking for ways to remedy personal problems and separate them from their professional lives.

15. **Focus and concentrate to achieve their goals.** They create an environment in which they can best avoid distraction and they focus steadily on their work.

16. **Spread themselves neither too thin nor too thick.** They strike a balance between doing too many things, which results in little progress on any of them, and too few things, which can reduce the level of accomplishment.

17. **Have the ability to delay gratification.** While they enjoy the smaller rewards that require less energy, they focus the bulk of their work on the goals that take more time but promise the most gratification.

18. **Have the ability to see the forest and the trees.** They are able to see the big picture and to avoid getting bogged down in tiny details.

19. **Have a reasonable level of self-confidence and a belief in their ability to accomplish their goals.** They believe in themselves enough to get through the tough times, while avoiding the kind of overconfidence that stalls learning and growth.

20. **Balance analytical, creative, and practical thinking.** They sense what to use and when to use it. When problems arise, they combine all three skills to arrive at solutions.

Make these characteristics your personal motivational tools. Return to them when you need reactivation. Use them to make sure that you move ahead toward the goals that mean most to you.

How can you *create and live* your personal mission?

If the trees are your goals, the forest is the big picture of what you are aiming for in life—your personal mission. To define your mission, craft a *personal mission statement*.

Dr. Stephen Covey, author of *The Seven Habits of Highly Effective People*, defines a mission statement as a philosophy outlining what you want to be (character), what you want to do (contributions and achievements), and the principles by which you live (your values). He describes the statement as "a personal constitution, the basis for making major, life-directing decisions."[19]

Here is a mission statement written by Carol Carter, one of the authors of *Keys to Success*.

> My mission is to use my talents and abilities to help people of all ages, stages, backgrounds, and economic levels achieve their human potential through fully developing their minds and their talents. I aim to create opportunities for others through work, service, and family. I also aim to balance work with people in my life, understanding that my family and friends are a priority above all else.

EXPLORE YOUR PERSONAL MISSION

get creative!

Work toward a description of your most important life goals.

As a way of exploring what you most want out of life, consider one or more of the following questions, which ask you to look back at the life you imagine you will have. Freewrite some answers on a separate piece of paper.

1. You are at your retirement dinner. You have had an esteemed career in whatever you ended up doing in your life. Your best friend stands up and talks about the five aspects of your character that have taken you to the top. What do you think they are?

2. You are preparing for a late-in-life job change. Updating your résumé, you need to list your contributions and achievements. What would you like them to be?

3. You have been told that you have one year to live. Talking with your family, you reminisce about the values that have been central to you in your life. Based on that discussion, how do you decide you want to spend your time in this last year? How will your choices reflect what is most important to you?

Thinking about your answers, draft a personal mission statement here, up to a few sentences long, that reflects what you want to achieve in life. Focus on what you want to do and the effects you want to have on the world.

_____

_____

_____

_____

_____

How can you start formulating a mission statement? Try using Covey's three aspects of personal mission as a guide. Think through the following:

- **Character.** What aspects of character do you think are most valuable? When you consider the people you admire most, which of their qualities stand out?
- **Contributions and achievements.** What do you want to accomplish in your life? Where do you want to make a difference?
- **Values.** How do the values you established in your work in Chapter 2 inform your life goals? What in your mission could help you live according to what you value most highly? For example, if you value community involvement, your mission may reflect a life goal of holding elected office, which may translate into an interim goal of running for class office at college.

Because what you want out of life changes as you move from one phase to the next—from single person to spouse, from student to working citizen—your personal mission should remain flexible and open to revision. If you frame your mission statement carefully so that it truly reflects your goals, it can be your guide in everything you do, helping you to live with integrity and to work to achieve your personal best.

Seeking experiences that broaden your horizons may be part of your personal mission. These students are learning both academic and life lessons during their travel in China.

Live with integrity

ETHICS

A system of moral values; a sense of what is right to do

Having integrity puts your ethics into day-to-day action. When you act with integrity, you earn trust and respect from others. If people can trust you to be honest, to be sincere in what you say and do, and to consider the needs of others, they will be more likely to encourage you, support your goals, and reward your work.

Living with integrity helps you believe in yourself and in your ability to make good choices. A person of integrity isn't a perfect person, but is one who makes the effort to live according to values and principles, continually striving to learn from mistakes and to improve. Take responsibility for making the right moves, and you will follow your mission with strength and conviction.

Aim for your personal best

Your personal best is simply the best that you can do, in any situation. It may not be the best you have ever done. It may include mistakes, for nothing significant is ever accomplished without making mistakes and taking risks. It may shift from situation to situation. As long as you aim to do your best, though, you are inviting growth and success.

PERSONAL TRIUMPH

JOE A. MARTIN JR. Professor of Communications, University of West Florida, Tallahassee

Growing up around people who've been hampered by difficulties can inspire a person to make different choices. Joe Martin made the effort to achieve as a student—but that wasn't enough for him. His main focus now is his life mission to use his abilities to help and inspire others. Read the account, then use a separate piece of paper to answer the questions on page 281.

I grew up in the housing projects of Miami, Florida. My mother didn't finish high school, and no one in my family even considered going to college, including me. My low GPA and SAT scores seemed to indicate I wasn't "college material."

While I was in high school, six of my friends died as a result of crime, drugs, or murder. At least 12 people I knew were in prison, five from my own family. I made a vow that if I survived the projects, I would do something constructive with my life and give something back to the community. I initially wanted to join the military, but after the recruiter told me I wasn't smart enough to go to college, I decided to prove him wrong.

I enrolled in college and, given my academic background, was shocked by my success. I ended up graduating at the top of my class, with a bachelor's degree in public relations, and was voted "Student of the Year" among 10,000 students. Competing against more than 400 other candidates, I landed a job right out of college working for the federal government. Within a year, I was able to move my mother out of the projects and afford almost anything I wanted. Life was great, but I didn't like my job and the person I was becoming.

Around that time, I heard a motivational speaker talk about the need for young professionals to give back to the community. I suddenly realized that I hadn't kept my vow. I was indulging myself, but I didn't have any passion or purpose for what I was doing with my life.

After his presentation, I asked the speaker for advice. I jotted down his suggestions on a napkin and began to implement his ideas. I discovered that I could make money doing what I do best—talking. I became a motivational speaker for students and found that my true passion was teaching. Through teaching, whether on stage or in the classroom, I discovered that I could make a difference in the lives of students who were growing up in poverty as I had.

I've given over 300 presentations and spoken to more than a quarter of a million people about student success. I've written books, recorded audio- and videotapes of my programs, and have my own television show. However, my biggest accomplishment so far has been the creation of a Web site called "Real World University." With the Web site, I'm now able to reach more than 100,000 students a month in 26 different countries.

I believe the reason many students fail is because they have no clue about their gifts and talents or about how they can use those gifts and talents to serve others. Many people are on what I call the "Treadmill Trench" of life—motivated to stay busy, but too scared to live their dreams.

My main question to students is: "If you knew you couldn't fail, what would you attempt to do professionally?" The answer to this question can help anyone find their purpose and passion in life. I also stress to students the importance of meeting a model of success—not someone you'll probably never meet, like Michael Jordan, but someone who is doing what you love to do. Then spend time with that person to find out how they did it. Once students have a clear vision of what they want to become, they're destined to succeed.

And life is what we make it, always has been, always will be.

GRANDMA MOSES

Aim for your personal best in everything you do. As a lifelong learner, you will always have a new direction in which to grow and a new challenge to face. Seek constant improvement in your personal, educational, and professional life. Dream big, knowing that incredible things are possible for you if you think positively and act with successful intelligence. Enjoy the richness of life by living each day to the fullest, developing your talents and potential into the achievement of your most valued goals.

Kaizen is the Japanese word for "continual improvement." Striving for excellence, finding ways to improve on what already exists, and believing that you can effect change are at the heart of the industrious Japanese spirit. The drive to improve who you are and what do you provides the foundation of a successful future.

Think of this concept as you reflect on yourself, your goals, your lifelong education, your career, and your personal pursuits. Create excellence and quality by continually asking yourself, "How can I improve?" Living by *kaizen* helps you to be a respected friend and family member, a productive and valued employee, and a truly contributing member of society. You can change the world.

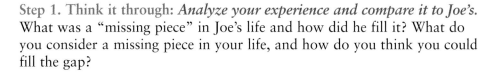

BUILDING SKILLS

FOR COLLEGE, CAREER, AND LIFE SUCCESS

Developing Successful Intelligence

PUTTING IT ALL TOGETHER

Learn from the experiences of others. Look back to Joe Martin's Personal Triumph on page 279. After you've read his story, relate his experience to your own life by completing the following:

Step 1. Think it through: *Analyze your experience and compare it to Joe's.* What was a "missing piece" in Joe's life and how did he fill it? What do you consider a missing piece in your life, and how do you think you could fill the gap?

Step 2. Think out of the box: *Imagine ways to contribute.* Think about the ways in which you could serve. How might your talents and skills give something to others? Brainstorm ideas about how you could use what you do well to make a difference.

Step 3. Make it happen: *Make a practical plan to get involved.* Decide on a specific way to help others, then form a plan to pursue this goal. As you think about your decision, consider your "missing piece": Is there a way to contribute that also somehow fills that missing piece? Write down what you intend to do and the specific steps you will take to do it.

create your future

Team Building

Building interview skills. Divide into pairs—each student will have a turn interviewing the other about themselves and their career aspirations. Follow these steps.

1. Independently, take three minutes to brainstorm questions you'll ask the other person. Focus on learning style, interests, and initial career ideas. You might ask questions like these:
   - If you could have any job in the world, what would it be?
   - What do you think would be the toughest part of achieving success in that profession?
   - Who are you as a learner and worker—what is your learning style?
   - What sacrifices are you willing to make to realize your dreams?
   - What is your greatest failure, and what have you learned from it?
   - Who is a role model to you in terms of career success?
2. Person A interviews Person B for 5 to 10 minutes and takes notes.
3. Switch roles: Person B interviews Person A and takes notes. Remember that each person uses their own questions that they developed in Step 1.
4. Share with each other what interesting ideas stand out to you from the interviews. If you have any, offer constructive criticism to your interviewee about his or her interview skills.
5. Finally, submit your notes to your instructor for feedback.

This exercise will build your ability to glean information from others and to answer questions during an interview. You will use this skill throughout your professional life. Probe deeply when interviewing others so that you develop the ability to draw out the best in someone. Be as interested—and interesting—as you can.

Writing

Record your thoughts on a separate piece of paper or in a journal.

Addiction. Many people have, at one time or another, had to cope with some kind of addiction. Describe how you feel about addiction in any form—to alcohol, drugs, food, sex, the Internet, gambling. How has addiction ensnared you, if at all? How did you deal with it? If you have never faced an addiction nor been close to someone who did, describe how you think you would work through the problem it if it ever happened to you.

Career Portfolio

Complete the following in your electronic portfolio or on separate sheets of paper. When you have finished, read through your entire career portfolio. You have gathered information to turn to again and again on your path to a fulfilling, successful career.

A Wheel for Life. In Key 9.11 you see a blank Wheel of Life. Without looking at the first wheel from the beginning of the semester, evaluate yourself as you are right now, after completing this course: Where would you rank yourself in the eight categories? After you have finished, compare this wheel with your previous wheel. Look at the changes: Where have you grown? How has your self-perception changed? Let what you learn from this new wheel inform you about what you have accomplished and what you plan for the future.

Continue to update your Wheel of Life so that it reflects your growth and development, helping to guide you through the changes that await you in the future. Add or change the categories as your college, career, and life priorities evolve.

If you realize that your attitudes may stand in the way of success in a particular job or career area, consider what specific steps you are willing to take to change them. You might also consider whether you want to rethink your career or company choice to find a position or area that suits you better. Finally, think about how your ability to set effective boundaries may affect your success in school. Working up to your limits, but not too far beyond, will help you become the person you want to be both at school and in the world of work.

Use this new wheel to evaluate your progress.

9.11

Rate yourself in each area of the wheel on a scale of 1 to 10, 1 being least developed (near the center of the wheel) and 10 being most developed (the outer edge of the wheel). In each area, at the level of the number you choose, draw a curved line and fill in the wedge below that line. Be honest—this is for your benefit only. Finally, look at what your wheel says about the balance in your life. If this were a real wheel, how well would it roll?

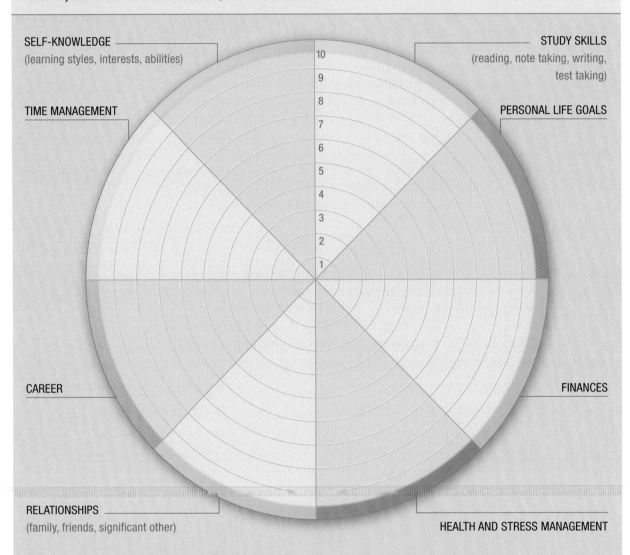

Source: Based on "The Wheel of Life" model developed by the Coaches Training Institute, © Co-Active Space 2000.

SUGGESTED READINGS

Adams, Robert Lang, et al. *The Complete Résumé and Job Search Book for College Students*. Holbrook, MA: Adams Publishing, 1999.

Beatty, Richard H. *The Resume Kit*, 5th ed. New York: John Wiley & Sons, 2003.

Bolles, Richard Nelson. *What Color Is Your Parachute? 2003: A Practical Manual for Job Hunters and Career Changers*. Berkeley, CA: Ten Speed Press, 2003.

Detweiler, Gerri. *The Ultimate Credit Handbook*, 3rd ed. New York: Plume, 2003.

Duyff, Roberta Larson. *The American Dietetic Association's Complete Food and Nutrition Guide*. Hoboken, NJ: Wiley, 2003.

Jones, Laurie Beth. *The Path: Creating Your Mission Statement for Work and for Life*. New York: Hyperion, 1998.

Kadison, Richard D. and DiGeronimo, Theresa Foy. *College of the Overwhelmed: The Campus Mental Health Crisis and What to Do About It*. San Francisco: Jossey-Bass, 2004.

Kuhn, Cynthia, et al. *Buzzed: The Straight Facts About the Most Used and Abused Drugs from Alcohol to Ecstasy*, 2nd ed. New York: W. W. Norton, 2003.

Selkowitz, Ann. *The College Student's Guide to Eating Well on Campus*. Bethesda, MD: Tulip Hill Press, 2000.

Tyson, Eric. *Personal Finance for Dummies*. Foster City, CA: IDG Books Worldwide, 2000.

Ward, Darrell. *The Amfar AIDS Handbook: The Complete Guide to Understanding HIV and AIDS*. New York: W. W. Norton, 1998.

INTERNET RESOURCES

Prentice Hall Student Success Supersite (fitness and well-being information): www.prenhall.com/success

Columbia University's Health Education Program: www.alice.columbia.edu

Federal Centers for Disease Control and Prevention (disease prevention and health information): www.cdc.gov

It's Your (Sex) Life: www.itsyoursexlife.com/

MayoClinic.com (medical information from this world-renowned medical center): www.mayohealth.org

HIV Prevention: www.thebody.com/safesex.html

U.S. Bureau of Labor—statistics: www.bls.gov/oco/

The Motley Fool (money and investment advice): www.fool.com/

1st Steps in the Hunt: Daily News for Online Job Hunters (advice on finding a job via an on-line search): www.interbiznet.com/hunt/

College Grad Job Hunter (advice on résumés, interviews, and a database of entry-level jobs): www.collegegrad.com

JobWeb (career information site for college students): www.jobweb.com/

Prentice Hall Student Success Supersite—Money Matters: www.prenhall.com/success/MoneyMat/index.html

Career Path: www.prenhall.com/success/CareerPath/index.html

Résumé Edge (résumé advice): www.resumeedge.com

ENDNOTES

1. Jennifer Jacobson, "How Much Sports Is Too Much? Athletes Dislike Conferences' Efforts to Give Players More Time to Be Students," *The Chronicle of Higher Education*, December 6, 2002 [on-line]. Available: http://chronicle.com/weekly/v49/i15a03801.htm (March 2004).

2. CBS News, "Help for Sleep-Deprived Students," Durham, NC, April 19, 2004 [on-line]. Available: www.cbsnews.com/stories/2004/04/19/health/main612476.shtml (May 2004).

3. "College Students Sleep Habits Harmful to Health, Study Finds," *The Daily Orange—Feature Issue*, September 25, 2002 [on-line]. Available: www.dailyorange.com/news/2002/09/25/Feature/College.Students.Sleep.Habits.Harmful.To.Health.Study.Finds-280340.shtml (May 2004).

4. Herbert Benson, M. D., and Eileen M. Stuart, R.N., C.M.S., et al., *The Wellness Book*. New York: Simon & Schuster, 1992, p. 292; and Gregg Jacobs, Ph.D., "Insomnia Corner," *Talk About Sleep*, 2004

[on-line]. Available: www.talkaboutsleep.com/sleepdisorders/insomnia_corner.htm (May 2004).

5. Kim Hubbard, Anne-Marie O'Neill, and Christina Cheakalos, "Out of Control," *People*, April 12, 1999, p. 54.

6. J. McGinnis and W. Foege, "Actual Causes of Death in the United States," *Journal of the American Medical Association (JAMA)* 270.18, American Medical Association, November 10, 1993, p. 2208.

7. H. Wechsler et al., "Changes in Binge Drinking and Related Problems Among American College Students Between 1993 and 1997," *Journal of American College Health* 47 (September 1998): p. 57.

8. Ibid, pp. 63–64.

9. National Institute on Alcohol Abuse and Alcoholism, No. 29 PH 357, July 1995.

10. Darra Clark, Arizona State Freshman's Comments on EssayEdge.com [on-line]. Available: www.essayedge.com/college/admissions/speakout/arizona.shtml (March 2004).

11. National Institute on Drug Abuse, Capsule Series C-83-08, "Cigarette Smoking," Bethesda, MD: National Institutes of Health, 1994.

12. David Stout, "Direct Link Found Between Smoking and Lung Cancer," *New York Times*, October 18, 1996, pp. A1, A19.

13. National Institute on Drug Abuse, "National Survey Results on Drug Abuse from Monitoring the Future Study," Bethesda, MD: National Institutes of Health, 1994.

14. Drug Enforcement Administration, U.S Department of Justice [on-line]. Available: www.usdoj.gov/dea/concern/mdma/mdmaindex.htm (February 2003).

15. Women's Review of Books, "Rebuilding a Life: Susan Davenny Wyner Replays Her Transformation from Singer to Conductor," December 2000, reprinted on the Web site for the New England String Ensemble [on-line]. Available: www.newenglandstringensemble.org/ (May 2004).

16. Laura A. Bruce, "College Kids' Credit Card Use Can Leave Them Drowning in High-Interest Debt," Bankrate.com, 2001 [on-line]. Available: www.bankrate.com/brm/news/cc/20000815.asp (March 2001).

17. Eric Hoover, "The Lure of Easy Credit Leaves More Students Struggling with Debt: Consumer Advocates Blame Lenders, Congress, and Some Colleges," *The Chronicle of Higher Education*, June 15, 2001 [on-line]. Available: http://chronicle.com/weekly/v47/i40/40a03501.htm (March 2004).

18. List and descriptions based on Robert J. Sternberg, *Successful Intelligence*. New York: Plume, 1997, pp. 251–269.

19. Stephen Covey, *The Seven Habits of Highly Effective People*. New York: Simon & Schuster, 1989, pp. 70–144, 309–318.

Index